S0-BLZ-049

WALKING
THE TIGER'S PATH

WALKING
THE TIGER'S PATH

YOLO COUNTY LIBRARY
226 BUCKEYE STREET
WOODLAND CA 95695

WITHDRAWN

A Soldier's Spiritual Journey in Iraq

PAUL M. KENDEL

Tendril Press

DENVER, COLORADO

Walking the Tiger's Path:
A Soldier's Spiritual Journey in Iraq

http://walkingthetigerspath.com/

Copyright © 2011 by Paul M. Kendel. All Rights Reserved.

Published by Tendril Press™
Copyright © 2011 All Rights Reserved.
www.TendrilPress.com
PO Box 441110
Aurora, CO 80044
303.696.9227

No part of this publication may be reproduced, stored in a retrieval system, or transmitted in any form or by any means, electronic, mechanical, photocopying, or otherwise, without the prior written permission of Tendril Press, LLC, and Paul M. Kendel. The material in this book is furnished for informational use only and is subject to change without notice. Tendril Press assumes no responsibility for any errors or inaccuracies that may appear in the documents contained in this book.

All images, logos, quotes, and trademarks included in this book are subject to use according to trademark and copyright laws of the United States of America.

First Publishing September 2011

ISBN 978-0-9841543-5-7 Paper

Printed in the United States of America
10 9 8 7 6 5 4 3 2 1

Cover Photo taken in Iraq with author's camera by fellow soldier.
Autor photo by Moreland Nicholson

Art Direction, Book Design and Cover Design © 2011.
All Rights Reserved by

A J Images Inc.,
www.AJImagesInc.com — 303•696•9227
Info@AJImagesInc.com

For Sakyong Mipham Rinpoche.
May his leadership, wisdom, humor, and smile,
change the lives of all those in pain

and

Margot, my spiritual advisor and friend

and

"The Immortal Eight" who paid the highest price

KIA-24 July 2005	**KIA-30 July 2005**
SSG. Carl R. Fuller	SFC. Victor A. Anderson
SGT. John F. Thomas	SSG. David R. Jones SR.
SGT. James O. Kinlow	SGT. Jonathon C. Haggin
SPC. Jacques E. Brunson	SGT. Ronnie L. Shelley

I hold my face in my two hands.
No, I am not crying.
I hold my face in my two hands
To keep my loneliness warm
Two hands protecting
Two hands nourishing
Two hands preventing
My soul from leaving me
In anger.

—Thich Nhat Hanh, a Vietnamese monk,
following the destruction of a village during the Vietnam War.

Religion begins with an answer, spirituality begins with a question.
—The Dzogchen Ponlop Rinpoche

...a frightening, uncomfortable place
is the knife that severs discursive thought.
—Padmasambhava

CONTENTS

FOREWORD

The letter, signed "SGT. Paul M. Kendel, Alpha Company, 2-121, 48th BCT, US Army, Iraq," addressed the problem of trying to meditate in a tent with 20 other soldiers. "The only quiet time is in the shower or a hot sweltering porto' potty," he wrote. "Neither are terribly conducive to meditation practice. However, riding around all day in a humvee waiting to get blown up provides one with unusual opportunities for contemplation."

That was my first introduction to SSG. Kendel. He had gone online from the base where he was stationed to seek help. It was the start of a journey that began in a war zone and brought him face to face with a leader he had no idea existed: the King of Shambhala.

This book is the story of that journey. It has now been five years since SSG. Kendel emailed his first cry for help. During that time, like many in the cauldron of Iraq, he tried to make sense of the carnage around him and the personal torment within. "It's hard not to grow angry and bitter," he wrote after failing to revive a dead soldier drowned in a ditch. "But I have gained a different perspective on the dignity of the human race. Thankfully, it has opened my mind, not closed it."

His first email, sent in July 2005, made its way to Shambhala, a worldwide network of meditation centers that draws its inspiration from the legendary Himalayan kingdom of that name. The mountain realm was said to have been a model society renowned for its wisdom and compassion. Although he could never have known it at the time, within two years, SSG. Kendel would be sitting in the presence of Sakong Mipham Rinpoche, the current throne-holder of that ancient kingdom's lineage.

"I send my greetings, prayers and blessings to you and those around you," wrote Sakyong Mipham Rinpoche after reading SSG. Kendel's first message from Iraq. "The Tibetan people have gone through persecution and tremendous hardship. It was their resolve not to abandon compassion and not to give into anger that ensured the survival of the Tibetan culture and people. As you mention in your letter, the contemplation that sentient beings are innately endowed with goodness and wisdom is always important to remember again and again, regardless of stupid and cruel behavior—for if we let their actions trigger our anger, not only will they have stolen our mind, but our dignity as well."

As the President of Shambhala, I had the honor of reading aloud those first messages exchanged with Margot Neuman to a gathering of hundreds of Shambhala warriors under a huge white tent in the Colorado Rockies. Many of us were weeping. I remember being almost unable to continue as I tried to read out this passage: "This place is like Vietnam, they kill you and slip away into the night. You never really see their faces. And because of that the anger expressed by my friends is misdirected toward the average Iraqi who is just trying to survive. We retaliate and our hate grows, simply perpetuating the problem. The only answer to the problem is more compassion, just like the Sakyong said to me in his letter. But how do you convince a group of people that just had their good friends blown to pieces that the answer is love and compassion?"

I remember thinking at the time that this sergeant, whose name was still only a signature on unbearably poignant emails, had just asked the central question of our age. At that point we were only four years into the "War on Terror," since re-named "The Long War." It is the question

that countless people—crossing all boundaries of geography, culture, and religion—have asked themselves: what do you say to those who have just had their good friends blown to pieces?

The diet of this decade, served up in the continuous reel of 24-hour news, has been the record of humanity's answer to that question. We are all witnesses to the long roll call of bombings, assassinations, massacres, and funerals. We have all listened to the voices raised in debate, in protest and appeal. No one knows the total number of casualties. Certainly, the toll taken on humanity's psyche has been incalculable.

In the wake of 9/11, I was in war-torn Sri Lanka as part of an interntional Buddhist delegation. I asked a conference of the country's leading monks if they had any message we should take back to the West. This was just after their own country's national airport had been the target of a terrorist attack.

Two of them spoke. The first said, "Please tell your people that the Buddha's teaching is that all humanity is one family. The only difference that matters is whether our minds are turned toward peace or toward war."

"Look at what has happened in America," said another, "and the impact it has had everywhere. Now people can see for themselves: this world crisis is the product of endless violence. More violence is not the solution."

Not everyone would agree. SSG. Kendel, now a civilian educator teaching world history and special education in Jacksonville, Florida, would not describe himself as a pacifist. But as his evocative writing makes clear at each twist of this remarkable story, he has lived his life on the razor's edge of the question that has haunted him. As he wrote while still in Iraq, "Just when I was beginning to think that my time here has been nothing but a horrible waste, to find out that my personal experiences and those of my friends around me—as terrible as some of them have been—may help make a difference in maybe just one person's life makes my existence here not seem like it is all in vain."

Richard Reoch
President of Shambhala

PREFACE

It was May 2005, Ft. Stewart, Georgia. At the conclusion of our training for deployment to Iraq, our battalion commander gave a big going-away speech to the troops and their families. He cited the huge sacrifices we were all making to preserve freedom at home and abroad. As I stood in formation, I heard the parting call from a father or brother to one of the men, bellowing loudly as he drove away, "Kick some ass!" It reminded me of the infamous comment President Bush made when the insurgency in Iraq began to grow. With a cocky swagger, he responded to increased violence against American forces with "Bring 'em on!" And of course they came on with a vengeance.

As the truck drove off, I couldn't help but think, despite the patriotic gesture, that "kicking some ass" against the bad guys, whoever they really were, wouldn't be what that guy thought.

The reality of events on the ground would prove to be less than patriotic and honorable at times. After a couple of months of deployment, the term "patriotic" no longer seemed to refer to winning anyone's hearts and minds; it just meant "survival," bringing your ass home alive. Then I started reading about the Shambhala warrior and the Tiger's Path in the meditation books of Chogyam Trungpa, Sakyong Mipham, and Pema Chödrön.

The Shambhala teachings of the Tiger's Path proved highly relevant to my situation. At times my mind (as well as those of my friends) seemed hopelessly ruled by anxiety and blind impulse. The tiger is used as a symbol because the tiger, according to Trungpa Rinpoche, "moves slowly and heedfully through the jungle," mindful and precise in its surveying of the landscape. Because of this gentle, alert approach, the tiger sees with clarity how to act. Knowing what action to take had life or death consequences in Iraq. "Without a strong motivation to use discernment," says Sakyong Mipham, "we buy into our habit of running around in circles of meaningless thought….making decisions becomes a matter of trial and error, based on mood…Wisdom and compassion begin with cultivating discernment, not just reacting to what happens." The tools of the Tiger's Path of discernment—the ability to be clear and aware of the emotional climate and the physical realities on the ground—were vital, not only for circumventing the effects of emotional rage, but also for cultivating a military conduct that avoids causing unnecessary harm. Most of my friends, though perhaps less alarmed by their aggression than I was at my own, nevertheless conducted themselves with courage and loyalty. Fear and anger were the most common reasons for soldiers to lose judgment and over-react.

The tiger is also characterized as "meek," referring to a lack of arrogance. Arrogance obscures the ability to see situations as they present themselves. Humility, on the other hand, is the ground for sufficient openness of mind to weigh choices accurately and to consider the needs of others, not just your own desires. I don't know if I was a "Shambhala warrior," but I couldn't ignore the suffering of the people around me. To simply kill them out of convenience or carelessness seemed a repugnant way to fight a war of "liberation." I couldn't avoid my own feelings of remorse at the violence inflicted on Iraqis—human beings who just wanted a life similar to the lives the soldiers hoped to enjoy upon their return home. I felt strongly that we had to consider the moral and physical consequences of our warfare strategy.

Commenting on Vietnam, Chogyam Trungpa once said, "Americans try so violently to be non-violent." Iraq wasn't a Hollywood movie where you could leave the theater and forget about it. Our actions meant something. Lives were changed forever. I couldn't avoid the emotions stirring within my own heart.

Sakyong Mipham called our mission in Iraq "wrathful compassion." If being "wrathful" meant we had to track down terrorists, it also meant that we had to see through our own selfish delusions. We had to face the reality of our own fear and discern who it was that we saw as we gazed down the barrel of our guns. I had to feign aggression at times to be respected, while inside my head I had to deal with the repercussions of my actions, as well as those of the soldiers around me. If the tiger of Shambhala warriorship, as Sakyong Mipham says, places his "paws carefully," knowing the need to "respect karma," and that "every decision we make has repercussions," then I struggled to walk a spiritual tightrope while carrying an M4 rifle in my hands.

Trungpa Rinpoche taught:

> The key to warriorship and the ultimate definition of bravery is not being afraid of who you are. Examine your experience to see what it contains that is of value in helping yourself and others. Warriorship is the opposite of selfishness. We become selfish when we are afraid of ourselves and afraid of the seeming threats the world presents. We want to build a little nest, a cocoon, to protect ourselves. But we can be much more brave than that. Even in the face of great problems, we can be heroic and kind at the same time.

I began writing this story about my tour in Iraq in an effort to chronicle its most poignant events. But as the story evolved and began to write itself, it quickly became something far more than an "Iraq War book." I became aware that I was examining my experiences in a war zone, as well as my homecoming, and discovering that my feelings contained a menagerie of fear, hate, ugliness, and at the same time, love, hope, and forgiveness. At first I resisted telling some of the more painful details of my story in an effort to maintain that little nest of privacy, a cocoon of self-protection. With the support of Margot and others, I was able to break through such impediments and tell the complete truth about my experiences in the hope that this book would ultimately help me, as well as others who found themselves with the same concerns. Exposing the truth that even a soldier in the throes of war can be "heroic and kind at the same time" has been a powerful healing process.

Acknowledgments

I would like to thank my mother for her love and support (which came in many different ways) while I was in Iraq. Thanks to my two young sons, Alex and Sean, for their cheerful, loving presence. My sincere gratitude to David and Susie Biddulph for their extraordinary kindness in providing me with a place of refuge in a time of need. Many thanks to Ric Dolan, who opened his home to me and tolerated my late evenings (I should say early mornings). To Cliff Neuman for all of his assistance. I am grateful to Moreland Nicholson for his friendship and his suggestions for the manuscript and to Emily Hilburn Sell for her editorial advice and support. My thanks to Pema Chödrön, Patricia Kelly, Jennifer Holder, Glenna Olmsted, as well as all those involved in the Shambhala community, especially to President Richard Reoch—whose friendship and advice helped guide me through difficult times. His words and teachings have been a gift, providing answers to even the most challenging questions. In particular I would like to thank Gary Allen who worked tirelessly editing this book from its genesis to its completion. Without the benefit of his friendship and guidance, both literary and spiritual, the book would not have reached its fullest potential.

MILITARY ACRONYMS

ACR — Armored Calvary Regiment
AO — Area of Operations
BCT — Brigade Combat Team
EOD — Explosive Ordinance Division
HE — High Explosive
FOB — Forward Operating Base
IED — Improvised Explosive Device
KIA — Killed In Action
NCO — Non-Commissioned Officer
OP — Observation Post
PSD — Personal Security Detail
PTSD — Post-Traumatic Stress Disorder
QRF — Quick Reaction Force
ROE — Rules Of Engagement
RPG — Rocket Propelled Grenade
SOP — Standard Operating Procedure
TC — Truck Commander
TCP — Traffic Control Point
TCN — Third Country National
TOC — Tactical Operations Center
VBIED — Vehicular-Borne Improvised Explosive Device

WALKING
THE TIGER'S PATH

INTRODUCTION

I met SSG. Paul Kendel through a series of emails he sent to me during his deployment to Iraq as a soldier with the 48th Infantry Brigade of the Georgia National Guard. He had been in Baghdad only a short time before he felt besieged with doubts and questions regarding the U.S. presence in that region—he saw little progress in "winning the hearts and minds" of the Iraqi people as he witnessed the hardships the military and its policies placed on their way of life.

I intend no derogation or harsh criticism of young soldiers who are thrust into combat. The military teaches them who their "enemies" are and that these enemies want to harm their families and friends. They are placed in a hostile environment where the enemy does indeed kill them and their comrades. Exhausted, enraged, stressed, and fearful, they are placed in harm's way, yet we hold them accountable to the standards of a peaceful, civilized society. When a particular case gets too much media attention, stigmatizing the United States and its policies, then that young soldier is sacrificed—branded as an abnormality. Not only is he shamed for his action, but his family and unit must also walk in the shadow of his disgrace. I respect our soldiers, as does SSG. Kendel. In this book he wrote what he witnessed, but it was always with an underlying sense of understanding for the situations and circumstances that confronted them all.

Paul's aversion to organized religion had muted his natural interest in Buddhism; but through the ravages of war, he found a voice that resonated with his own sensibilities. Out of frustration and seclusion, he sent an email to Shambhala International, expressing his appreciation of the teachings in the book and requesting further guidance for the difficulties of his situation.

The Sakyong's executive secretary forwarded SSG. Kendel's email to me. As a 33-year student of Tibetan and Shambhala Buddhism I'm trained as a teacher and meditation instructor in that tradition. My husband Cliff and I founded and direct a non-profit charitable organization now known as Ratna Peace Initiative. Its mission is to provide meditation instruction and materials to prison inmates, who are often themselves traumatized by violence and a violent history, and many of whom are incarcerated veteans. A soldier in Iraq seemed a logical next step, so, touched by Paul's situation, I accepted his inquiry and responded to his email, which marked the beginning of an on-going correspondence through his ten-month tour of duty.

Paul's experiences and reflections don't place him on a moral pedestal above other soldiers—they simply make him all the more extraordinary for the discovery of his own compassion. What he accomplished psychologically and spiritually throughout his involvement in the Iraq conflict was nothing short of amazing. Wrestling with his own anger, fear, and deaths of many friends, he maintained the views and sensibilities of a peaceful, civilized society, and also the sensitive intelligence of a scholar aware of the culture in which he was operating. U.S. Ambassador Ryan Crocker, who has spent his entire career in the Middle East, commented, "One thing I learned a long time ago is you don't go into someone else's complicated society armed with your own preconceptions."

Paul demonstrated a unique combination of knowledge and an inclination toward kindness that guided his actions. In the face of extreme violence and turmoil, he maintained his integrity and his convictions. For his efforts to spare and protect the lives of innocent civilians, including women and children, he was often berated. He chastised himself for the rare times his own anger momentarily overcame his convictions; nevertheless, he employed the experience of these intense, emotional situations as self-reflections that furthered his sense of awareness.

With considerable trepidation, I pondered my qualifications for providing spiritual advice to a soldier in combat. I, after all, had never been in combat. But I'd also never been in prison, a distinction my incarcerated students seemed not to mind. In the end, I drew on years of experience working in the prison environment, where dehumanization, pain, and despair are the norm—an environment eerily similar to the challenges of military combat, where compassion for others is seen as weakness and where an individual who desires to separate his sensibilities from the stark ruthlessness of his surroundings has no choice but to expose himself to the taunting ridicule of his peers. The ultimate guide for selecting relevant materials for SSG. Kendel came from Buddha's wisdom. His teachings are presented not as dogma or "religious" dictates, but rather as spiritual and philosophical guides to daily life experiences. Such a life based on openness and clarity of insight affords the student an opportunity to make informed and skillful decisions.

I sent Paul materials attached to emails, as well as several relevant books. One teaching in particular seemed relevant to his situation: the *charnel ground* principle. Unlike western cemeteries, Indian graveyards leave their dead above ground. Buddhist scholar Judith Simmer-Brown in *Dakini's Warm Breath* describes charnel grounds:

> [Charnel] grounds were unclean places of terror and anguish. In portions of the field, bodies wrapped in cloth shrouds were burned in large bonfires and reduced to tangled piles of charred bones. In other portions of the charnel ground, uncremated bodies were simply left to rot. The cremation grounds were full of foul odors…and also full of many kinds of beasts of prey.… no attempt is made to mask the horrors of decay.…Symbolically, it is the landscape or the psychological environment in which one can commit to things as they are.

Traditionally, Buddhist yogis went to charnel grounds to confront the truth of impermanence and develop equanimity toward death and conditioned existence. In this charged atmosphere, their practice matured quickly. The wisdom gained from the charnel ground is usually accompanied by an intense personal experience, most likely an unpleasant one. To absorb the true power of the charnel ground, one must be willing to embrace painful events and all of the horrors they represent.

Paul clearly faced a charnel ground in Iraq, including even the gruesome reality of dogs roaming about, looking to consume remains of soldiers' bodies torn apart by IED (improvised explosive device) explosions. The charnel ground teachings are shocking—but teachings presenting the nature of reality would be incomplete without addressing the horrors inherent in the human condition. Through contemplation of this wrathful principle, one is encouraged to let go of his usual thoughts and assumptions to face the harshest facts of existence—and few things are more harsh than war. When one has a tool to employ in accepting such savagery as a presentation of reality in a horrific form, the possibility of insight and understanding arises from what would otherwise be a blanket rejection of a situation that clearly cannot be negotiated or ignored. To perceive the reality of life and death accurately in a situation empowers one with the clarity of vision necessary to begin to discover the warmth of human compassion.

Paul told me that without my guidance and that of the Shambhala teachings, his experiences in Iraq would have been very different—that he might have given in to anger and aggression, losing himself and his humanity.

I am touched by his kind words and affirmation, but I feel that I am the fortunate recipient of an immeasurable gift as a result of my interaction with the war in Iraq. Our relationship inspired further work with veterans, and since Paul's return, our Veterans Peace of Mind program has reached out to offer veterans meditation instruction and the gentle,

healing benefits of mindfulness practices as powerful psychological tools for coping with post-traumatic stress.

I'm honored to have met this courageous soldier, a true Shambhala Warrior. May his path of awakening compassion for himself and others be an inspiration to all our returning soldiers.

—Margot Neuman

CHAPTER ONE

CURFEW AND CUCUMBERS

If you want to make enemies, try to change something.
—Woodrow Wilson

We killed our TVs, shut off our IPods, put away the video games; it was ten p.m.—time for war.

We donned our armored vests loaded down with ammunition and grenades, grabbed our M4s and M240 machine guns, and connected our AN/PVS-14 night vision devices to the fronts of our helmets. This would be the first time our section went outside "The Wire," the protective wall that surrounds American bases in Iraq. I took one last look around our air-conditioned tent. *So this is it*, I thought. *We're really going out.* As the Georgia National Guard, most of us had never entered a war zone. After two weeks of sitting around the base with its very American amenities, we packed into our humvees to face the enemy.

We drove along the high brick and cement wall surrounding Baghdad International Airport. Lamps on the wall cast an intermittent, orange glow over the road, creating the ominous feeling of going through a tunnel taking us closer and closer to the inevitable. When we reached the gate, we rolled to a stop and piled out of the humvees to lock and load. I pulled the charging handle back on my M4, got a magazine from my vest pocket, and slammed it in tight, releasing the bolt forward, chambering a round with a loud *thunk*. Around me echoed a cacophony of metal on metal as bolts hammered bullets into place. Re-entering our humvees, we settled in to wait for a tower guard to descend the steps, cross in front of us, and open the huge metal doors in the wall. Sitting there in anticipation, we watched as he laboriously opened first the left door, then the right. It reminded me of those towering doors in *King Kong*. I felt my heart beating. We moved forward into the night as the doors closed behind us.

Adjusting the night vision device on my helmet, I scanned the area—a clear night with the moon's soft glow. Most Iraqis were fast asleep, only occasional lights, like fireflies bobbing in darkness, illumined their homes. It seemed quiet and peaceful, but it was a world where men waited to kill us.

Our combat mission included enforcing a curfew imposed upon the residents from midnight to five a.m. in an area southwest of Baghdad, part of the Sunni Triangle or "Triangle of Death." After a six-month train up, we saw ourselves nailing a top al-Qaeda or Sunni militant leader, capturing a massive cache of explosives and weapons, and hauling them victoriously back to the base. We were looking for action and we found it, but it was not *exactly* what anyone had expected.

We set up our patrol of humvees off on the side of the road in the dark, waiting for unsuspecting cars breaking curfew. We didn't issue tickets for breaking curfew; we wanted to catch insurgents operating at night, carrying weapons or explosives in their cars. VBIEDs (vehicle born improvised explosive devices) posed a legitimate threat; the cars we encountered, especially those out after curfew, could be rigged to explode.

A friend lay on the ground nearby, trying to get some sleep, while I stood in the gunner's hatch of our vehicle, scanning through my night vision device. Through the monocle covering my right eye, I looked out on a hazy green world and saw the outline of fields and homes. My naked left eye saw the surrounding fields cloaked in darkness, punctuated by lights from a few homes nearby. I glimpsed a ray of light and noted headlights coming down the road behind us. Here was our chance! A small white Toyota pickup truck approached, its bed stacked high with crates. It slowed down as it pulled closer to another of our humvees that was parked on the other side of a small canal that went under the road. It stopped, still a good distance away.

I watched CPL. Aaron Gibbs, a short, stocky African-American, flash the truck with a spotlight. He moved the light up and down. The truck made slight movements forward, and then stopped again. Once more, Gibbs moved the spotlight up and down. The truck made another slight movement forward. I turned back in the direction that I was supposed to be watching. Seconds later I heard a burst of machine gun fire and a number of small arms shots from an M16. *What the hell is going on? The car seemed to have stopped. What caused them to fire?* I jumped down to investigate.

Gibbs kept the spotlight beam on the driver, whose frozen face stared at the approaching soldiers, their weapons trained on him. By now I was following behind them, my M4 ready. The man got out of the truck with his hands up. Appearing confused, he moved away from the vehicle. We edged close enough for me to see a small bullet hole in the windshield's bottom left corner. How the hell that bullet didn't hit the driver in the chest, I do not know. Another round had struck the engine; fluid was leaking onto the ground. The driver, apparently unfazed by the fact that he'd missed death by about an inch, reached into the back of his truck. We tightened the grips on our own weapons, ready to tear him apart with our fire.

But no, he pulled out a cucumber—he just felt like a snack.

Surrounded by armed American soldiers, he gnawed on that cucumber as casually as though he'd been stopped for a minor traffic violation. I walked up to the man, motioned for him to move a few feet away from his truck, then went around to the back and began to examine his dangerous contraband. A brief inspection revealed this man as a despicable curfew violator traveling with a dangerous cache of terrorist tomatoes and cucumbers—clearly a threat to the American way of life.

Standing there, munching on his cucumber, he seemed to exude a sense of *This is Iraq, and this is nothing but a minor annoyance.* We detained him since it was at least fifteen or twenty minutes past curfew, and then moved him on to Camp Stryker, our base near Baghdad International Airport. The army sent him home a day or two later after a thorough interrogation for the treasonous act of transporting vegetables after curfew—or maybe it was for munching on a cucumber in the presence of American soldiers. Whatever his crime, they soon released him. When they dropped him off at his house (as my friend described it), his family came running out to greet him; they probably thought him dead. Before he walked into his home, he turned back to the American humvees and gave them the bird.

After the incident that night, I realized that when CPL. Gibbs had moved the spotlight up and down, the poor tomato farmer had interpreted that as a command to pull forward. As a result, we shot at and nearly killed him over a simple miscommunication. There would be a lot of miscommunication while we were in Iraq, and not all of it had to do with electronic devices.

The Iraqis are resilient people—they have to be. They take a lot in stride and don't seem to get that upset even under extremely adverse circumstances. The problem was that the average Iraqi farmer didn't own a computer, so he failed to receive an email from the United States government declaring when he could or could not drive around his own country. Any farmer in America knows that he has to get up early to have his produce ready for market. It's the same in Iraq. Of course there was no way a farmer could expect to have his produce delivered and set up in Baghdad on time if he didn't physically leave his home before five in the morning. So he naturally encountered obstacles—namely *us*.

Pulling over every random farmer would quickly become a daunting task for a limited number of soldiers on patrol. I suggested to my platoon sergeant, SFC. Janes, that yes, the official curfew was five in the morning, but it was clearly not realistic. Since we were the individuals being affected, it was up to us to modify it to conform to reality. The response I received was "Fuck 'em!"

A week or so later, we set up another checkpoint to catch curfew violating tomato/cucumber farmers. We got all excited when the first curfew breaker came driving down the road. Fortunately, we didn't shoot at this one. We inspected his vehicle and searched the trunk for weapons of mass destruction, where I made the mistake of sticking my hand into mounds of okra, searching for hidden weapons. PVT. Ross, the driver of my vehicle, laughed at me. "It's okra, man, you don't want to get it all over you or you'll itch like hell."

"How the hell was I supposed to know that?" I said. "I'm from southern California. I've never even *heard* of okra."

While we were detaining this farmer, another car came down the road, and then another and another. We tried to search all the vehicles, but soon fifteen or twenty had lined up.

With this going on, I stopped traffic from a different direction with fewer cars, forcing a silver mini-van to sit and wait at least forty-five minutes. Finally, I began to feel bad for the van's occupants and called the vehicle up, waving my spotlight. As the van pulled forward, my former squad leader, "SGT. T," and I started to walk up to the vehicle. When I got there, I looked around and realized I was alone. What happened? I glanced back and noticed him hiding behind the humvee door, protecting himself from a potential VBIED explosion. Resigned to going it alone, I peered inside the van at what appeared to be a large family. In the back, a woman doubled over in pain. I assumed she had suffered a miscarriage or some stomach-related problem. The men in the van seemed indifferent to her plight, while the women tried to comfort her.

The driver, probably her husband, casually informed me that they were on the way to the hospital. I shook my head and allowed them to drive on. *Another successful evening fighting the global war on terror.* Once the ridiculously long line of curfew breakers had grown to a length beyond reasonable control, SFC. Janes relented in his "fuck 'em" views and let all the vehicles continue. After this incident we rarely bothered the tomato/cucumber farmers at this time in the morning.

In the weeks following the two incidents, I began to question our purpose in Iraq. Were we there to just harass and possibly kill innocent Iraqis? How was preventing them from getting to the emergency room helpful? I wanted to believe our presence meant something more.

When we first arrived, we were introduced to the locals, the people we were there to protect. We visited schools and local shops, met Iraqis known to be friendly to Americans, as well as various tribal elders. But once our company was given autonomy, we settled into a routine in which we were simply conducting regular daily patrols of our sector, making our presence known while circumventing the major buildings and avoiding the population.

I arrived wanting to use my experience of the Middle East to assist the mission. I held out hope that my knowledge would have a moderating influence on the violence and occasional over-eagerness of other soldiers. I imagined interacting with the locals by providing security, medicine, food, and water, while talking to and understanding them in an effort to improve the overall situation. Without success in attaining those goals, I saw no reason for us to be there.

In those first few weeks, when we'd return from patrol, my squad leader SGT. Moore, a former Marine with an attitude to match the image, would have his bunk stacked with letters or packages, sometimes five or six, from his wife and parents, while my bunk often remained empty. I would then sit down on it and watch Moore open up his mail. Sometimes he'd give me packages just so I'd have something to open. My wife eventually did send me some things, but in those first critical weeks when I was stumbling into my disillusionment with our mission in Iraq, I felt especially lonely and isolated.

When a former member of Alpha Company who worked in the Stryker detention center told me how he'd returned the tomato farmer to his family and gotten the middle finger, I wondered if this was the kind of thanks we'd always get. I could accept leaving my wife without a husband and my children fatherless, as long as it was for a higher purpose. I'd signed the paperwork. But would I waste my life on this absurd duty where nothing was ever brought closer to a genuine resolution? We'd drive around and around in the darkness, hoping to avoid being shredded by an IED, never confronting the "enemy," the amorphous evil that threatened our lives on a daily basis. We weren't establishing a democracy, we were just providing a target for people who hated us.

Even though our presence in Iraq often did little more than hassle and oppress the daily lives of Iraqis, leaving them resentful and sometimes dead as they tried to go about their business, many soldiers that I came into contact with never seemed to give it a thought. Though we nearly shot some random tomato farmer, they regarded it as a joke, something amusing, forgotten by the following day. It was only some incident with a "Hajji" ("Hajji" is military slang for Middle-Easterners, either from the traditional Muslim pilgrimage called the Hajj, or perhaps the Indian character in the *Johnny Quest* cartoon).

In my frustration, I began to look for some kind of guidance in dealing with my feelings and experiences. One day, after coming in from an eight hour patrol, putting down my gear, and taking a shower, I found myself sitting on my bunk, looking at the books I'd brought. There was the *Iliad*, the *Koran*, a couple books on Middle-Eastern history, and Thomas Mann's *The Magic Mountain*. Looking at their spines, I thought, *I just don't have the energy.* Then I recognized *Turning the Mind into an Ally.*

I'd impulsively thrown Sakyong Mipham's book on meditation into my bag while packing in Florida. I pulled it off the shelf and started reading.

I began to feel comforted. Here was somebody well-respected, whose voice and teachings resonated in a way that touched me deeply. His words provided clear, concise insight into my situation. They articulated my feelings, as if I were reading my own thoughts in someone else's book:

> From a Buddhist point of view, human beings aren't intrinsically aggressive; we are inherently peaceful. This is sometimes hard to believe. When we're angry or upset, our untrained mind becomes belligerent and we routinely strike out at others. We imagine that reacting aggressively to the object of our emotion will resolve our pain. Throughout history we have used this approach over and over again. Striking out when we're in pain is clearly one way we perpetuate misery.

I had found the support I was looking for. Being in an environment that encouraged aggression brought out the raw impulses—the "untrained" quality—which led to our situation. An Iraqi subjected to bombs, check points, interrogations, search and seizures of his home, the death of his wife, the crippling of his child could quite easily develop the rage that planted IED's on the roads we patrolled. Getting lied to, shot at, or blown up would just as easily provoke normal American guys with families and hometown values to express the darker aspects of human nature.

After the first few chapters, I started researching Shambhala Buddhism on the Internet. This effort led me to the teachings of the Sakyong's father, Chogyam Trungpa Rinpoche, particularly his famous book, *Shambhala: The Sacred Path of the Warrior*. The less religious, more secular approach of Shambhala appealed to me. One day after a patrol, I impulsively fired off an email to the Sakyong in care of Shambhala International, describing my situation and requesting assistance:

June 29, 2005

WALKING THE TIGER'S PATH
PAUL M. KENDEL

I am currently serving in Iraq with the 48th Infantry Brigade out of Georgia. We are a National Guard unit deployed for a year...I do not subscribe to any organized religion, but I do consider myself a spiritual person, and have been interested in Buddhism for some time. I am currently reading Sakyong Mipham's book, and it is helping with the stress of my job. We go out of the base every day where we have to worry about roadside bombs and other dangers. One of our humvees was blown up the other day, but fortunately no one was seriously hurt. I am having problems dealing with the mind-sets of some of my fellow soldiers who do not think the way I do. Many crave violence and wish for opportunities to shoot someone.

I do not. I just want to return home to my wife and two young sons in one piece. I am constantly singled out because I prefer to see the Iraqis as human beings and would like to treat them with respect, rather than as nameless entities. I understand the threat here; I'm no pacifist. They claim to be Christians, but their actions and attitudes toward the people here are often appalling. I guess the hundreds of years separating the Crusades from today haven't made that big of a difference in basic human compassion. I was hoping maybe you could recommend someone I could speak to, or literature to read that might help me deal with my current situation. Thank you for your time.

Sincerely,

SGT. Paul M. Kendel

CHAPTER TWO

EASY CORRUPTION

*You corrupt very easily, he thought. But was it
corruption or was it merely that you lost the naiveté that
you started with? Would it not be the same in anything?
Who else kept that first chastity of mind about their work
that young doctors, young priests, and young soldiers usually
started with?*

—Ernest Hemingway
For Whom the Bell Tolls

I had never really expected a response to my email. It was a shot in the
dark, and I could not know that this little note would change my life—in
Iraq and beyond.

Shambhala International forwarded my email to Margot Neuman, head
of the Ratna Peace Initiative, a charitable, non-profit organization providing materials on meditation and meditation-instruction to prison inmates
under the auspices of Shambhala Buddhism. The logo for Ratna Peace
Initiative is a treasure vase, which connotes the idea of a *wish-fulfilling*

gem of wholesome, sane awareness, able to provide unceasingly for the needs of others. The vase remains perpetually full, an inexhaustible source of abundance and generosity, no matter how much is withdrawn.

Meditation can be employed as a method for developing greater insight into one's chosen faith, Buddhism or otherwise. Meditation can also be stripped of its religious trappings and employed as a psychological tool for dealing with stress and conflicting, painful emotions. The Veterans Peace of Mind, a program within Ratna Peace Initiative, supports veterans suffering from post-traumatic stress with secular mindfulness practice as well as providing programs for youth-at-risk and troubled teens.

Thinking that I'd never hear a reply to my message, I was surprised to find an email from Margot (pronounced *Marget,* not *Margo)* waiting for me a couple days later:

> I'm happy to say we do not have any experience in a war zone, but we certainly sympathize to say the least. Since you are reading the Sakyong's book, perhaps you could tell us some aspects of the book that are helping you cope. Have you tried meditation—is this even a possibility in your situation? Do you have any questions that have come up based on the book that I could possibly try to address?
>
> It seems you have realized a perspective which is entirely incompatible with your environment, but entirely compatible with basic human dignity. If there is anything I can do to help, I am more than happy to do so.
>
> I can write to you and provide you with books and other written material. I can also email you a substantial amount of reading material that would probably be very helpful. I'm a senior student with over thirty years of study and meditation practice under the guidance of the Kagyu lineage of Tibetan Buddhism. Of course, I would be happy to speak with you over the telephone if that is a possibility for you.
>
> Sincerely,
>
> Margot Neuman

By this time, I'd finished reading *Turning the Mind into an Ally*, and began ordering other books such as *Shambhala: The Sacred Path of the Warrior* and *Great Eastern Sun* by the Sakyong's father, Chogyam Trungpa Rinpoche. Much like *Turning the Mind into an Ally*, these two works provided a sense of comfort and support and furthered my interest in Shambhala Buddhism. But it would be my correspondence with Margot that would provide me with a personal and intimate exposure to the dharma and the Shambhala community. She was able to assist me in numerous ways: as teacher, a source for Buddhist materials, and most importantly of all, as a friend. I might have been alone in my views toward the war in Iraq and my views toward the Iraqis, but now I had a support in the teachings as well as a friend who understood my problem and was there to help in any way possible.

The words of the Sakyong had resonated deeply, making me feel less alone and alienated. I felt more secure from the inside. But the mission of the Sakyong isn't to act as a Tibetan Dr. Phil in a combat zone, providing pearls of wisdom for someone such as myself in the hope that his teachings will provide the necessary comfort to ease another's pain. His teachings aren't a self-help guide to finding happiness; they awaken you to the world as it really is, with its beauty, ugliness, joy, and pain, and its charnel grounds. The message is that only through embracing, not avoiding, every aspect of life—even the most painful and disturbing—can you begin to realize the importance of basic goodness in yourself and others:

> With a trained mind, a stable mind, a mind with a larger motivation than its own comfort, we find another way to work with the difficulties of daily life. When we're in a difficult situation, we maintain our seat. Instead of perpetuating misery by acting out aggression, we learn to use the rough spots to spark the courage to proceed on our journey. Eventually we may actually be able to turn the mind of anger into the energy of love and compassion.

I'd only been in Iraq a few weeks, and I was looking for a way to bring some kind of sanity into a war zone. The teachings offered a way of applying centuries-old, time-tested methods for working with the confusion I felt in myself and those around me. The first hint of disillusionment had cropped up, questioning our romantic, Hollywood-influenced notions of this war. The tomato farmer and other incidents seemed like temporary, trivial problems; I felt hopeful that we would still serve a greater purpose, that being to fulfill what we'd traveled 10,000 miles from our homes to do. There is no purpose served in leaving your family for a year and risking your life for nothing.

*****

Following the nationwide invasion of Iraq in 2003, the U.S. military acted like squatters, taking over the various buildings that formerly had been used by the Iraqi military and police. Displaced Iraqi civilians also moved into some of these buildings and made them into homes. A short distance outside Baghdad International Airport sat a building we at first called the "Crack House" due to its dilapidation. Later known as the "Safe House" because it was just outside the base wire, we used it as a place where we could rest and recuperate during patrols without having to worry about being blown up.

According to the 3rd ACR (one of the units we replaced), this building had belonged to Uday Hussein, Saddam's son. Though not large, at one time it must have been a relatively plush palace. They told us that Uday had used it as his own personal "pimp," palace where he had his way with local village girls. Like many buildings that had belonged to Saddam Hussein, locals had literally gutted the place after the fall of Baghdad, removing everything from the electrical wiring to the stucco decoration.

Families who had taken over some of the deteriorated buildings near the Safe House sent their children to the Safe House every morning.

Four, maybe five kids would hang out all day, selling cold drinks, chips, and candy to the soldiers stationed there on a regular basis, as well as the patrols that stopped in to rest. These kids were good little capitalists. I enlisted one to go into town for me and bring back some cans of Dutch beer. If we wanted beef or chicken kabobs, the children's mothers would make lunch and the kids would deliver it. We would pay these kids a few dollars to clean-up trash around the building and fill sand bags when we wanted to reinforce something. The income from the sale of drinks and clean-up jobs helped feed their families.

One evening we drove to the Safe House, not for a break, but to save a life. Our patrols usually departed either at noon or around eleven in the evening. A standard patrol consisted of three to four humvees. It would take the driver an hour to prep the vehicle—filling the tank, checking the engine, and getting the radio working—and then we'd load up. Our infantry company (Alpha) was known as the "Animals." When we first started our patrols, I carried an M4 rifle (a newer version of the M16 with a collapsible stock and a shorter barrel), modified by having an M203 grenade launcher attached. Pouches attached to my vest held a basic load of ammunition: seven thirty-round magazines totaling 210 rounds, and four or five rounds of high explosive grenades. We all wore the new Interceptor Ballistic Armor vests that allowed us to insert protective chest and back plates that (at least in theory) would protect us against a 7.62 mm round fired from an AK47. The thick plates added another thirteen pounds to the overall load. I also had other basic necessities such as a knife, flashlight, and first aid equipment.

We left the wire for our patrol around eleven-thirty. We would usually stop at the mess hall, navigate our way past the chow hall Nazis (a suicide bomber blowing himself up during lunch in a Mosul chow hall led to an increase in chow hall security at all American bases—though the ID checkers tended to be over-zealous), and grab some food to go. The chow hall had the usual assortment of fast food: burgers, hot dogs, fries, egg rolls, etc.

At first, the evening seemed ordinary: we drove around, set up a couple of OPs (observation posts), and tried not to get blown up. Simple. After less than an hour, we received a call over the radio. A Bradley Fighting Vehicle had rolled into a ditch near the Safe House. When my section reached the scene, SGT. Mercer's friends were pulling him out of the muddy canal and up the side of the embankment. They had removed his uniform and body armor while still inside the vehicle, so he was naked from the waist up as they placed him limply on the ground. I heard one of Mercer's men say something about his condition. The soldier's response was, "What do you think? He's fucking *dead*, man!" Then I watched in shock and confusion as his companions turned away. *Maybe he wasn't dead*, I thought; you never know. Our medic went over to SGT. Mercer, then moved on to the others, leaving Mercer alone a short distance from the ditch.

I walked over to see if there was anything I could do—I felt impotent and worthless just standing there. I called SGT. Moore and SGT. T to help me provide CPR. The medivac helicopter had yet to arrive, and it seemed obvious to me that we should continue to try to revive him until it landed. Moore and SGT. T began CPR while I checked for a pulse. Mercer was a tall, solidly-built man, whose large hand seemed enormous compared to my own, as I held it and waited anxiously for a sign of life. After a number of chest compressions and mouth-to-mouth resuscitation, nothing but grey mud came out of his mouth. For a moment I thought I felt a pulse, but it was just a reaction from the chest compressions. Though I still didn't know it, Mercer had died when the Bradley had flipped as he stood in the turret, thrusting him, head down, in mud to his chest. His legs kicked wildly as the crew attempted to dig him out. Eventually, they dragged him from the mud, but his legs had stopped kicking. A horrible way to die—upside down, disoriented, drowning in cold, wet blackness.

At last the medivac helicopter arrived. Looking up at the dark sky as it circled, I began to grow angry. *Land, damn you! Why don't you just land?*

A horrible way to die—upside down, disoriented, drowning in cold, wet blackness. SGT. Mercer's over turned Bradley. Southwest of Baghdad.

This man's dying—he needs your help, now! When the helicopter finally landed, the medic rushed out. With my flashlight on Mercer's face, he took one quick look, realized that Mercer was beyond saving, and went off to check for other casualties. When he returned a short time later, we placed Mercer's body on a stretcher, but when we lifted it to put him into the helicopter, his body slid right off into the dirt. We looked at each other in disbelief—could it truly be this hard to help someone in their last moments on earth? The whole set of circumstances—life and death in Iraq—suddenly struck me as being a string of mishaps. We lifted him once again and this time loaded him without incident into the helicopter, and they took off.

SGT. Chad Mercer was 25 years old, married, and had three children: Alanna (8), Amber (5), and Gavin (2). The day before his death, he'd been hurt slightly when a roadside bomb disabled his Bradley. He could have removed himself from the next night's mission, but he didn't. Second Lt. Nathan Childers, Mercer's platoon commander, remarked, "That's not the kind of soldier he was. It never would have occurred to him not to go." His death was more than an accident. It woke a lot of us up to the realities of the war. Not everyone would be going home alive. As the first soldier from the 48th Brigade to die in Iraq, SGT. Mercer will always be remembered and honored.

Once the helicopter carrying his body departed, my section continued to maintain security until morning, when a recovery crew could remove the Bradley from the ditch. After trying to recover weapons and night vision devices from the vehicle, most of us milled around with nothing else to do. I walked over to the ditch and made a closer examination of the vehicle. There I encountered the driver who had made the fateful mistake. He told me he was following the vehicle in front of him, but as it swerved to avoid the ditch, it turned up a cloud of dust—apparently enough to obscure his vision. When he saw the ditch, it was too late to react. The tracks showed how the Bradley in front of him had skimmed the edge of the ditch.

Although obviously in shock, the driver of Mercer's Bradley seemed relatively cognizant of everything that had taken place, but he was also detached, as if nothing serious had happened. I asked him how he'd gotten out of the Bradley after it rolled. Calmly, he pointed to the driver's hatch, half-submerged in mud; he'd been just barely able to crawl out. He appeared confused about events, yet he seemed to be in control of his emotions. But as I walked back to one of our humvees, I turned and watched the young man suddenly sit down on the ground and begin crying, his face in his hands. His crew consoled him. Our patrol kept its distance—we were outsiders. A short time later the entire crew of the Bradley got transported back to Camp Stryker, leaving us to pull security on the Bradley.

For weeks, I felt angry and upset over the incident, believing the medivac crew had taken their sweet time with the evacuation of SGT. Mercer.

But they hadn't. They'd done their job exactly as they were supposed to, and I'd let rage get the best of me. Months later, we were stationed in southern Iraq. Prompted by a medivac helicopter's taking nearly three hours to arrive for a soldier, I told the story of Mercer's death to a friend. A helicopter pilot who assisted wounded soldiers overheard our conversation and asked how long it had taken for the helicopter to arrive. I reiterated the time-line. He replied that he'd be fired if his helicopter was not off the ground within twenty minutes of being notified of an incident. The problem lay in radio communication. If it took two hours for the helicopter to arrive, most likely it had taken an hour and a half to get the grid coordinates from the accident or attack site up the chain of command to the base from which the medivac helicopters operated. I also learned that circling around the site before landing is standard operating procedure for helicopters because they need to test the area first to be sure they won't be blown out of the sky by a rocket or shot up by a barrage of AK47 rifle fire the minute they touch down. Despite having had the procedure explained to me, I held on to my anger. I had held Mercer's hand, waiting for help to arrive. I could not see the big picture.

* * * * *

When the sun rose, the farmers and general population began driving to their various destinations for the day. The recovery crew arrived and began attaching tow cables to pull the Bradley out of the ditch. At that moment a car drove up to our security checkpoint and came too close. I was still pissed off over Mercer's death. I thought things should've been handled quicker, that the helicopter should've arrived sooner and landed faster. At this point we were still recently deployed; I'd yet to fire my weapon. I walked toward the car with my hand in the air motioning for him to stop. I waited a couple of seconds, but the car inched closer. This was precisely what a suicide bomber might do: find a congregation of soldiers that he could drive into and detonate his explosive-packed trunk. I thought I might have to fire, but wondered if I'd be seen by the leadership above me as over-zealous. The car then inched ahead a little further. Suddenly feeling that it would relieve me of my anguish and anger over Mercer's death, I decided to fire. I discharged three rounds in the dirt to the left of the car to make it stop. PVT. Baker, standing guard next to me, fired off two rounds of his own as insurance. For a fleeting moment I believed firing at that car had placated my anger over Mercer. The violent gesture created an instant of relief. Behind me the Battalion Commander's PSD (personal security detail), who'd accompanied the Colonel outside Camp Stryker to view Mercer's Bradley, began cheering and shouting things like, "*Fuck*, yeah!"—"Shoot the fucker!"—"That's what I'm talking about!" My aggressive outburst was clearly well-received. Suddenly I was surrounded in approval. I felt exultant. However, none of these people had held Mercer's hand the night before, hoping for him to spit out enough mud so he'd breathe again, so he'd open his eyes and live—they were just excited to see a little action.

I looked at the Iraqi's face, his eyes wide with fear. He quickly put the car in reverse, backing away about two hundred feet, wheeling around, and driving off down a different road. This man was just a farmer trying to get to work, nothing more. My high began to recede. I returned back up the road with Baker toward the humvees and the rest of my section. My platoon sergeant, SFC. Janes, looked at PVT. Baker and asked, "Which of you fired first?" He clearly assumed Baker was more likely to have taken the aggressive action against the driver.

Baker shrugged at Janes. "It wasn't me. It was SGT. Kendel."

Janes looked a little taken aback. He didn't expect a "California liberal" to take such aggressive action. I felt pleased that I'd dispelled some preconceptions about me, but I felt hollow. I remembered a passage I'd just read in the Sakyong's book, *Turning the Mind into an Ally*, where he's in India trapped behind a truck, ground to a halt in traffic, frustrated and angry that the truck ahead of him isn't moving as the traffic grinds on for hours—and then finally the traffic opens up. As he passes the truck, he sees that truck driver, also stuck in traffic, was just trying to make a living. The pointlessness of his anger at this innocent guy going about his life hit home. Even though I had to fire on the man for genuine security reasons, the thrill of the gunfire dissolved into guilt. I'd directed all that anger and frustration at an innocent man. What if I'd hit him by mistake? I realized I'd succumbed to aggression easily and automatically, and I wasn't proud of it. Erroneously, I'd believed that I was a cut above others, that I wouldn't so easily slip into the pitfall of hatred. I thought I was more balanced and rational than that, but I wasn't. In my first email to Margot I wrote:

> Thank you for responding to my message...the Sakyong's book has certainly helped in dealing with some recent events. Meditation is difficult here; I live in a tent with 20 other soldiers and we have to walk with someone wherever we go. The only quiet time is in the shower or a hot sweltering porto' potty. Neither are terribly conducive to meditation practice. However, reading [the Sakyong's teachings] on contemplation has been very helpful. Riding around all day in a humvee waiting to get blown up provides one with unusual opportunities at contemplation, but it has been the issue of anger that has really made a difference. Most of the soldiers around me GROW ANGRIER AND ANGRIER AT THE IRAQIS EVERY DAY...

This particular day, however, was just beginning.

While the recovery people were removing the Bradley from the ditch, we got a call from the "Viper" element, instructing us to drive out and investigate two bodies they'd spotted lying in the middle of the road in a small village a few miles away. "Viper" was the codename for the Apache helicopters that flew daily missions around our sector to provide air support. It took some time finding our way to the site because it was out of our normal sector. The area consisted of fields and dirt roads, crisscrossed by irrigation ditches. Even with the modern Blue Force Tracker computer system installed in the humvee to aid in navigation, it was difficult finding our way at times because of the irregularities of the landscape. The Apache circling above guided us to a small village. We could see the bodies in the road ahead. We stopped our patrol a distance away because we didn't know if we were getting set up for an ambush, or if the bodies might be booby-trapped. After they were gunned down, some kind villager had come out of his home and placed a sheet over both bodies. We dismounted the humvee and walked toward them with caution.

We motioned over a young man standing nearby. He explained through our interpreter that the men had been carjacked, murdered, and their vehicle stolen. He made a point of saying that they weren't from the village but most likely from Baghdad.

We removed the sheets. The men were fat, clearly well fed. In fact, they had to be the fattest Iraqis in the whole country. Maybe that explained why they were shot full of holes from an AK-47 at a distance of about two feet. SGT. Moore named them *Chico* and *Esteban* because they looked like dead Colombian drug lords. Not a lot of blood for having been gunned down by an AK-47. Both Chico and Esteban had their eyes wide open, just staring blankly at us. The shells from the bullets lay scattered around them. Both wore the white ubiquitous *gallabya* that most men wore in Iraq. We just called them "man dresses" because the loose fitting outfit that went down to their feet looked like a woman's dress. After inspecting the bodies and taking pictures for evidence, we called the Iraqi police to come and recover the bodies. We would wait *three hours* with poor Chico and Esteban rotting in the hot sun. By this time, the presence of our patrol in the small village had drawn the interest of local villagers and a number of children. Eventually we were told the Iraqi police refused to come and collect the bodies because they considered the area "too dangerous." So much for investigating the crime scene. After all the spin-offs from C.S.I, *C.S.I. Baghdad* would make a great show, assuming you could get the Iraqi police to lift a finger.

We went through their pockets and found a wad of bloody dinars on Chico. None of us wanted the money, and we offered it to the young

Iraqi. His eyes got wide, and he shook his head, clearly viewing the cash as tainted with misfortune. SGT. Moore replaced it in Chico's pocket.

SGT. T was in charge of the patrol that day but refused to have the bodies in his humvee and left it to us to take care of them. By the time we began to put Chico and Esteban in body bags, rigor mortis had begun to set in. No longer just fat, they were stiff as hell. And old Chico wasn't just stiff from rigor mortis—he was stiff in another way. As most doctors and medics are aware, when a victim suffers a spinal injury, one place poor Chico had clearly taken a bullet, the victim will sometimes develop an *erection*. PVT. Scott Ross, the gunner on our humvee, came over to take a look at the bodies. "There's no way I'm riding in the gunner's seat near a dead Iraqi with a hard-on," he said, reaching down and flicking Chico's penis with his finger, making his last erection on earth quickly disappear.

As fabulously well-fed as Chico and Esteban were, it took four of us, struggling, to carry each body to my humvee. It was just our luck that out of all the skinny Iraqis in the country, we had to come across two that were in desperate need of an Atkins Diet. To help me get Chico into a body bag, Moore, Ross, and the Iraqi interpreter each took a limb and started to lift. As I pulled up on his right arm, blood shot out of a bullet hole, splattering my leg crimson. I dropped the arm, shouting, "Fuck!" Everyone laughed. Reaching down, I got the arm again, and we lifted him into the bag. We zipped it up, grabbed the bag handles, and lugged the stiff, rotting, enormous weight of Chico to the rear humvee door. Then we did the same for Esteban.

Transporting the body bags would be the least of our problems—it was getting them into the humvee that would prove the greatest challenge. After an extensive discussion of mechanics, we decided the only solution was to lay both bodies over the rear seats and the platform where the gunner stood, one piled on the other. The shear mass of Chico's body bag fit awkwardly through the door opening. Struggling to hoist it high, we got him in just far enough to drop his head down on the seat with a thump. We laughed, breathing hard. "It's OK," I said. "It's not like the guy's feeling any pain." We maneuvered him forward in six-inch jerks, thumping his head along until he was in halfway. Then the other guys reached from the opposite side and pulled him in the rest of the way. Esteban was worse because we had to get him up even higher to lie on top of his friend.

When the bodies were stacked and we were ready to leave, PVT. Ross, who had re-assumed his position as gunner, said, "Where the hell am I supposed to sit?" He could no longer sit down on the plastic cooler we removed to make room for Chico and Esteban. We told him to make do. Then he said, "Hell with it!" and sat down on top of them both, using their bodies as a makeshift gunner's seat. We didn't leave right away, and after a time Ross said desperately, "We have to get moving, these bodies are really starting to stink!" If only Chico and Esteban could have seen themselves being used as furniture for an American soldier.

We drove back to Route Tampa, the main supply road, and dumped the bodies in the dirt near an Iraqi checkpoint, leaving the Iraqi police to collect them after we said our goodbyes to poor Chico and Esteban. With any luck, they were already enjoying their 72 virgins in paradise. As we drove down the highway, we crossed under an overpass. Sitting in their newly purchased American pickup trucks provided by the American taxpayers, avoiding the sun with the A/C blowing, were the Iraqi cops who had refused to come out and collect the bodies.

Chapter Three

The More Force, the Greater the Compassion

Violence is the last refuge of the incompetent
—Issac Asimov

If our naiveté about the war began to crack with the death of SGT. Mercer, the hole would only grow larger with subsequent events.

After writing only a single email to Margot, I was shocked to receive a personal email of support and advice from Sakyong Mipham Rinpoche himself. The Sakyong's executive secretary made it clear that it was highly unusual for the Sakyong to write such a email, the first one he knew of in months. His advice would prove prophetic and instrumental in dealing with the emotional fallout from future events:

July 19, 2005
Shambhala Mountain Center

Dear Paul Kendel,

I received your letter this morning. Reading your moving and realistic portrait of how life is there makes me feel extremely glad my book has been of some use in a very trying situation. The Tibetan people have gone through persecution and tremendous hardship. It was their resolve not to abandon compassion and not to give into anger that ensured the survival of the Tibetan culture and people.

As you mention in your letter, the contemplation that sentient beings are innately endowed with goodness and wisdom is always important to remember again and again, regardless of stupid and cruel behavior—for if we let their actions trigger our anger, not only will they have stolen our mind, but our dignity as well.

Since the purpose of your being there is wrathful compassion, the more force you have to apply, the greater your compassion should be. Human beings through their actions bind themselves to seemingly intractable and convoluted situations. It's not brain power alone, but rather the weight of genuine compassion that will resolve this. I'm currently in our retreat center in the mountains of Colorado guiding people in meditation over the next month, with the result—hopefully—of having more compassionate and open-minded people on earth. I send my greetings, prayers and blessings to you and those around you.

Yours sincerely,

Sakyong Mipham

After such a brief correspondence with Margot, I was truly stunned to receive this email. Only now do I fully grasp how much of an *honor* it was to personally hear from the Sakyong. It would prove to be a truly fateful or, maybe I should say, *karma*-induced occurrence. During a phone conversation with Margot I told her how every time I went outside the wire I thought about the advice the Sakyong had given me in his email. I tried to use his profound and timely words as a guide, as a method of discernment in the hostile environment that is Iraq.

Soon after receiving the email we had our first encounter with the "enemy," something no one from my section had yet experienced. SGT. Mercer's death was a tragedy, but it had been an accident. The tomato farmer doesn't count, nor does an Iraqi coming too close to a checkpoint.

Chico and Esteban, sadly, proved a source of amusement. On this night however, an actual threat, even if invisible, became a sudden reality with a crack and a bright red flash.

Operation Scimitar was the name given to the operation involving the 48th Brigade and the Marines. The Marines' task was to root out insurgents to the south of our area of operations. The 48th Brigade was to operate in a support role, providing security and checkpoints to prevent all hostile elements from escaping. During the course of this operation, which would last over a week, my section had been sent out to get an injured member of 3rd Platoon ("Thugs") to medical treatment. A patrol from the TCP (traffic control point) left the perimeter shortly after eleven in the evening to set up at an intersection in order to stop traffic and personnel out after curfew. A car tried to run the roadblock, and they fired at it. A ricochet wounded SPC. Jeff Brand in the left arm, which was treated on the spot. The car barreled into a ditch and the drunk driver received treatment for gunshot wounds to both legs and right foot. A convoy was assembled to take Brand and the wounded Iraqi to the medical facility at Abu Ghraib prison.

My humvee was chosen to lead the convoy of four humvees to Abu Ghraib. On this night, I was acting as a dismount, sitting behind the driver, PVT. Gilley. PVT. Ross was the gunner. We had our Iraqi interpreter with us as well. Once organized, we drove away toward Abu Ghraib to get SPC. Brand there as quickly as possible. Like most sections, we drove at night wearing night vision devices instead of driving with white lights. We figured we stood a better chance of survival this way. If someone were to set off an IED, it would be harder for them to gauge our position with the lights off. In Iraq, the killing of American soldiers is not just about religion or removing an occupying power—it's also about money. According to reports, the destruction of a Bradley Fighting Vehicle netted about a thousand dollars and a humvee netted about five hundred from insurgent groups willing to pay—pretty good money for someone who probably makes less than twenty dollars a month. Planting an IED involves more than one man. The night before, or earlier in the day, one or more persons dig the hole and then conceal it. Someone else arrives later to plant the explosives. Sometimes there's a spotter, often a child who aids in the attack. The final person in the process is the man holding the detonation device. Someone can detonate an IED from a distance using anything from a cell phone to a garage door opener. The success of an IED ambush hinges on the timing. Missing the target by a few seconds can make the difference between life and death—or success and failure, depending on your point of view.

That night we drove to Abu Ghraib with white lights on because we were anxious to get SPC. Brand and the wounded Iraqi to the medical facility. To reach Abu Ghraib, we had to pass through a small town. We rushed into town and made an immediate left at an outdoor market with the usual mosque in the center. As we passed the mosque, neon lights on the building cast a green glow down the dark road in front of us. Past the mosque on the right was nothing but blackness. The road dropped off into a small field. Behind us the mosque's illumination receded into a kind of green mist, while straight ahead looked like a dark tunnel. I thought to myself, *This would be a perfect place for an ambush, but that won't happen*. I tried to dismiss the idea from my head. The lead vehicle is usually the one that does *not* get hit, we'd been told in all those briefings at Ft. Stewart.

Immediately, an explosion struck the humvee's right front, rocking the vehicle and shattering the windshield. A large piece of shrapnel tore through the engine block. I remember hearing a loud *crack!* and seeing a bright red flash of light. Hit with dust, rocks, and shrapnel, the gunner Ross (the same one who used Chico and Esteban as a gunner's seat) cried out. If he had been standing up higher in the gunner's hatch he might have had his head ripped off, but he suffered only a small laceration to his chin. Standing up in the hatch, Ross yelled, *"Fuck you, you motherfuckers!"* As we drove on out of the dust and debris from the explosion, SGT. Moore and I yelled at him to get down.

The vehicles behind us had been hit by two other IEDs, but they had not done any serious damage. Following the IED blasts, insurgents armed with AK47's fired upon our patrol. Our gunners returned fire. Behind us, SPC. Bourquin went crazy, firing dozens of rounds into the dark.

The insurgents' goal was to cripple our vehicle, creating an obstacle to the vehicles behind us. Once we were all jammed up and unable to move, they'd be able to open up with RPGs (rocket propelled grenades). If that had happened, we'd have been sitting ducks in the middle of this dark, narrow road.

With the power steering failing, and our vehicle slowly dying, we made our way out of the kill zone. SGT. Moore ordered driver Gilley to turn off the paved road onto a dirt path that led through a field to Route Tampa, the main highway. I took a small flashlight out of my pocket to determine the extent of Ross's wound. Blood covered his chin and his vest.

Wanting to reassure him, I said to Ross, "You're okay, there's just a little chunk missing, you'll be fine."

I should have said it was just a nick, because Ross became even more outraged, believing a large piece of his face was gone.

Gritting his teeth and using all his strength, Gilley managed to wrench the wheel and get us out of the farm field and onto Route Tampa. Another humvee quickly pulled ahead of us and stopped. As we sat in the middle of the road, the engine completely dead, I saw SGT. T run toward us with a tow cable that would take us a mile down the road into Abu Ghraib prison and safety.

While Ross was getting his chin stitched, Moore and I went back outside to get some fresh air, needing to decompress from nearly dying in an ambush. Out in the darkness, we found a place to lay down in the dirt and tried to relax, talking about what happened. Suddenly the bright lights of a humvee swept over us. It slammed on its brakes, send-

THE MORE FORCE, THE GREATER THE COMPASSION

ing up a cloud of dust, and stopped a couple feet away from us. Startled, we looked up as the driver jumped out, snapping at us but also laughing, "Hey you guys, get out of the way! This is not a place to lay down and rest! You're going to get run over!"

Moore and I looked at each other in semi-disbelief. Having survived a furious insurgent attack, an hour later we willingly placed ourselves right in the path of death in a parking lot.

After a couple hours, Ross' chin was stitched up, and we rejoined our section, setting up an OP not far from the "Lion's Den," where the Iraqi army was based. The place was surrounded by concertina wire and large dirt-filled containers erected by our engineers to protect the compound. We were anxious to get back to search for the insurgents who'd attacked us.

PVT. Ross was particularly fired up to get some payback. "That's what we need to do! We need to roll back in there and find those who knew what the hell was going on!"

"The lights were on at that mosque when we drove by," I replied. "You know there were people inside at the time with a perfect view straight down the road. They knew exactly what was going to happen."

"Hell, yeah!" Ross continued. "Let's cordon off that mosque and go back in there. I bet they've got an arms cache."

It was morning when we rode back into the center of town and blocked off the four roads into the hub, setting up near the mosque across from the market. The people there seemed shocked by our sudden appearance with weapons drawn, ready for a fight. Glaring at us, irritated by our presence, they knew what had happened the night before and we knew it. We interviewed some bystanders, and then went to the mosque where the imam and a couple of other men stood at the gate, not wanting us to enter. Everyone said the same thing: "No, we have no idea what happened."

Lies! How could anyone have driven trucks down the road in the middle of town, dug three huge holes, and planted explosives without somebody having witnessed it?

After a fruitless effort to uncover facts, we reorganized our patrol and drove down the road where we were ambushed, looking for the holes where the bombs exploded. We found them next to a cucumber field. A farmer was out there, hoeing the soil in order to better irrigate his crop. We called him over.

"Is this your field?" we asked through our Iraqi interpreter.

"Yes, it's my field."

"Do you know who was responsible for attacking the Americans last night?"

"No, I don't know anything about it."

He was obviously lying. We debated detaining him and taking him to Camp Stryker, but because we were supporting the Marines, we didn't have the manpower to drive all the way back. We made a token effort to search the buildings across the street from where we were attacked, but no one we talked to knew a thing.

An hour later, after setting up another OP, we discussed what had happened in the town.

Clearly angry, Ross said, "What the hell was that? We roll all the way back in there for nothing! To ask a few questions and that's it? Why didn't we detain anybody or break down some doors? We didn't do a damn thing! All those bastards were lying!"

Like Ross, I thought we'd roll back into town with force, making more of an effort to find those responsible. "Setting up in the center of town like that, just asking a few questions, expecting the obvious lies, what the hell did we hope to accomplish? All we did was send the signal that it's OK to ambush Americans and simply deny it the next day. It encourages them."

"You saw the looks on their faces! Every one of those bastards standing around wanted to cut our balls off!" Ross complained.

"We should've detained every one of 'em, every man, woman, and child. Maybe then we could've gotten some answers," said Moore.

"If you detain the whole lot of them, all the women and children,

THE MORE FORCE, THE GREATER THE COMPASSION

you're only going to alienate the whole populace further," I pointed out.

"True, but screw 'em!" Hatred grew in Ross' voice. "They all want to kill us anyway!"

"I'm going home in one piece! I'm not that concerned what happens to a fucking Hajji!" said Moore.

Later I wrote Margot about the incident:

> ...Of course I would like to have caught the individuals responsible, but I didn't feel any hate or desire for revenge. What happened was just something that is part of the horrible nature of where we are. It was odd though, when I think about the incident. Some individual who doesn't even know me had so much hate and pain inside him that he sat in the dark and TRIED TO KILL ME. I never did anything to this person or persons, and yet he wanted to leave my two young sons without a father. It's just so strange when I think about it. So much hate. So much anger. Fortunately, the incident didn't end tragically, but it did make me realize how important it is, just like the Sakyong said in his letter, to maintain your dignity and not let anger destroy you. Because if I do, if I let this place and the hate that is all around me, fill me with aggression and anger, I will only become like the men who wait in the darkness in the hope of inflicting death upon another human being. It's all nothing but a vicious cycle. Ignorance and hate drive some men to kill us, and we perpetuate the problem by seeking the same in return.

Margot wrote to me:

> Dear Paul,
>
> My experience with the dharma, with the way of life cultivated through the practice of Buddhism, has permeated every aspect of my life and every pore of my being. There have been good times and bad times—really bad times!—but I'm relieved to say, nothing that matches the intensity of your present experience. I have heard stories from prisoners that are close, or maybe equal in a different way, but you have an ability to describe the world

you presently inhabit in a way that really communicates the horror. I really have to say that I am very impressed with your ability to hold on to some clarity of mind in the midst of this…You have articulated some temptation to shut down, but the clarity of your mind won't allow you to do so—you seem to be able to flirt with shutting down your sensibilities, but you just can't accomplish it because you don't have the disposition to ignore the reality and subtleties of the situation. I admire you immensely for this ability and encourage you in the bravery you possess to hold your mind in a deluge of emotions. Please accept this as a view from the other side of the world—you are demonstrating a great deal of sanity.

I appreciated Margot's words, and I was certainly trying to live up to them, but sometimes extreme situations make one forget one's humanity—an abnormal predicament where traditional morals and judgments, the kinds of things taught in most churches across the nation on any given Sunday, are quickly abandoned—a state in which one resorts to the most primal urges, such as the desire for revenge—a nightmare where the true horrors of war and of death suddenly became something that guy who yelled out "Kick some ass!" before we left for Iraq could never have imagined.

Chapter Four

Bombs and Obituaries

Our enemy is our greatest teacher.
—The Dalai Lama

As trying as my life in Iraq was at times, my experiences may have helped others in some small way. According to his executive secretary, the Sakyong read one of my letters to his audience during a summer retreat at the Shambhala Mountain Center in Colorado, and a couple of them were reproduced in Shambhala community publications.

A few days later, I wrote to Margot:

> Thank you for responding to my letter so soon. Once again I am shocked that the Sakyong has taken an interest in me and my situation. I know he is an extremely busy man. I feel quite privileged to have had him read my letter to his meditation members. I consider it a real honor. Just when I was beginning to think that my time here has been nothing but a horrible waste, to find out that my personal experiences and those of my friends

around me, as terrible as some of them have been, may help make a difference in maybe just one person's life, makes my existence here not seem like it is all in vain.

For a brief moment I felt a sense of accomplishment for what I and my companions were doing in Iraq. As some members of the meditation retreat listened to the email about SGT. Mercer's death, they wept. Their response to the violence in Iraq demonstrated for me a much larger vision of his violent death. I not only saw the rage and rawness of Mercer's death in myself, but also its connection to the world—that something so horrible could result in compassion and sadness for humanity itself.

On the evening of July 26th, 2005, before the sun had set, my section had walked over an area once used by the Iraqi military under Saddam as a fighting position for their tanks and other equipment. Scattered around the field we found the remains of Iraqi army uniforms, helmets, parts of gas masks, and a number of unexploded rockets. To combat boredom, we used some of these discarded items for target practice. As per SOP (standard operating procedure), we'd called for EOD (explosive ordinance division), waiting for them to come out to inspect the field and either remove the most dangerous items or blow them up in place. We'd been waiting about six hours standing around the humvee—bored and bull-shitting amongst ourselves—when another section from our platoon arrived to replace us. They looked stunned. CPL. Derek Mack spoke first: "We lost Fuller, Kinlow, Brunson, and Thomas."

We were all confused. One soldier in my section said, "What do you mean 'lost'?" He must have thought they were simply missing somehow, maybe captured.

Mack said flatly, "They're KIA. They're dead."

"Dead?" I said. "How could that be? We haven't heard anything about it."

With a three vehicle patrol, they'd just come off Route Aeros and passed through a TCP (traffic control point)—which usually meant a secure area—ten minutes from the base and safety. The first two vehicles got through, but not the third. It was a FIVE HUNDRED POUND BOMB. Meant more for a tank, it left a hole almost seventeen feet deep. The blast easily tore through the vehicle's relatively soft underbelly and literally blew the humvee apart, blowing open its heavy armored doors. The bulk of the humvee lay in ruins, smoldering and charred. Fuller, Brunson, and Thomas died instantly. Only the driver, Kinlow, was still alive following the blast. He still had his limbs, but the blast's intensity had pulverized his body to a jelly-like state. He succumbed to his injuries before a medic could arrive. SGT. Rousseau led the patrol that night. When the explosion went off, he heard a loud "thump." The "thump" he heard was a friend's severed head, helmet intact, bouncing off their humvee. The human remains still inside, it lay next to the tire. Rousseau and the other surviving members of the patrol fired their weapons into the dark in an attempt to kill whoever had detonated the bomb. Rousseau lobbed grenade after grenade from his weapon, but to no avail—the trigger man was gone.

It was a FIVE HUNDRED POUND BOMB. Leaving the shattered remains of the humvee which belonged to Fuller, Kinlow, Brunson and Thomas.

The death of SGT. Mercer had been a horrible tragedy, one that had opened a few eyes as to the reality of where we were, but SGT. Mercer was not from our unit and none of us had known him personally. Although his death was the first from the 48ᵗʰ Brigade, it was an accident that could have happened anywhere. These friends from my own company were the first soldiers from the 48ᵗʰ Brigade to die in combat since WWII.

SSG. Carl Fuller, an African-American, was the senior member of the patrol. He was forty-four years old but looked ten years younger. Fuller's body was identified by the remains of his chest. His arms and legs had been blown away, his bullet proof vest had shielded his chest from the explosion and his vest was blown open revealing the remains of his uniform with Airborne badge and Combat Infantry Men's badge with a star. A portion of his head remained intact. SGT. Fuller had served in the first Gulf War in 1991, as well as the initial invasion of Iraq in 2003 while serving in the National Guard; he'd volunteered to return this time. I didn't know him well, but he seemed very quiet and reserved. According to the men under him, he was a good leader.

During the training at Ft. Stewart, I went through a class on the Army's new navigation system for the humvee, known as Blue Force Tracking System. The course involved working with a computer system, not exactly my forte. Both Fuller and I struggled throughout the course. When it finished, some of us, including Fuller, snuck away from the base, called a cab, and went to a *Hooters* near Savannah. When we got to the restaurant, we all changed out of our uniforms. When Fuller came out of the restroom he was in a nice pair of dress pants and a polo shirt, while the rest of us had on nothing but shorts and t-shirts. Fuller had class; I'll never forget him.

SGT. James O. Kinlow, an African-American, was the humvee's driver. Kinlow had spent eighteen years in the Georgia National Guard and married his high school sweetheart, Daphanie, with whom he had two daughters, Chelsea, age ten, and Chauncey, age fifteen. Before our deployment and our train up at Ft. Stewart, he tore off sheets of notebook paper and wrote out a summary of his life, as well as his own obituary as a beginning, complete with blanks for the newspapers to fill in. "Mr. James O. Kinlow, 35, of Holt St. Died ___ in Iraq." Seven months later the missing date would be added. Before his departure for Iraq, he told his wife, "If two men in military uniforms ever come looking for you, I'm gone. I'm dead." According to her, "It was almost as if he knew he would die." He served in Iraq for only six weeks, during which he kept a diary. His final entry, the day before he was killed was elated. "Got my leave!" He was scheduled to come home on leave from Iraq at the end of August with me.

On the night he died, SGT. John Thomas, thirty-three, was acting as a dismount, sitting in the back of the humvee. Before we departed from the armory in Valdosta for the train up at Ft. Stewart, Thomas had introduced me to his eighty-three year old grandfather, an Air Force retiree who'd grown up in an orphanage. He'd buried his own son years earlier and would have to suffer the pain of burying his beloved grandson as well. After being informed by the military that they were the beneficiaries of their grandson's death benefits, Thomas' grandfather said, "I'd give everything if I could get my grandson back. He was like a son to us." Thomas had served in the Marines years earlier. He was always respectful toward rank, even for someone like myself who didn't take it that seriously. When he spoke to me, still a Specialist, he always referred to me by my rank and would usually stand at parade rest with his hands behind his back. While at Ft. Irwin, California, a month before leaving for Kuwait, I sat with him for a few hours late at night. He told me about his wife and their marital problems and about the time he spent in the Marines. I got the impression that Thomas was at heart a very gentle person who would prefer not to harm someone if he could help it, someone who would do whatever he could for a friend. Thomas was promoted posthumously, as were the others.

Herodotus, the ancient Greek historian who had witnessed the effects of war, said, "In peace, sons bury their fathers; in war, fathers bury their sons." SPC. Jacques "Gus" Brunson, thirty, was acting as a gunner on the humvee. He would be buried by his father. A devoted father himself with two young children, "it really pained him to leave them" when he deployed to Iraq, according to friends. He had a reputation as a dependable and caring friend. I was told later by Ronnie Shelley, who would himself die less than a week later, that SPC. Brunson's father was so distraught over the loss of his son that he refused to believe he was dead. When the casket arrived back in the United States, he insisted on having it opened to confirm that the body was in fact that of his son. He was informed that the body was unidentifiable; the explosion had been so massive it was impossible at the time to know what body parts belonged to whom.

The following day was a somber one. In 2nd Platoon's AO (area of operations—where our tents were located), the mood was a mix of anger and frustration directed at an unseen enemy. Alpha Company, mourning the loss of our soldiers, wondered aloud why the leadership of the 48th Brigade didn't approve an in-depth, methodical operation focused on clearing every house and field and checking the identity and intent of every male between fifteen and sixty-five in order to cleanse the area of any hostile elements. Our patrols continued—business as usual—as if nothing traumatic had occurred. This inaction or apathy on the part of the 48th Brigade staff would prove to be catastrophic.

Nearly everyone who could make it from our company attended their memorial service. We sat on long metal bleachers under a setting sun and listened to the rifle salute and the playing of taps. The "lost man" ceremony was conducted, where a chair is left empty for each soldier killed. His name is called out twice and then the speaker moves on to the next "lost" soldier. Tears welled up in the eyes of many sitting for the ceremony, especially those who had known the men personally. I fought back my own tears. We all left hoping that something like this would never happen again. Maybe the incident was just an unlucky occurrence—we were wrong.

Following the deaths of Fuller, Kinlow, Thomas, and Brunson, going outside the wire, especially at night, became a very different experience. Every dirt mound and trash pile on the side of the road could be hiding a bomb; every freshly covered hole in the road could be concealing a newly buried artillery round wired to explode. During one patrol I realized that I'd forgotten a small beaded leather bracelet my eldest son Alex had sent to me. I'd carried it for over a month when going outside the wire, hoping it would bring me luck and keep me safe, and it had. That whole night I actually believed I might die due to the fact I'd forgotten the bracelet. I survived of course, but I never forgot the bracelet again.

Our section would convene for an hour or two in the middle of various palm groves in our sector to seek shade and a little rest from the threat of hidden bombs. During these periods of relative tranquility, I had an opportunity to reflect on recent events and often read *Awakening Loving Kindness* by Pema Chödrön, not your typical combat zone reading. I thought about the deaths of our friends and the amorphous figures responsible for them. Who were they? Had we just passed them on the road? What about that man tending his field—did he have a night job digging holes for an IED? There was no way to tell. And why did they want to kill us? How could another human being be so hateful that he was willing to take another life? What were his motivations, his dreams? What about his religion? How did these men justify their actions when they claimed to be religious? I had studied Islam, and as many moderate Muslims claim, Islam is a peaceful religion for the most part. In the Bible you can find passages where Jesus speaks of turning the other cheek, and by the same token you have passages where he says he is not here to bring peace, but the sword. In America most people claim to be Christian, but often many of these professed Christians can be aggressive and judgmental toward those who do not share their beliefs. These kinds of questions entered my head as I began reading from *Awakening Loving Kindness*.

By the way that we think and by the way that we believe in things, in that way is our world created. In the Middle Ages, everyone accepted the idea, based on fear, that there was only one way to believe; if you didn't believe that way, you were the enemy. It was death to all forms of creative, fresh thinking.... When a belief system is threatened, people may even become so fanatical that they kill and destroy...people find it quite easy to have beliefs and to hold on to them and to let their whole world become a product of their belief system. They also find it quite easy to attack those who disagree. The harder, the more courageous thing, which the hero and the heroine, the warrior, and the mystic do, is continually to look one's belief's straight in the face, honestly and clearly, and then step beyond them.

Her words did not help identify an insurgent or change the nature of the world I was in, but they certainly explained the dangers of adhering to a rigid belief system, both for the Islamic terrorists and insurgents, and for the American soldiers reacting to them. The courageous, the truly heroic thing is to look beyond those beliefs we erect in order to hide our fear and try to see the real human beings on the other side.

* * * * *

On the evening of July 30th, our patrol had just departed Camp Stryker and set up an OP a short distance from Route Aeros and Route Tampa, the main supply road. I hardly ever suffer an upset stomach, but on this day, before going out on patrol, I felt nauseous. Having eaten nothing out of the ordinary, I told myself I was probably just being superstitious. After sitting in our humvees shooting the shit for about an hour, we heard a loud explosion. In Iraq, "boom" sounds are not exactly uncommon. Following the explosion, we heard automatic weapons fire; it sounded like a fire fight, but after a few minutes there was nothing but silence. Once again, radio communication didn't give away what had happened. We heard some chatter about a humvee being hit, but that wasn't unusual. And then a call came from our TOC, ordering us to move a short distance from our position to block all access to Route Red Sox, a road we used regularly to re-enter Camp Stryker. Still unaware of what was going on, we moved to our new position; minutes later a patrol of humvees raced past us. Sitting there blocking the road, bored, listening to the radio with no updates, we assumed it was nothing serious.

However, after we finished pulling security in the area off Route Red Sox and got back to Camp Stryker, we heard the news. SSG. Howard poked his head into my and SGT. Moore's accommodations while we were beginning to relax, and said matter of factly, "We lost Anderson, Jones, Shelley, and Haggin." That was it.

"You've got to be kidding me!" I yelled as I swung around to face him. One look told me he was serious. We'd lost another four. If our naiveté wasn't destroyed with the deaths of the first four, it was now. How the hell could we lose eight men in less than a week? We were just the National Guard, for Christ sake. This shit was only supposed to happen to the real soldiers, those on active duty. Times had changed; forget floods and hurricanes—we were now expected to die just like anyone else.

Like the previous explosion, the men were returning to Camp Striker after a routine patrol. Driving down the paved road pock-marked with IED's, the first two humvees had crossed an irrigation canal with high reeds surrounding it, allowing excellent cover for a bomber to sit and wait with clicker in hand, just hoping an American patrol would drive past. The first two vehicles passed through without incident, but the third wasn't so lucky. Explosives had been placed inside the culvert, just a few feet below the passing vehicles, and were detonated just as the last one reached the canal. Unlike the earlier attack, the humvee was literally torn apart, the intensity of blast hurling the front axel and tires over fifty feet from the rear tires. The heavy armored doors were cast aside the way a child would discard a used toy, leaving only twisted metal and charred human remains. The "bomber" slipped away into the night, an amorphous figure who quickly returned to his normal life. He could have been a doctor or even a teacher. He was probably under ordinary circumstances a decent and caring person. I had to wonder what drove him to sit among the reeds of an irrigation canal, knee deep in water, while his family slept—maybe a brand new baby in a cradle waiting for its father's love—to plot the deaths of fellow human beings. The answer can't be a simple one; but for me and others, it *was* simple: he was the enemy and needed to die for us to live. Unfortunately, on this night, it was us not him.

Little evidence left of humvee belonging to Anderson, Jones, Shelley and Haggin.
—Photo by Scott Courdin.

Following the explosion, the remaining vehicles moved away from the shattered humvee and established security down the road. Afraid of a secondary IED if they tried to get back to the other side of the ditch, they radioed for EOD who had to wait until sunrise to finish clearing the blast site of any further potential explosives. Once the site was deemed safe, SPC. Courdin and SPC. Royal, friends and fellow members of my platoon, were ordered to drive around the shattered vehicle and across the irrigation ditch to the far side in order to secure the road there. Steering around a human torso that lay in the middle of the road and through other smaller body parts, SPC. Courdin made his way safely to the other side of the blast site. He later remarked about the pungent smell of burning fuel and human flesh that hovered in the air.

A formal investigation would ensue, but more important was recovering the remains of the dead. The massive blast had deposited body parts, large and small, all over the area surrounding the smoldering humvee. The results of the "firefight" we thought we'd heard a short time earlier lay all around; now came the painful job of recovering the dead. Once the complete area had been secured, the surviving soldiers of the patrol, as well as other members who arrived to provide security, began the process of retrieving what remained of their friends. They found most of the body parts throughout the fields surrounding the canal. A fully intact pair of pants was fished out of the water. The body seemed to have vaporized into thin air without leaving so much as a blood stain on the pants. They discovered a lone combat boot, laces severed from top to toe—a perfect, clean slice as though cut open with a razor. No blood splattered the boot, like the foot in it simply vanished. Photos of the scene mirrored the previous explosion. Anderson's severed head, helmet intact, sat upright on the side of the road; they found his legs a short distance away. SPC. Courdin's most poignant memory of that day was watching a fellow soldier casually walking by, carrying a severed hand. The hand looked like it had been removed by a doctor, sliced cleanly off with a surgical instrument, no blood or tendons visible, like a wax hand. He spent his time walking around the area, pulling security, and identifying remains, mostly just small pieces of flesh. Of Jones and Haggin, they could locate nothing recognizable. Shelley was identified by a wedding ring on the severed hand—he was the only one who wore one.

With dawn they noticed the dogs. A pack of mongrels attempting to run off with pieces of our dead friends forced Bopp, Royal, and others to fire at them. Not a pleasant task, but they did their job, collecting all the human remnants that could be found, placing the larger pieces in body bags and smaller ones in trash bags. Meanwhile a team went with Lt. Donaldson and SPC. Courdin to search a nearby house, looking for the bomber. Clearly the occupant—possibly an Iraqi policeman whose unit patch and a magazine from an Iraqi police issued Glock pistol they found—had fled hastily after the explosion. Left on a bed, undoubtedly a meal for the family dog, they discovered the remains of a human spinal column, nearly licked clean of flesh. Enraged over their discovery, Courdin, Bopp, and others lashed out in anger by ransacking the building, smashing dishes, breaking furniture, smashing windows with rifle butts, and urinating on the beds.

The patrol was led by SFC. Victor Anderson, thirty-nine, married, and a father of two: Tyler, age nine, and Jessica, age fourteen. In January 2005, when the Brigade mobilized, the Guard told him he couldn't join his men because of his diabetes. Undeterred, he exercised, dieted, and lost weight. He would join the Brigade and Alpha Company in time to deploy to Kuwait in May 2005. SFC. Anderson had an interest in history, and when he learned that I had an M.A. in the field, he came to my tent one evening in Kuwait, a week before flying to Baghdad. We spoke for a while about our interest in history, and I told him I'd taught American history at a Florida college. He gave me a book called *The Last King*, about the famous Mithradades, one of the most feared enemies of the Roman Empire. The night before he died, Anderson gave away a number of personal possessions to surprised members of his platoon, including his TV, his DVD player, and his radio, as if he knew he wouldn't be needing them.

SSG. David R. Jones, forty-five, was married and a father of two children. He loved history as well, especially military history. During his memorial service, the Rev. Mike Klaus said SSG. Jones could talk about every ship and every battle in every war going back to biblical times. He was a master of facts and trivia. After learning of the deaths of Fuller, Kinlow, Thomas and Brunson, Jones had said he found it really hard to go back out on patrol.

"But they went," his wife said later. "That's what courage is, when you know what can happen and you go anyway."

SGT. Ronnie Shelley, thirty-four, had wanted desperately to be promoted to SGT. He deserved it, having spent eight years in the Marine corps and serving in the first Gulf War in 1991. Unfortunately, getting promoted in the National Guard often depends on who you know. Shelley would get his promotion, but it came at a horrible price. He left behind a wife and three children, ages thirteen, eight, and four. Like SFC. Anderson, he could have avoided going to Iraq, but he was determined to serve. In order to be eligible to deploy, Shelley had all his rotting upper teeth removed, replaced with dentures. The night he died he volunteered to take the place of another soldier who was suffering from a stomach ailment.

At the time of his death, SGT. Jonathon Haggin, twenty-six, had reconciled with his ex-wife, who was pregnant. The couple married young. She was seventeen; he was twenty-two. They had a two-year-old child. On the morning of July 30, 2005, his wife went into the emergency room, complaining of pain and bleeding. She feared she might lose the baby. The doctors told her she was fine. The next morning a pair of U.S. Army officers arrived at her door and informed her of her husband's death. Haggin had learned of his wife's pregnancy while in Germany, recuperating from wounds suffered in an IED attack a few weeks earlier. He persuaded the doctors to let him return to Iraq even though he wasn't fully healed. He would die on his first mission back. After the 48th Brigade returned from Iraq, Haggin's wife, Anna, wondered how to tell her two-year-old about her father. During an evening dinner with family and friends, oblivious to her father's death, the little girl told them proudly, "My daddy's in Iraq."

We had certainly suffered the pain and loss of friends to the enemy, and for many, their hatred and bitterness would grow. After this, the need to blame others—such as those who decided to drive that night with white lights on instead of using night vision, which was the norm—would play an important role. Brig. General Rodeheaver, commanding the 48th Brigade took a lot of heat over the incidents and dodged responsibility by claiming that both 500 pound bombs had been buried *before* the invasion of Iraq. There was really no point in blaming others for the unfortunate deaths. It could have happened to any of us. Anger and resentment would not bring our friends back. You have to let go because if you don't, you will exist in a cage of perpetual anguish and pain. Yes, we'd suffered a great loss, but if we gave in to hate and anger, we'd become no better than the shapeless figures that waited in the darkness to kill us.

The loss of the eight soldiers from our company hit everyone hard. We tried to write off the first four deaths as simply a fluke. The bad guys had gotten lucky. But with the second explosion, it appeared that they could kill us whenever they wanted. I slipped into a feeling of dark resignation. If eight could die in a week, what about next week? A sense of imminent death enveloped us.

The killings had the greatest impact within the 2nd Platoon itself. PVT. Mann, nineteen, a close friend of Haggin, had been on the same patrol when Haggin died. Upon returning to his tent, he overturned his cot and grabbed books and equipment, flinging them away, lashing out with anything at hand in his anger. When the chaplain tried to console him, Mann launched into a tirade: "Fuck that! We need to try and find these fuckers now and kill them all!" He wanted to charge back outside the wire right then and there.

Another close friend of Haggin, fellow marine SGT. David Grimes, also lost it when he heard about Haggin's death. Like PVT. Mann, he tore up his tent, trashing everything in sight, and charged outside, bellowing for revenge. His friends, seeing him incoherent with rage, grouped around him and wrestled him to the ground, pinning him down until his wits returned.

I thought about what Sakyong Mipham had written to me: *"For if we let their actions trigger our anger, not only will they have stolen our mind, but our dignity as well."*

Grimes' and Mann's reactions highlighted how easily we can succumb to fury and resentment and lose control of our mental faculties. I could understand their anger, but their breakdowns showed how it was a trap, a black hole I or anyone else could easily slide down. The Shambhala meditation teachings I'd been learning, called "the Tiger's path of discernment," reminded me to watch my step. They emphasized not giving in to emotional impulse, but seeing clearly what was going on both inside and outside of yourself so you could recognize the best way to act—like a tiger moving through the jungle with strength and sensitivity. When I arrived, I'd thought I could somehow stay above these harsh feelings, but I immediately realized that my mental situation was far more fragile, that I could collapse just like they had. Once you begin down that dark path of frustrated hatred, as many war vets have experienced, it's hard to pull yourself back and regain your dignity and self-control.

For many of the soldiers, the deaths led to seeing the Iraqis as the ultimate threat—the ultimate enemy. There was absolutely no desire to understand the bigger picture. Their minds shut down, preventing any chance of seeing more deeply. War, I learned, creates a narrow, tunnel-like vision of our existence. Haggin had learned of the first four deaths while recuperating in Germany, which probably motivated him to return to Iraq rather than remain in the hospital. He came back unexpectedly and soon after departed for his first, and last, patrol, Grimes said to him, "If you see one, and you have a chance, you take the shot." Haggin couldn't wait to get back out on patrol and make those who had killed our friends pay for it. The problem of course was finding them, whoever "they" were. Haggin never found an opportunity to "take the shot" to avenge our friend's deaths. Instead, death found him.

August 7, 2005

Dear Margot,
    Dealing with anger is certainly the most important issue confronting myself and my companions. I lost another four friends a few days ago to another massive explosion. That's eight dead in six days. I'm sorry if these letters are so depressing, but it is nice to have someone to talk to. In your letter you mentioned doorways to perception that can be opened during wrathful situations. As ugly as this place is, I have been able to gain a unique perspective on human nature that I might never have experienced in any other situation.

The second memorial service in less than a week was definitely surreal. *Weren't we just here?* I thought. It was real alright—four sets of boots and rifles topped by helmets represented our lost friends. Well, not exactly *real.* The boots and the rifles had been borrowed. They weren't the real ones; those had been obliterated. For some reason the second memorial service seemed less emotional. I think most of us were in a state of shock. The first four deaths were clearly not a fluke, like the bad guys had our number. And the big question loomed: *Who's next?* We'd only been in Iraq for two months—*eight dead from one company in six days? What the hell did we have to look forward to for the next ten months?*

    When I called my wife to tell her about the loss of another four friends, I received bad news from the home front. Before I could even begin to talk about their deaths, she informed me that she'd suffered a miscarriage. She was obviously distraught, and I decided not to tell her about the deaths. I'd been unaware of the pregnancy and tried to be as kind as I could to her, but unfortunately, from 10,000 miles away there was little I could do. I told her how sorry I felt, and even said that if she wanted another baby, we could try again when I returned home. Clearly death was the norm, and my life at home did not seem to be immune either.

CHAPTER FIVE

THERE WAS DANGER...

An eye for an eye makes us all blind.
—Mahatma Gandhi

Iraq always carried the imminent threat of death, but the real danger to us would be the long-term consequences. Our experiences would affect us for the rest of our lives. Most of us will live another forty years, but the war issues we faced were not about *time*, not about the future, they were about living in the now. Many Vietnam War veterans continue to suffer bitterness and hate. As tragic as those experiences were, many vets made the mistake of allowing them to destroy the remainder of their lives.

Margot wrote to me:

> ...It seems to me, as a life-long student of the human mind, that wars must feel like one has been transported to another planet inhabited by strange, ferocious beings. My cousin, who I mentioned to you as a "walking-wounded" Vietnam vet (and who

drank himself to death by age 45) was my best friend in my young childhood. He was absolutely as close as a close brother and he was a very sweet, gentle person, loving—and loved by his family. He didn't grow up with a particularly penetrating and curious mind, so he was easily, hmmm, trained and indoctrinated by the army when he was drafted. When he found himself in Vietnam, he took part in atrocities (he never confessed it openly to me, but somehow managed to communicate his participation in killing children—). It wasn't who he was, but I suppose somehow according to maturity or karmic predisposition, one can melt into the environment and go along with it while others, karmically, like yourself, are able to maintain human sensibilities...

Margot had a unique ability to send me reading material that fit the unusual nature of my situation, helping to provide comfort and answers during difficult times. One such book, *Good Life, Good Death* by Gehlek Rinpoch, tells the story of a Tibetan monk released from a Chinese prison in the 1980's after a harsh life where he was likely tortured. When asked by His Holiness the Dalai Lama what was the greatest threat he'd encountered in prison, he said simply, *"There was danger..."* The monk wasn't referring to the *physical* danger, but the danger that he might have succumbed to *hate and anger*. I found this story especially relevant to my situation in Iraq. After the deaths of our fellow soldiers, my life became a daily practice of working with the issues of hatred and anger. All this death made the Buddhist teachings on impermanence especially vivid. And I found that one of the best ways to overcome negative emotion was to appreciate the environment I was in.

I wrote Margot:

> I regularly have to walk up to cars when we set up roadblocks and I always wonder if the car is about to explode. The other night, around one in the morning, an hour past curfew, a car pulled up to our checkpoint and stopped, but made a move to keep moving forward. That's always a bad sign. My friend fired a bullet in front

of the car to make it stop, which it promptly did. But sometimes when cars make a sudden move, we just shoot the driver.

On a lighter note, your last letter nearly got me killed.

While I was at the computer trailer, a mortar round landed nearby while I was reading your letter. Needless to say, they closed down the computers and I wasn't able to respond to your letter. Don't worry, I don't blame you, I was going to the computers to check the news as well. But the timing was a little amusing.

That's the other important thing I've learned from the readings, as well as my time here: RESPECTING THE NATURE OF IMPERMANENCE. When you're woken up nearly every morning by the sound of mortars and rockets impacting nearby, you learn to value just being alive. I've gotten so used to it that I usually just roll over and go back to sleep. If it lands on our tent and kills me, well, that's just the impermanence of life here. There's no need to worry or stress out about it. If it happens, it happens. But I have certainly grown to truly appreciate the love of my wife and children. They are all that matters. So I have gained something from this place, even if it's come at a cost. There is much beauty here, I see it almost everyday. When the sun sets it is a magnificent sight; a bright orange ball spreading itself out behind lush green palm groves. People think its all desert here, but it's not; it's the cradle of civilization, and it is remarkable. I just wish my fellow soldiers would take a moment to look past the ugliness and hate, and see what a beautiful land it is with genuinely good people, who are only trying to exist in a hard and challenging world.

"There was danger…" Yes, a real danger. The physical threat was short term, but the venomous emotional threat could poison our humanity.

The case of a 23-year-old U.S. Army soldier convicted of raping and killing a 14-year-old Iraqi girl and her family is an ugly, tragic example of how hate and anger toward others can destroy lives. When asked by the judge during the soldier's trial why he committed these crimes, his answer was, "Iraq made me angry and violent." He told the judge flat out that he hated Iraqis. He was sentenced to 90 years in prison. Alexander

Hamilton once wrote: "War is as much a punishment to the punisher as it is to the sufferer." The soldier was a member of the 101st Airborne Division, the unit that replaced the 48th Brigade when we moved to the south of Iraq. The rape and murders occurred in the same area the 48th Brigade once patrolled. Different units, different men, different outcomes. Controlling our rage in a hostile environment was undeniably one of the most difficult challenges we faced.

* * * * *

Finally, the opportunity many of us had been waiting for arrived—seeking revenge for the deaths of our unit's eight soldiers. Some local Iraqis passed information to the upper levels of the 48th Brigade, identifying specific targets where those responsible were believed to reside.

Personally, I was not looking for *revenge* per se, but if we could capture and put away the men responsible, I would be very happy for this bit of justice. And honestly, if one or two of them were to be, how should I say, *injured*, during the confusion that might ensue, I would not lose any sleep over it. As in most wars, it's the collateral damage that can leave the most scars. Lashing out in anger can make you feel like you "got something off your chest," but the feeling is only temporary.

Before we departed Camp Stryker, Brig. General Rodeheaver gave us words of encouragement. "Be safe," he told us. "I'm sure you know we lost some more soldiers tonight." Eleven days, eleven dead. Earlier that evening, before our raid on the target houses, we were informed that three other members of the 48th Brigade who belonged to an engineer unit had been killed when a suicide bomber blew himself up at their checkpoint. Not a terribly auspicious beginning to an important operation where we'd likely suffer even more casualties.

Nonetheless, we were ready for a fight, and this was our chance to have one. We set out on the raid about 2 A.M. It was not a far drive, but at night, wearing night vision devices, all the villages and homes looked the same. Fortunately, we had the modern Blue Force Tracking system to guide us. Even with this sophisticated equipment, the map of the area wasn't exactly up to date. The illuminated screen did not always correctly depict the reality on the ground around you.

This night, SGT. Moore's excellent sense of direction led us directly to the target house. My section was not the only one involved in the raid; a number of other houses in the area were targeted. Alpha Company had suffered a tremendous loss, but on this night the whole 2nd battalion 121st Infantry would be assisting us. Members of our battalion would search over 14 houses and detain 45 people, but I was only concerned with the houses we had to search. The goal was to surprise them while they were sleeping. My vehicle led the raid, and I was acting as a dismount. Once at the target house, my job was to stay close to the humvees and organize the detainee collection point. We reached the target house without incident and quickly dismounted the humvees. The world around us was one of confusion and chaos.

We called the strobe lights attached to the back of each vehicle "crickets" because they flashed on and off. The purpose of the "crickets" was to assist other patrol vehicles in recognizing each other at night when driving without white lights, but the crickets disrupted the vision of the gunners on the humvees, who were our main source of protection. Shortly after stepping out of my humvee, SPC. Eric Fleming yelled down to me from the gunner's hatch to remove the cricket on my vehicle so he could see.

We could hear machine gun fire from other teams raiding target houses nearby. SGT. T was leading the team assigned to clear the main house. When they neared the front door, he grabbed SPC. Felix, a short, stocky veteran of the first Gulf War, and pushed him inside ahead of him, minimizing the risk to his own life. Two men were immediately brought out. At the same time, another team led by SGT. Moore and two soldiers, including PVT. Ross, went to search the building out back.

I could hear Ross' voice. "Get down! Get down!" he yelled at someone in the dark. What they found was a boy, around fourteen, sitting on the ground. In Iraq, with the obvious dearth of air-conditioning, most Iraqis sleep outside in the summer months, where it's cooler. The boy had been sleeping outside when we arrived and had woken to the sounds of our voices and vehicles. Unresponsive to their commands and gestures to get down on the ground, Ross punched him in the face to make him do it. The stocky boy didn't fall down and didn't respond, but he just stood there, looking confused. His failure to comply incited Ross to knee him in the groin. He dropped to the ground. Ross then grabbed him by the arm and dragged him fifty feet to the collection point.

I'd been called by SGT. T to assist with a detainee in front of the main house and found him resting his knee on the back of a prone man's neck to prevent him from moving. Both SGT. T and I dragged the man from the house to the humvees. After we placed him on the ground against the side of a house, which had become the detainee collection point, things moved quickly. Another man from the main house was cuffed and placed against the wall. Ross came up with the boy and shoved him into a sitting position on the dirt.

He complained that the boy wouldn't listen to his commands to get down on the ground and had resisted being dragged away. The boy never spoke; he just made soft whimpering sounds. While he was on the ground at Ross's feet, I noticed something wrong with the boys' facial features. I shined my flashlight in his face. Having taught special education, including children with severe disabilities, I quickly realized that the boy was mentally challenged.

I told Ross, "I think he has Down Syndrome."

He looked shocked. It turned out that Ross has an older brother, with whom he is very close, who also suffers from a mental disorder; nothing as severe as Down Syndrome, but one that affects his ability to function at normal levels. Ross tried to soothe the boy by stroking his head with

his hand, repeating, "I'm sorry buddy, are you okay?" The unresponsive boy just sat there, staring at the ground. He was obviously suffering from shock and fear at having been dragged away in the dead of night, beaten, and now surrounded by American soldiers. While the rest of the family resided in the main house, it appeared that he was kept in the small shed-like building like a dog in a kennel. Ross appeared genuinely sorry for having hurt the boy. The reality of what he'd done, however justified from a military standpoint, hit him hard. Aggression and revenge don't always result in the satisfaction you might expect.[1] We helped the boy up and placed him against the side of the house with the other detainees.

Our group of detainees soon totaled four. I distributed blindfolds. An older man, heavy set and seemingly in his late forties or early fifties—probably the senior member of the family—began to give us some trouble over being blindfolded. SPC. Felix solved the problem with a knee to the man's face. The rest of the men were then blindfolded without resistance, and we started gathering names through our interpreter. He wrote the names of each individual on a tag and affixed them to the detainees. A fifth man was detained because we found him outside his small house a short distance from the target house. We took photos of each man as evidence. A short time passed before the truck from Camp Stryker arrived to collect the Iraqis.

The Down Syndrome kid was very unresponsive and lethargic. He wouldn't, or couldn't walk, so I dragged him for a short distance. If I had let him go, he would have crumpled to the ground. He was so heavy that I requested assistance, and eventually we got him to the back of the truck

---

1. In *The Myth of Freedom (1976)*, Trungpa Rinpoche believes that even if one's aggression was so intense that you killed someone one would only achieve a small degree of satisfaction from the act. Because, when it is over, that "aggression still lingers around you. Even if you were to try to kill yourself, you would find that the killer remains; so you would not have managed to murder yourself completely. There is a constant of aggression in which one never knows who is killing whom." He makes the following analogy: "It is like to trying to eat yourself from the inside out. Having eaten yourself, the eater remains and he must be eaten as well, and so on and so on."

where there was a ladder. I had one hand around his leg and one hand against his left buttock. His gallbaya hitched up, and I found myself pushing on his big bare ass, adding insult to absurdity. With the other guy on the opposite side, we strained to lift him up and into the truck. He was whimpering and crying—he must have been so scared. While I was struggling to get him on the truck, he continued to whimper, but he made louder grunting noises when he realized he was being taken away from his home and family. At that moment, I felt what it must have been like to be an ordinary German soldier just following orders, rounding up Jews in Krakow.

Unfortunately, that was not the end of the sad story. Once the truck with those we had captured departed, we had to wait awhile before leaving. The daughters, of the last man detained, ranging in age from four to eight, were in the yard crying and screaming for their father. I had to stand there for twenty agonizing minutes, listening to their screams of *"PAPA, PAPA, PAPA!"* Those children had no idea why their father was being taken from them in the middle of the night. I could only think: *What if I was being taken away with my two young sons screaming for me, "DADDY, DADDY, DADDY!"?* We did what we had to do; these were bad men, but it hurt to hear their children cry. The wounds our hatred and anger created would take a long time to heal.

At Camp Stryker, a facility had been set up to receive anyone detained or captured during patrols or raids. After writing the required statement concerning what transpired at the raid, I headed to my tent, air conditioning, and a good long sleep. Walking past the detainee tent, I saw the kid emerge. The medics had been very kind, blowing up a rubber glove and giving it to him as a balloon with a smiley face drawn on it in black marker. He walked out of the tent seeming happy and content. I was told later that he was taken to another medical facility to determine if there was anything that could be done to improve his condition. He would later be released to his family. As for PVT. Ross, who took his frustrations

out on the boy, I think he learned something valuable, as did I—anger can have unforeseen consequences. It shattered whatever we thought we could accomplish so simply—capturing and roughing up the bad guys. We pursued our mission that night through aggression, but I will never forget forcing that poor kid onto that truck as he whimpered in pain and terror. It was a consequence of our actions. A consequence of anger.

As I continued on to my tent, the Sakyong's words echoed in my head: *The more force, the greater the compassion.*

WALKING THE TIGER'S PATH
PAUL M. KENDEL

Chapter Six

Compassion as a Sign of Weakness

*Compassion is perceived and felt as genuine even by
the most confused mind...when a confused mind is face-
to-face with genuine compassion, awareness happens and
opens the gate for their own compassion to come forth.*
—Dane Sadler, former inmate

"Compassion as Weakness?"

During the ten years that Margot visited people in various prisons throughout the United States, she's heard a common complaint from prisoners who'd embraced the Buddha's teaching: *Others see compassion as a sign of weakness. To survive in prison you have to be aggressive—compassion will only make you a target.* The army is very much the same. As a soldier, you are expected to be aggressive. Showing compassion toward the Iraqis made you look weak, suspicious, potentially untrustworthy to defend yourself and others in a moment of crisis. Showing compassion in Iraq was a challenge that I never quite mastered.

But I did try to feel compassion, however unsuccessfully, under very difficult circumstances. The Sakyong's letter offered me enormous aid. As my situations became more intense, his advice became more relevant. The use of force typically incites greater levels of rage. Once the war became more intimate and personal, whatever reservations we might have had about accidentally killing innocents started to vanish. Hence, the need for compassion grew as the application of force intensified.

I wrote to Margot:

> This place is like Vietnam; they kill you and slip away into the night. You never really see their faces. And because of that, the anger expressed by my friends is misdirected toward the average Iraqi who is just trying to survive. Their anger needs an outlet, and unfortunately most do not know how to channel it in a non-destructive way; we retaliate and our hate grows, simply perpetuating the problem. The only answer to the problem is MORE COMPASSION, just as the Sakyong said in his letter. But how do you convince a group of people who just had their good friends blown to pieces that the answer is love and compassion? Unfortunately, in America, especially in the Army, these types of attributes are considered a sign of weakness, not strength. We can launch a space shuttle that shows the brilliance of human ingenuity, but we can't find a way to solve the most basic ills that plague society.

The military establishment expected the American soldier to appear stoic under duress in war; you do your job without complaint—they don't want you to think. You have an objective, and you carry it out. Feelings and compassion open up a can of worms that is counter-productive to single-minded military aggression. It's a John Wayne world where you trust, without ambiguity, the righteousness of your mission: you're the good guys and they're the bad guys. Yes, there was this black and white thinking they trained us to have, and then there were the actual realities—the gray areas—we faced on a daily basis.

I compared it to traffic. Iraqis are like everyone else in the modern world—they do stupid things while driving. In Baghdad, when an American patrol rolled down a road, most drivers would pull off to the side. But for some mysterious but typically human reason, one driver would invariably attempt to jockey for a better position to get ahead of the others. On one occasion, three or four drivers pulled onto the shoulder to allow the American patrol to pass, but the last driver in line suddenly pulled out in an effort to move ahead of those in front of him. When he swerved out into the middle of the road, Eric Fleming, on orders from the T.C., raked the vehicle with a burst of machine gun fire.

That driver's impatience proved to be the biggest mistake of his life.

The car continued across the road and came to rest in a ditch. The driver was mortally wounded, but the patrol, en-route to the Safe House, didn't stop to verify if it was a suspected suicide bomber or just an innocent civilian in a rush to get home. Instead, it rolled on, passing the man who lay slumped over in his car on the side of the road. *Just another day at the office in Iraq.* The patrol did return to check on the man half an hour later. According to an Iraqi bystander, he'd been taken to a hospital in Baghdad, but apparently he'd died before he got there. Would his life have been saved if the patrol had stopped?

In the beginning of our deployment I'd tried to emphasize to other soldiers the need for understanding the complexity of our situation. I'd volunteered to be part of the Company Commander's personal security detail, thinking my knowledge of Islam and the Middle East could be helpful, but it wasn't. He was the captain of an infantry unit going to war; he knew what he needed, and he certainly wasn't going to take advice from someone who'd voted for John Kerry over George W. Bush.

I tried the same tack with SGT. Moore and others once we were in Iraq. But many saw our deployment in very simple terms: we were going to fight the "enemy," the perpetrators of 9/11. I saw things very differently. Like the soldier during training who asked to borrow my copy of the Koran simply to find passages that confirmed his anti-Muslim bias, many soldiers around me were there for one thing and one thing only: to kill the enemies of the United States. But this wasn't a simple goal—something I tried to articulate during the first months of our deployment, that was quickly dismissed. This "war" was to be used by certain people to give them their fifteen minutes of fame.

Many, like Moore and Bopp, thought their knowledge was superior to all those around them. Certainly, to their way of thinking, listening to me was unnecessary, unwanted, and unheeded. One day at the Safe House, we got a report of a suspected insurgent driving a generic, ubiquitous vehicle with a specific license plate number. I knew the Arabic numerals and could read the license plates. I got the number and wrote it with a non-permanent marker on the inside windshield of Moore's humvee. This way he could look at vehicles we passed and try to match up the numbers I'd written for him on the windshield.

"That's a great idea," a fellow soldier said. With reluctance Moore accepted my suggestion. But then I offered more. "I'll write all the Arabic numbers on the windshield, so in the future when we have different license plate numbers to look for, you'll have them written down for reference."

He gave me a condescending look. "Just write the numbers down for the car we're looking for." We were the same rank but he was technically my superior, so I had no control. I walked away with the realization that any effort on my part that might threaten his innate belief in his own superiority would be a mistake.

Shortly following that incident, SFC. Janes and Moore told me I would be in charge of the patrol for the day. This would mean navigating around our sector. Up to this point I'd simply ridden along as a dismount, never having to respond to radio calls or read a map and determine where we needed to go. Janes and Moore did this with the expectation, or simply the hope, that I would prove incompetent and need their assistance, confirming their preconceptions about me.

As it turned out, I navigated brilliantly around the sector that day, even escorting a different unit into Baghdad International Airport. Once

Inspecting the inside of a former Saddam palace.
From left to right: The author with SPC. Youngblood, SGT. Moore,
SFC. Janes and SPC. Petty near the Safe House.

the patrol concluded for the day, Moore said hesitatingly, "You did a good job today, SGT. Kendel." He turned and walked away, looking a little embarrassed. That was the last time Janes or Moore put me in charge of a patrol until Moore went home on leave. Their egotistical belief in their own superiority had been broken. I could function as well as they could, and they didn't like it. But my desire to view the Iraqis as human beings, not as objects of our resentment, would lead to incidents where my ability to function in combat would be questioned.

One day, as we were heading back to Camp Stryker at the end of an ordinary patrol, we passed the road leading to the Safe House, then came around a sharp bend to the left where there were a few mud huts among trees. Directly in front of me, on the other side of the road, I noticed children, ages three to eight, as they played in the front yard of a small house. I then focused on a small white car stopped in the right lane ahead. I had to make a split second decision whether or not to fire on the vehicle. It was not completely off the road, as was the normal Iraqi procedure. My thoughts ranged from *perhaps the man was unaware of our sudden appearance* to *maybe he was the father of the children and had stopped in for lunch.*

He seemed to be waiting for someone from within the house. SGT. Moore bellowed from below, "Shoot the fucking car! Shoot the fucking car!"

With one eye I could see the car, and with the other I could see the kids playing in the front yard. Deducing that the car wasn't an immediate threat, I concluded that we'd simply surprised *him*. If I shot and hit the car the bullets could very well ricochet, cutting down the children.

I chose not to shoot. We passed the car without incident.

From below came Moore's voice: "Why *the fuck* didn't you shoot that fucking car?"

I sat back down in the gunner's seat where I could see Moore's livid expression. I said, "I couldn't shoot. I didn't want to take the chance of a ricochet killing those kids playing in the yard."

"I don't care about any fucking kids!" he responded. "Next time you shoot!"

I stood back up in the gunner's hatch, thinking, *What the hell have I gotten myself into? If I do something like that again, they're not going to trust me.*

I think it was at this point where conflict began to develop between myself and some of the other soldiers in our company. I clearly saw the war and our role in it as something far different than some of those around me.

As we continued down the road, I watched the children playing happily in the front of their house, oblivious to the conflict raging over my decision not to shoot. I realized I'd have to feign aggressiveness in order to placate those around me. I'd fire in the other direction if I had to. I'd pretend that I was playing the game. The last thing I wanted was to spend the rest of my tour behind a desk doing paperwork, the fate of soldiers not trusted to perform as the Army saw fit under duress. But in those few seconds where the lives of innocents hung in the balance, I'd controlled my fear and rage, made the right decision, and chose not to pull the trigger.

CHAPTER SEVEN

SNAPSHOTS FROM A WAR ZONE

The privilege of absurdity; to which no living creature is subject, but man only.

—Thomas Hobbes

The majority of our time in Iraq was boring and monotonous, but life in that country could get very interesting, very quickly. Suicide bombers were an obvious threat, but not all suicide bombers were effective. One day while driving to the rundown former motor pool nicknamed the Lion's Den, where the Iraqi army was stationed, we got a call over the radio to look out for a small crater in the road at the foot of the overpass that ran across Route Tampa, the main supply road. Apparently a lone individual with a vest full of explosives had blown himself up when a convoy drove by. His attack proved a complete failure as far as American forces were concerned, but a complete success in killing himself. When we drove over Route Tampa, I tried to get a look at where the man had exploded himself. Sure enough, in the road was a small crater surrounded with a dark red stain. All that remained of the man rested innocently next to the blast hole: one white athletic shoe with the foot still inside—it gave a whole new meaning to the phrase "road kill."

I questioned the IQ of the average suicide bomber. If he was going to kill himself, you'd think the individual would plan his attack a little better, especially if he intended to attack an armored vehicle. One suicide bomber/Rhodes scholar decided to ram his car into a Bradley Infantry Fighting Vehicle. A highly effective explosion, it completely obliterated the car and the man, but didn't even make dent in the Bradley. Like the other suicide bomber whose only remaining body part was his foot in a shoe, one part of this man's anatomy remained intact—his genitalia. Sitting about thirty feet from the bomb crater was the man's severed privates. Nothing else remained. If he went straight to paradise, where his reward of 72 virgins awaited him, he'd realize the stupidity of his action. He left an important item behind.

* * * * *

In Iraq, you had to find laughs in strange places and at unusual times to get you through each day. My cigar buddy, SPC. Daylon Brown from 3rd Platoon, was out on patrol one day and drove behind the small town of Al-Salaam, a former military housing complex under Saddam Hussein. A number of IEDs had previously been discovered in the area. In one incident, a patrol from 3rd Platoon narrowly missed setting off an IED. At the last second, the T.C. and driver of the humvee noticed the sun reflecting off a string of fishing wire that stretched across the dirt road, eye level with the windshield. Stopping on a dime, they missed the wire by inches. They called EOD, who, sure enough, discovered fishing wire attached to an IED buried on the road side. A few days later in the same area, they discovered something odd lying off to the side of the road in thick knee high grass. The patrol stopped and quickly identified a body. Determining that it was not booby trapped, they bagged the body and drove into Al-Salaam, but no one was willing to accept it. Stuck with unwanted human remains, the higher chain of command ordered them to take it to the nearest police station. Like my patrol had been forced to do with Chico and Esteban, they covered their noses against the rotting fragrance of death and strapped the decomposing corpse to the hood of a humvee with bungee cords and rope.

With the body firmly attached to the hood, like a freshly killed deer, the patrol set off with their prize—a human hood ornament. Not wanting to drive into unknown areas searching for a police station at two in the morning, they unceremoniously dumped the body at the doorstep of a local police officer that lived nearby. Not surprisingly, the officer and his wife who answered the door were shocked and refused to accept the body. Their eight-hour duty to the War on Terror was nearing its end, hungry, with the chow hall soon to close, Brown and his section simply drove off into the night, leaving the poor officer and his family to contend with their discarded hood ornament.

* * * * *

An average day on patrol involved trying to avoid boredom and the heat. After driving around for a couple of hours, we'd usually set up our patrol in a palm grove and relax, leaving the gunners up for protection. I've never had a problem sleeping in unusual places, but for some reason I couldn't sleep well sitting inside a humvee. I'd lean over the steering wheel when we stopped and try to sleep that way, but my legs would get stiff, awakening me after fifteen minutes or so. During one patrol in August 2005, the largest sandstorm to hit Iraq in nearly fifty years blew in just as we left Camp Stryker for a routine patrol. I couldn't see even a few feet into the intense brown haze. To avoid an accident, we pulled into a palm grove to wait it out. We weren't going anywhere for a while, and since I didn't have a Snickers bar, I leaned over the steering wheel to get some rest.

After a time I drifted off, then some feeling caused me to wake and lift up my head. There, like a mirage in the brown haze a few feet in front of the hood, an old man herded his goats. I just stared in shock at the herder, who stared in shock right back. No doubt he didn't expect to find an American vehicle sitting in a palm grove in the middle of swirling sand. For a moment, I thought I was dreaming: we in our twenty-first century gear and humvee and this old man herding his goats as his ancestors had done since time immemorial, both caught up in a blinding sandstorm. As dangerous as Iraq could be, it always provided one with unique opportunities to say to oneself, *"Did that just happen?"*

* * * * *

Every section from our company had an Iraqi interpreter who traveled with them. One, however, was not an Iraqi. His name was Jackson, a Christian from the Sudan. By a strange twist of fate, he'd fled his war-ravaged country years earlier. Saddam Hussein had allowed a number of refugees such as Jackson to settle in Iraq. Married to an Iraqi woman, Jackson had a young child. However, he hated Iraqis, and this made him an excellent interpreter because he had no problem roughing them up to get answers for us. Jackson stood out—there were not many large, black Africans who worked as interpreters for the Americans. He slept in our tent and had a section to himself next to my makeshift room. He received death threats because he worked for the Americans. Still, he never seemed afraid. He should have. While going home on a four day pass to Baghdad to see his family, he was attacked by insurgents who slashed his throat and dumped his body on the side of the road.

* * * * *

A late night raid on a suspected VBIED (vehicle borne IED) factory epitomized the absurdity of some of our missions in Iraq. As any soldier has known since the beginning of warfare, bad intelligence and poor communication can lead to disaster.

Our platoon initiated the attack on the suspected VBIED factory. Machine gun and small arms fire preceded an assault team that entered shortly after the barrage of bullets. Somehow, after firing dozens of rounds at a group of men who had been milling about in front of the building—bullets impacting into cars, the ground, and the walls of the building—no one, *not one single* person, got hit. Everyone involved said the incident reminded them of a scene from the movie *Matrix,* the way the men seemed to move in slow motion trying to avoid the hail of bullets.

When the assault team entered, they found a large group of mourners attending a *funeral.* At the head of the room, on a large table, sat an open wooden casket with a young woman's body on display—no insurgents, no explosives, only a corpse. Outside, Bopp and the others were detaining suspects. Due to bad intelligence, they'd just raided and nearly killed an entire family and their friends who were gathered to mourn a lost life. The man Bopp had thrown to the ground and cuffed after the initial assault was in fact the *husband* of the dead woman. Informed of the situation, Bopp cut the cuffs off the man and said, "Sorry, my bad."

There really wasn't much to say after something like that. In the end, there most likely was an actual VBIED factory, probably just a few blocks down the road.

These types of mishaps occurred all the time in Iraq (the VBIED factory debacle, however, had to have been unique). Unfortunately, I must place myself on the list of bad decision makers on another occasion.

During the first Gulf War, as well as before our invasion in 2003, Saddam Hussein had erected large anti-aircraft emplacements—some possibly a hundred feet tall—outside the walls surrounding the airport. Anti-aircraft batteries once sat on top of these large mounds but had since been removed. We were out patrolling our sector, and on this day, we decided to stray from our usual route and drove over to one of the large emplacements a short distance from some homes.

This may sound cruel, but at one point we received orders to shoot all stray dogs in our area. In Iraq, dogs acted as a home security system. Whenever we got close to a home, a dog would invariably appear, letting people know that someone approached. This was a problem when it came to sneaking up on suspected insurgents in their houses: the damn dogs would give us away by barking long before we had a chance to get close. So the "shoot all stray dogs plan" made some sense, except for the fact that the average Iraqi used them for personal security; getting robbed at night or being killed by insurgents for refusing to support them were the greatest threats to most Iraqis. A dog-borne advanced warning system was a necessity.

Dogs in Iraq aren't the cute, lovable pets they are in the U.S.; most are dirty, grungy animals. That said, we were driving right in front of a house with the kids playing in the front yard. The family dog ran after our humvee barking like any dog would in the United States. He stopped before leaving the edge of the yard, tail wagging and tongue hanging out, what had to have been the most well-groomed, well-fed dog in all of Iraq, clearly a real family pet. SPC. Felix, M16 rifle in hand, popped up out of the gunner's hatch and *Bang!* —the dog took a bullet in the chest, right in front of the children. And we drove on, another successful day of winning those Iraqi hearts and minds.

But back to the anti-aircraft emplacement…while driving up to the base, we saw a lone dog hanging around. Since this was as good a time as any for target practice, SGT. Moore got out of the humvee, aimed his weapon, and fired. The usually bored, lethargic Iraqi dog can move with incredible speed if properly motivated, and this one clearly was. SGT. Moore missed with the first shot and kept firing. The dog zigzagged his way around behind the gun emplacement with lightning speed. In the end, he escaped death by the grungy fur on his head. We parked our vehicles at the base of the gun emplacement and walked to the top. Our perch gave us a panoramic view of the entire area. Agricultural fields spread out below us. We could see the walls surrounding the airport and the large figure of Saddam's palace just inside the walls—now used by American Special Forces as a command center with high tech communications gear sprouting from the rooftop. A lone dog ran along the ground, perhaps the same one that had just escaped with its life. SGT. Moore shot at it but missed again. The distance was too great. Then I got the wonderful idea to use the dog as an excuse to fire my grenade launcher.

I had no intention of actually hitting the poor dog, but I got permission from SFC. Janes to fire an HE (high explosive) round at the animal. Unfortunately, I failed to factor in the elevation of the anti-aircraft emplacement. The dog scampered along while I pointed the barrel upward. I aimed and fired. The round went up and up and up. After a time, I wondered if it was a dud. Then I saw the explosion and its impact—about a hundred feet from a house. A short distance away at another house, children played in the front yard. *Oh shit*, I thought. It was a good thing no one was playing in the front yard of the house where my round hit. How would I have explained the death of a few children from my HE round? *Sorry, but I was just aiming for a stray dog.* After the explosion, I glanced around. Everyone gave me a look that said, "Time to get the hell out of here." We fled down the cement ramp, climbed into our humvees, and drove away. That was the last time I made any pretense of attempting to shoot a dog.

Apparently, I hadn't learned enough lessons about carelessness and the subtleties of aggression. One day in late September, my section was pulling security along Route Aeros. All vehicular traffic was banned due to the elections for the new Iraqi government. Overall, Election Day was boring; VBIEDS remained a threat, but nothing occurred; only a few

Iraqi kids hung around us. Sometimes the Iraqi kids were cute; some-times you just wanted to shoot them.

On this day, I felt inclined toward the latter. Robert Sheets—he liked to be called "The Sheets"—and I, along with Ross, walked down the road toward a small bridge erected over a canal. A group of kids frolicked in the water. We watched, amused by their antics. I had some candy and a few other items to pass out. I tried to distribute the items evenly, but as usual the boys forced themselves in ahead of the girls. While I tried to give something to his sister, one boy kept jumping up and down in front of me in order to get my attention. His interference got really annoying. Apparently I'd had enough because I raised my weapon with the grenade launcher attached and pointed it directly at the boy.

Snot began pouring from his nose. His face became an image of shock and fear. I hadn't expected this reaction; I just wanted him to get out of the way. When I lowered my weapon, he turned and walked off—mov-ing as though his life depended on it and leaving behind his bucket of water that I assumed he was meant to bring home from the canal. As he walked behind his older sister, he kept looking back at me—I guess he was afraid I'd shoot him in the back. After this incident, I had some seri-ous negative karma to remove, so I started by inviting myself into Iraqi homes for tea and bread.

Chapter Eight

As Simple as Tea and Bread

Peace cannot be achieved through violence. It can only be achieved through understanding.

—Ralph Waldo Emerson

Many of my fellow soldiers in Iraq found my attitude and actions at times to be inexplicable, particularly my interest in inviting myself into random Iraqi homes and asking the families to make tea and bread for me. The tea was damn good, as was the bread. This may sound peculiar, but I felt unafraid when I was around the local people with whom we interacted on a daily basis. The ones you had to fear were those you never saw—the ones who tried to blow you up at night. Of course it's possible that some of these people who offered me tea and bread (or their relatives living elsewhere) had spent some evenings lurking in the dark.

In the past, I had traveled extensively throughout the Middle East. For the deployment to Iraq, I brought a very diverse selection of reading material. I had a copy of the Bible and the Koran, as well as a number of fiction and non-fiction books. Since I'd studied the history of the Middle East as well as the Islamic religion in college, I'd planned to finish reading the Koran. One day during the train up for Iraq, a soldier in my unit saw the Koran among my books. He asked if he could borrow it. I watched him laughingly read a few passages to a couple of other soldiers. I realized he didn't ask to borrow the Koran to understand Islam; he wanted ammunition that would support his existing anti-Muslim beliefs—that Islam is inherently a violent religion and so forth. Since 9/11, Islam had certainly become a target.

The majority of Arabs I've met throughout my travels have been kind and helpful. When I went to Iraq, I had no reason to believe the average Iraqi would be any different. Nor did I see my service in Iraq as a patriotic effort to expunge terrorism. I felt a loyalty toward those with whom I served, and I had something to prove to myself—that after seventeen years in the military, I could acquit myself honorably in a real war. But I also looked at my deployment as an opportunity to visit the cradle of civilization. I was never that excited over the possibility of shooting someone; I hoped instead to interact with local Iraqis, see as much of the land as possible, and visit some of the world's most important archaeological sites, such as Babylon, the Ziggurat of Ur, and Hatra. Maybe I was a little naïve about what I was getting myself into; but as a whole, it proved to be an unusual experience, and all the more so when I invited myself into random homes.

I looked forward to meeting the local people, whether Sunni or Shia. I wanted the experience and I wanted to gain an understanding of other cultures, but I would be considered an "idiot" who lacked "common sense" because I didn't wrap myself in a blanket of fear and hatred. Other soldiers considered me suspicious and somewhat untrustworthy because I didn't see the same "reality" they did. To me, seeing humanity as a whole is the only way conflicts are going to be resolved; we must understand the other person's perspective. If we go in assuming we're right, we're either going to be wrong, or the other person's not going to listen. We have to understand that everyone is patriotic for his/her own country and will die for it. But Americans assume that everyone wants what we want.

* * * * *

Maybe I was a little too trusting at times, but it was worth it to combat the universal mistrust and ignorance of the people around us, who, at least in theory, relied on us for their protection. I tried to see them as human beings and wanted to interact with them whenever I could. Walking up to random homes and inviting myself in was a unique way of doing this.

Sometimes I would ask for tea, or *chai*, but usually people in the house would offer it to me. (It wasn't very likely at the time that a major al-Qaida figure was using their squatter home as a safe house.) Usually, whether Sunni or Shia, the whole family would come out. It seemed to be a big occasion for them, as though in hosting American soldiers, they were receiving important guests. I found the intimate interaction with Iraqis a truly rewarding experience, one that helped me gain a better understanding of the people around us. It opened a window into a completely different world, one which very few soldiers serving in Iraq ever chose to see.

We'd set up at OP1 on occasion, just for something to do. It was safer than driving around. OP1, a large concrete slab along Route Aeros, had been the base of a sizable building that was blown up and stripped clean. Concertina wire surrounded it but provided little protection. We used OP1 to stage our Bradley Fighting Vehicles as well as our humvees. If something occurred in the sector, these vehicles responded, but sitting around OP1 was boring duty; hence, we had time to explore the run-down neighborhood filled with displaced, squatting Iraqi families.

With limited income sources, many of the families throughout our sector lived in relative poverty. Both Shia and Sunni families occupied a number of houses scattered around OP1. The buildings weren't really homes, just make shift shelters made out of what was left of the original buildings. We often brought them medicine and drinking water. A group of young boys who lived near OP1 made money like the kids at the Safe House. They sold cold drinks and candy. Like members of the British Raj in India, these boys would prepare tea at home and serve it to us on a big metal tray with small glasses. Along with the tea they brought some of the ubiquitous flat, soft, round bread found all over Iraq. Both were delicious. Once, while leading a night patrol, I had an incredible urge and diverted the entire patrol to OP1 just for the tea and bread.

Not long after our arrival, we heard from the departing unit that a building nearby was a whorehouse. Being curious and social, we decided to investigate this suspected house of ill repute. While none of us believed a bevy of scantily clad women waited for us inside, it was worth a look. When we got close, the dogs began barking, alerting the people inside that they had visitors. We'd been led on. Our evening mission to explore the suspected bordello left us disappointed, but it did provide an opportunity to erase some of the guilt I felt about nearly blowing away a family in their front yard and scaring the living hell out of that boy.

Instead of a whorehouse, we found two separate families occupying the dilapidated former military structure, and they came out to greet us. The father of one of the families pulled the dog back from the fence and invited us into their yard. Their home had most likely been inspected by American soldiers in the past, as they seemingly had no reluctance to admit us inside. Small rooms belonged to each family—in actuality, only one large room for the whole family that had been sectioned off. A father, mother, a grandmother, and two young children lived in a room the size of most American one car garages. All of them smiled when we walked inside. Usually, the women will hide themselves by moving into a different room, or just turning their backs. These women really had no place to go, but they smiled at us and seemed unafraid.

I decided not to make our visit a waste and asked one of the men who lived in the adjacent home if he could make us some tea. He responded enthusiastically and invited us into his home. Being my sometimes over-trusting self, I walked straight in, leaned my weapon against the wall, took off my vest, and sat down on the family couch, making myself right at home. This section of the building had a sizeable dining and living area. Short on amenities, the dining area consisted of just the couch. The family was forced to stand. Even in relative poverty, they managed to possess a television with a satellite dish, with *Animal Planet*—a very popular program in Iraq—on screen.

My friends, including CPL. Gibbs and PVT. Ross, hesitated going inside and removing their gear. After a time they relaxed. For most sol-diers, this kind of friendly, informal social encounter with local Iraqis was unusual, to say the least. We usually spoke with Iraqis only about security matters, something that affected American forces in our sector; we did not hang out and share a pot of tea. Most soldiers wanted nothing to do with the locals for various reasons, the most obvious one being that they didn't trust them. Our job was to patrol our sector and stay alive. We encountered the average Iraqi, an amorphous figure, passing him on the side of the road, driving by, or when something was wrong. We passed out candy and other items to people, but the average soldier did not venture into Iraqi homes for the social experience.

This particular family—a young father and mother and their two year old daughter—welcomed us warmly. While the mother prepared tea, I attempted a conversation with the non-English-speaking father, but smiles and hand gestures can say a lot. When I asked them if they were Sunni or Shiite, the father, looking a little sheepish, replied that they were Sunni. The Sunnis had held a privileged status under Saddam. Not anymore. Like this family, many were now just squatters living in the remnants of the Saddam years, trying to survive. We stayed for about an hour. I gave the father a little money before I left. The mother held her young daughter in her arms. She was a beautiful child with dark hair that fell to her shoulders and big brown eyes. As I was leaving, the mother stood in front of me asking, "Toys?"

"No," I said. "But I will try to return soon with something if I can."

The issue of potable water was important in these homes. Before we left, the father asked if we had any water we could give them. I told him we had a few bottles in the vehicles back at OP1 that we would drop off before we left. These weren't enough, so I told him I'd come back with more. Fortunately, I was able to return the following day and make good on my promise. On this second visit, we drove up to the house. We received the same reception from the dog as we walked up to the barbed wire. The family seemed shocked that I'd returned so soon. The Iraqis are used to the Americans making pledges to them about security, medical supplies, water, and such, and not following through on their claims. I handed them two crates of water bottles and a big box full of candy, toiletries, and school supplies. And yes, I even brought a small Barbie doll for the little girl. When I held out the doll, she reached for it eagerly. The entire family responded with big smiles and genuine looks of gratitude. It must have been like Christmas for all of them, going through the mounds of gifts that I brought. I left feeling good. It was far more pleasurable to help the Iraqis than shoot at them—or cause snot to pour out of their noses.

* * * *

However, my forays into Iraqi homes did manage to get me into trouble. From the top of the Safe House, we had an excellent view of the surrounding area, which included large date palm groves. I led a foot patrol out of the Safe House one day, and capitalizing on an opportunity to explore, I deviated from the expected route and led the patrol down a road through a palm grove about a kilometer away. Large chicken coops sat all over our sector, and we'd usually search them while driving around. We'd never been in the one near the Safe House, so I decided to check it out. Once we encountered the family who ran it, I began socializing with them. After nearly an hour my Platoon Sergeant, SFC. Janes, began to worry, afraid we'd been killed or captured. I had no radio with me, so he couldn't contact our patrol. I finally realized we should head back, but not before Janes decided to send my friend Sam Bopp out to find me. Before Bopp left the Safe House though, my Platoon Sergeant spotted us walking down the road and called him back. The Sheets tried to reassure him, saying, "Don't worry, SGT. Kendel's probably just hanging out in some Iraqi home, having tea."

And that's exactly where I ended up. Before we finished our foot patrol, I stopped into the home of a young kid who hung out at the Safe House on a regular basis. The kid's name was George, or at least that was the name he wanted to be called. I invited myself into his home and spent at least half an hour drinking tea and socializing with his father. George told me later that without the work at the Safe House—selling food and drinks, as well as being paid to clean up the place—his family would have nothing. When I returned to camp, Janes regarded me coldly, not pleased by my disappearance.

I wasn't the only one to gain something from these personal experiences. After a subsequent visit to another Iraqi home near OP1, this time a Shiite family, PVT. Ross had another eye-opening experience. The boys who hung around OP1 were friendly and sociable. Most of the soldiers from the Bradley platoon got to know them very well because they saw them almost daily.

One night we set up at OP1 for a few hours to take a break from driving. I asked one of the older boys if his mother could make us some tea. He and one of the younger children, most likely his brother, ran happily away with our order. About twenty minutes later, both of them returned with a large metal tray on which sat a pot of tea, glasses, and bread. We spent the next hour, and another pot of tea, talking and joking. The kids were great, and I suddenly felt like inviting myself into their home to meet their father. The boys treated my request with enthusiasm, and after receiving permission from SFC. Janes, I recruited some guys to accompany me. PVT. Ross was less than excited about the venture. Since I couldn't go alone, I made him join me. Cpl, Gibbs, as usual, came reluctantly, but he was getting used to being dragged along.

The younger boy had raced ahead to let his family know they were about to have unexpected guests. His father met us at the door and held his hand out as I walked up to him. We firmly shook hands in a warm embrace. In his early forties, he had a big, broad smile and made us feel welcome right away. He motioned for us to enter. Like the Sunni home, the building consisted of one large room separated into two, making a living area and a dining/kitchen area, with some anterooms in the back. Clearly doing better than most, this family had the obligatory satellite dish, but also an actual dining table with chairs and an entertainment center against the wall. The man motioned me toward the couch, where I immediately made myself at home by stripping off my gear. As before, my companions surveyed the home with suspicion, but soon relaxed. Family photos and other personal items decorated the walls and shelves. The place felt like a real home, not a temporary squatter's residence. The mother began preparing tea while the father offered me a cigarette, which I declined. He spoke English well enough to carry on a conversation. They were certainly better off than most Iraqis in the area. I soon discovered the reason was us. The money the family made selling tea, beef kebabs, cold drinks, and candy provided an income that supported them. Without us, they would starve. I learned from the father that his family had been threatened because they were friendly to the Americans, the very reason they were surviving. He was very open and honest with me by letting me know that he believed when the Americans left Iraq, he and his family might be killed. The only thing preventing that now was our presence near his home. After that single serious admission, he kept the conversation light. His family included a young daughter, maybe twelve years old, who had a large growth in her throat that an American medic diagnosed as a tumor. She would need surgery to remove it, but he didn't have the money to take her to a hospital in Baghdad.

The older boy brought out some pictures, photos of the boys with members of the unit we'd replaced. They'd made the decision to link their survival to the Americans long before my platoon arrived, for good or for ill. As I relaxed on the couch and smoked a cigar, I was suddenly aware of the scene before me. I could have been sitting in any home in the States because of the resemblance to an American family Christmas—relatives gathering a little awkwardly with each other, but then warming to a genuine glow. After about an hour, Gibbs and Ross had become attached to the two boys, having them sit next to them or on their laps while they looked at the pictures. We all got together for a group photo with the family. As we were leaving, I gave the father some money.

Author Southwest of Baghdad giving pencils and other school supplies, sent to him by his father, to the Iraqi children.

We turned to look back and saw the family standing at the door, waving. We all waved back and seemed to share the same eye-opening feeling.

During the course of an average day of driving around our sector, the gunner of each humvee, especially the lead vehicle, would fire at least a dozen rounds at cars to make them move to the side of the road or to stop them, with PVT. Ross usually acting as the gunner. After spending more than an hour with this family, hanging out with their kids and taking pictures, Ross reflected, "After today, when I drive around shooting at cars, I don't think I'll be able to see the Iraqis the same way again." A brief visit with one family and he was able to see them as they really were: *human*. He realized that they were just people trying to make it through life, just as we all do; and he experienced the sudden insight that comes to us as part of our true human nature. If we allow ourselves to have an open state of mind, we discover that compassion and gentleness are always present within us—just below the surface.

Trungpa Rinpoche uses the term "warriorship" because in order to open our hearts and minds to this kind of gentleness, it's necessary to drop our habitual defenses, allowing the vulnerability that always accompanies to come forth. It takes courage to open ourselves to vulnerability. Trungpa Rinpoche emphasized that when a human being first gives himself up to the "tender heart of warriorship," he may feel extremely awkward or uncertain, but he eventually understands that he no longer needs to feel shy or embarrassed about being gentle. "In fact," Rinpoche states, "your softness begins to become passionate. You would like to extend yourself to others and communicate with them."

That evening's interaction with the Iraqi family offered a temporary escape from the horrific sensibilities that arise in a war zone. During our time with this family, Ross and I experienced "the tender heart of warriorship." We overcame our anxiety and nervousness, and most importantly, we overcame the animosity we may have harbored towards the average Iraqi due to the deaths of our friends. For a moment in time, viewing them as human beings rather than as targets of aggression and hatred, we experienced the relief and softness of compassion.

We'd started our mission in Iraq with sympathy for the local Iraqi people. A number of us had items such as toiletries, toys, and school supplies sent from the U.S. to distribute among local families and children in our sector. Schools and individuals we didn't know who wanted to show their support for the war effort sent numerous care packages. My father mailed a box of hotel soap that cost nearly fifty dollars to ship to me. He also sent a huge box of pencils to give to some of the local schools in the area. This generous altruism in time piled up in the middle of our tent. Countless items such as baby wipes, Germ-X bottles of hand soap, toothbrushes, and toothpaste sat undistributed and collecting dust. It didn't take long for an interest in "winning the hearts and minds" of the locals to fade away.

WALKING THE TIGER'S PATH
PAUL M. KENDEL

Chapter Nine

"Shoot Him, He's Sunni"

We have just enough religion to make us hate, but not enough to make us love one another.

—Jonathan Swift

The growth of civil strife in Iraq became obvious to nearly everyone from my unit not long after we arrived. The only reason religious and ethnic issues hadn't flared up during the Saddam years was because he, like Tito in Yugoslavia, put a lid on all the age-old resentments boiling beneath the surface of Iraqi society. With that lid removed—just like it did in Yugoslavia after Tito's death—all hell broke loose.

The man who had been taken away during the raids to capture those responsible for our friends' deaths and forced to listen to his young daughters screaming for him was in fact *not* connected to the individuals responsible. He had just happened to live near the home we raided and picked a bad time to walk outside to see what all the commotion was about. I don't know whether the innocent man we dragged away that night was a Sunni or a Shia—he could've been either. Sunni and Shia lived close to one another without ever associating.

All the homes appeared similar, and none of them had a flag waving above the doorstep, announcing that family's particular religion. I discovered quickly that when you entered a home, the best way to tell a Shia household from a Sunni one was the obvious portrait of the famous Shia martyr, Imam Hussain. Hussain was the grandson of the prophet Mohammed, the offspring of his daughter, Fatima, and his cousin, Ali. When Mohammed died in 632, leaving no obvious successor, prominent Muslims chose Abu Bakr, a close advisor of Mohammed, to take his place as symbolic head of the Muslim community throughout the world. This decision led to the division of the community into two sects. Different people within the early Islamic community rejected the choice of Abu Bakr to succeed Mohammed, favoring Ali, who died in battle against Sunni troops outside Karbala in A.D. 680.

We also distinguished a Shia home by the portraits and posters of the Grand Ayatollah Al-Sistani, a revered Shiite cleric who attempted to work with American forces in the past. But the most obvious evidence was a picture of radical young cleric Muqtada Al Sadr. He heads the Mahdi Army, a loosely organized group consisting of thousands of armed men who followed his orders and rose up against American forces in 2004. It gave me such a feeling of futility to walk into one of these homes and see posters of Al Sadr on the refrigerator or wall. We sacrificed American lives for these same people, spent billions of dollars to "liberate" them, and yet their "hero" is a radical Muslim who hates the United States.

Following the discovery of a number of IEDs in our sector off Route Alaska, a paved road not far from the Safe House, we conducted a series of coordinated sweeps through the area in conjunction with Iraqi army units based out of the Lion's Den. Not long after our arrival in Iraq, they began asking for volunteers to act as advisors for the Iraqi troops, a duty similar to the U.S. advisors during the Vietnam War who went out with South Vietnamese forces. At first that position seemed interesting, but once we began to recognize the Iraqi Army's questionable competency, no one coveted this position. Insurgent infiltration of Iraqi troops became a bone of contention. Iraqi interpreters working with American forces had been caught on cell phones right before a mortar attack, though most of them proved to be loyal.

The Iraqi Army's soldiers were motivated, but they possessed poor leadership and lacked a clear agenda. Composed primarily of Shiite soldiers, the new Iraqi Army's job was to confront the predominately Sunni insurgent threat.[1] They had no sympathy for the Sunni for obvious reasons. But that presented a problem for a fledgling "democracy." Sunni/Shiite distrust and hatred had been a part of life in the region for hundreds of years. The clear separation between the two sects became obvious when we conducted our sweeps through the small villages off Route Alaska. The operation (in theory) was supposed to be a surprise, but like most operations conducted by American forces, the bad guys already knew we were coming.

The Iraqi Army doesn't exactly move at lightning speed. We'd arrive early, not long after sunrise. The Iraqi units would eventually show up. Then it took half an hour to forty-five minutes before order was imposed and the Iraqi soldiers organized themselves in seven to ten man squads assigned to an American soldier. They'd stand and argue amongst themselves, and after a time I would find seven or eight Iraqis assigned to me. Once this was accomplished, we spent another ten or fifteen minutes getting them in line so we could sweep across the area and search all the homes in the vicinity. However, I'd never end up with the same Iraqi soldiers I started out with. Invariably, I would have more or less.

This will sound intolerant and insensitive, but the only way to operate with the Iraqi Army was to view them as children. If you instruct a child

---

1. This would change however. By early 2007, the majority of American deaths were caused by Shiite militia members backed by the government of Iran.

to clean his room, he will probably begin, but the minute you turn your back, he'll screw off. Likewise, I'd tell Iraqi soldiers to search a house, and they would, but the minute I turned my back, they slipped out of sight and started messing around. I had two or three Iraqi soldiers who decided to wander off and join another section that was clearing a different area simply because they wanted to hang out with their friends. The Iraqi officers just stood there, impotent. Exasperated at first, I eventually accepted it as it was and just laughed.

During these sweeps, the predominately Shiite troops would ransack the homes belonging to Sunni families. I'd have to tell them to stop throwing things around and keep moving. On one occasion, an Iraqi soldier handed me some souvenirs he'd discovered—a commemorative plate representing the power of the former Baath party and a wad of former currency and coins used during the Saddam years, which were now worthless. For many of these Shiite soldiers, this was payback for the Sunni soldiers who had ransacked Shiite homes in the past.

On the other hand, when they entered a Shiite home, they would hang out and have the family cook them breakfast (never mind the fact our operation had *time constraints*). The Shiite sect of Islam makes up 60% of the population in Iraq, with the Sunnis accounting for 20% of the total. The Shia are now reasserting their power after years of oppression under Saddam's rule. There's no sympathy for the Sunni, nor do they expect it. The balance of power has shifted. The Sunni who had a privileged status under Saddam know that "democracy" in Iraq will not benefit them in any way. As it is in all democracies, the majority rules, so now the Shia have the power and control. If you intend to "liberate" a country, you're going to encounter problems when a large segment of the population never wanted to be "liberated" to begin with. For the Sunni, it's about survival. They know they will never have a true say in the government, and the Shiite-dominated government know they have the power and no intention of giving it up. The division between the two sects of Islam has widened with our invasion.

The young boys who hung out at the Safe House all came from Shiite families. One day the water pipes next to the Safe House broke, creating a small lake right outside the concertina wire. An Iraqi construction crew was brought in to repair the damage. It took about two days to finish the job, but on the first day, our patrol happened to be at the Safe House. I and another soldier got the boring job of pulling security, basically standing in the hot sun and watching the men work. On this day a number of the kids from the Safe House hung out with us. After awhile, another group of boys about the same age walked out of the palm grove nearby and joined us. The newcomers were Sunni. The two groups of boys, separated by the concertina wire, confronted each other. The Shiite boys considered themselves privileged because of their monopoly on the Safe House. However, I couldn't tell the difference between them—they all looked alike. To me they were just a bunch of kids hanging out before going home for dinner.

In *Ruling Your World*, the Sakyong warns against planting the wrong seed in our deepest consciousness, an act that can have long-term consequences for us as well as others. The Tiger's discernment means we have a choice in life: what kinds of seeds get planted and whether they're watered with love and compassion or hate and anger. A negative environment such as Iraq provided fertile ground for planting seeds of resentment and blame, sentiments common among the adult population of Iraq affected by the war's violence, but it was the impact on the children, the next generation where the seeds of hope might flourish, that mattered most.

One of the boys on my side of the wire quickly informed me with a tone of disgust that those boys on the opposite side were "Sunni." The whole scene was a bizarre dichotomy of cultures, and I was caught in the middle. All these kids should have been playing happily together, except at some point their parents, religious leaders, or friends told them that they were "different," and that misguided logic separated them. It made them see one another as either inferior or superior to the other. The same concept holds for children in America. When they are young they don't recognize a color line separating them between black, white, or brown; then at some point they are indoctrinated into recognizing a "difference" where one had never existed before. In Iraq, abstract concepts of "democracy" and "freedom" meant nothing to these boys. Freedom, at least for the Shiite children, meant an opportunity to be bullies because they had become the privileged group. While we stood and watched the men work on the broken water pipe, a lone car drove down the dirt road near the Safe House. One of the Shiite kids from my side of the wire came close to me, pointed at the car, smiled mischievously, and said, "Shoot him, he's Sunni." I shook my head and laughed in disgust. Saddam was gone, but the fundamental mentality and awareness necessary to appreciate and comprehend democracy didn't exist. Respect for human decency and compassion, at least as we in the West understand it, was something completely alien to these children. And they are Iraq's future.

CHAPTER TEN

DEATH BEFORE LUNCH

They wrote in the old days that it is sweet fitting to die for one's country. But in modern war, there is nothing sweet nor fitting in your dying. You will die like a dog for no good reason.

—Ernest Hemingway
For Whom the Bell Tolls

After only three months in Iraq, I made the decision to come home on my two week leave. It was early in the deployment, but I missed my wife and children. The trip home involved flying to Kuwait and then taking a commercial airliner to the United States. It felt great to be able to sit at a bar in Atlanta's airport and drink a cold beer. Many travelers at the airport were helpful and friendly, offering the use of their cell phones. One man thanked me and shook my hand as I exited the men's bathroom. It was all a little embarrassing, but definitely better than being berated like many soldiers returning from Vietnam.

According to Claude Thomas Anshin, a Vietnam veteran (now a Zen Buddhist monk) and author of *At Hell's Gate*, a young woman spit on him at the airport when he returned home from his tour of duty. I had an hour layover at the airport before my flight to Jacksonville. As I sat at the bar, I watched the TV screen bordered by the bright red, white, and blue colors of Fox News where the huge swirling monstrosity of Hurircane Katrina slowly moved toward New Orleans and the Gulf Coast. After only two beers I began to feel a little tipsy, but it was time to head to my gate. I couldn't wait to get home and see my wife and kids.

After the brief flight, I exited the gate with my desert-colored backpack over my shoulder. I walked down the long corridor where I hoped my family would be waiting. I saw them—my wife Robin and my young sons, Alex (6) and Sean (4). Now, some say my boys look just like me, but others think they resemble their mother. Both definitely got her beautiful bright blue eyes. Alex is thin and eats little, while his younger brother is stocky and eats like a pig. As I got closer to them, I slowed down. I wanted to draw out the moment, but then I heard my wife yell, "Walk faster!" I picked up the pace. A female security guard had prevented my family from moving past her, but when she saw me, she told my wife it was okay for my boys to run to me. My wife was crying, and my boys ran to me as fast as they could. I put my backpack down and embraced them as they collided with me. My wife watched as I hugged and kissed them. She came to me, and I kissed her as well. We were a family again.

The joy of the moment did not last long. As Hurricane Katrina started to wallop New Orleans, my own storm began. My wife had convinced her mother to let us stay at her mobile home for the first couple of days before driving down to Coco Beach to enjoy the time share condo my father had given us for the week. We only stayed with my mother-in-law for one night. That first night after returning from Iraq I woke suddenly. The loud noise and bright red flash of an IED brought me back to the night I'd narrowly escaped death in the ambush—a classic PTSD nightmare. I looked over at my wife and put my hand to my forehead. I was home and safe, at least for the moment. After a time, I managed to fall back to sleep.

We left the following day. My relationship with my wife's mother wasn't exactly amicable, and I wasn't comfortable staying with her. She'd been divorced four times, and she often took out on me the deep resentment she harbored toward her ex-husbands. I'd agreed to move my family into the house she had purchased after following us out to Florida from California in the naïve belief that it would bring us all together as a family. However, she at once began to treat me as an outsider and worked to turn her daughter against me.

In Coco Beach, we had a great hotel room and terrible weather. I chose August for my leave because I wanted to spend time on the beach. Having lived in Florida since 2003, I should have anticipated hurricane season. It rained the entire time. Not that it mattered much—I was happy just to be home. However, it became obvious that my wife expected more. She'd failed to save money for our trip and for my two weeks home on leave, so we encountered financial problems that escalated into stress and conflict. It came to a head when we didn't have enough money for gas just to get back to Jacksonville. The week in Coco Beach was a complete failure, and we spent the last four days of my leave in Jacksonville. We hung out with friends and seemed to have a decent time. But something about my wife had changed. It was as though she'd come to some sort of conclusion in her head, and I had no idea what it was. I just tried to enjoy the last bit of time before returning to Iraq. When she dropped me off at the airport, we hugged and kissed, but our goodbyes were stiff and emotionless—far different from the feelings we shared when I had arrived two weeks earlier.

Once again, I dismissed these negative thoughts. I was headed back to Iraq with the possibility of returning in a coffin. I watched with resignation as my wife pulled away from the curb and drove off without looking back. I threw my backpack over my shoulder and walked inside the terminal. Within a few days I would again be on patrol, driving around our sector and waiting to be blown up, all thoughts of the disheartening week at Coco Beach gone from my mind.

* * * * *

Shortly after I returned from leave, we were ordered to launch an air assault on a defunct Russian-built power plant along the Euphrates River. Our infantry battalion was nicknamed "Devils," so they titled the operation "Devil Strike." For some reason, the American military likes to name operations in Iraq and Afghanistan with action-packed names. Maybe the generals at the Pentagon think naming operations in Afghanistan "Mountain Thrust" and "Mountain Fury" will scare the bad guys into submission. Then again, naming a military operation "Desert Blossom" would probably not instill a lot of motivation in a soldier.

We received a briefing on the mission a few days before the raid. Operation "Devil Strike" was intended to rout out 150 to 200 insurgents who were using the defunct power plant as a base of operations near the city of Yusifiyah, a predominately Sunni stronghold hostile to U.S. forces. According to our briefing, they stored a large number of weapon caches there.

After we sat on the airport tarmac for nearly four hours, the UH-60 Blackhawk helicopters finally arrived. We ran toward the waiting birds and climbed in for a flight south into one of the most dangerous areas in all of Iraq. The original plan included driving all the way down to the power plant. Fortunately, someone with sense realized that if we had done that, we most likely would have had our assess handed to us. The insurgents would have known when we were coming and created an IED alley all the way to the Euphrates River. In addition, we wouldn't have gotten a cool ride on a helicopter, affording us an opportunity to see more of the country. Lifting off from Baghdad International Airport, we flew over various villages. I could see the rooftops of the houses and was surprised at how low we were flying. Someone with an AK47 could fire up at us and take us out with a lucky shot, but I had to assume that the Black Hawk pilots knew what they were doing. Throughout the flight, the helicopter pilots shot red flares into the darkness in case someone fired a surface to air-missile at us. The flares prevent a rocket from striking the helicopter by diverting it toward the flare's heat signature. I considered the distance to the buildings below us. If we did take fire, it was unlikely the pilot would have to time to react, but what did I know? I was just some "Joe" along for the ride.

The flight was brief; before I knew it, we were preparing to land. Not that I could recognize a damn thing in the darkness because we had only the intermittent lights of a few surrounding buildings to guide us. I noticed the compound wall first, then a small house nearby. The helicopter touched down in a field just outside the walls. Bear in mind that this was the dry season; nearly every field I'd encountered outside of the irrigation canals was relatively parched—except for one. Of all the fields in Iraq we had to land in, this one was the wettest, muddiest, most ill-suited field in the whole country. The second we touched down, I jumped out of the helicopter. Big mistake.

I suddenly found my boots stuck in thick mud up to my ankles. This would not have been a serious problem—except I had at least a hundred pounds on my back, a load of ammo on my vest, an M4 rifle, a number of high explosive rounds for a grenade launcher, *and* I was trying not to fall over as I extricated myself from my helicopter with a four-foot AT4 rocket launcher in my hands. The only sound I heard as I landed was an ominous *thunk* as my feet sunk into the wet field. I was stuck. Hell, we all were. This was obviously going to be nothing like *Apocalypse Now* and a lot like *Keystone Kops* in a war zone. Once I got my boots released from the muck, I ran a short distance. And believe me, it *was* a short distance.

After about a hundred feet, I was done. *Smoked.* I was so exhausted that I didn't care if someone did shoot me. I fell to my knees, threw my pack down, and tossed the bulky rocket launcher down in the mud next to me. I got behind my pack for cover, loaded a magazine, and aimed my weapon toward the house a few yards away. That's when I noticed the barrel of my gun had filled with muck, preventing me from firing. Unfortunately, I wasn't the only one with Iraqi mud shoved up his gun barrel.

A friend to the right of me looked at the area through his night vision goggles, raised his weapon and pointed at a movement a short distance away. I saw the enemy too—a cow tied to a tree—so I told him not to fire. We lay there for a few minutes, exhausted and confused. The cow continued to stare at us with a bemused look on its face, the ringing of a small bell around its neck piercing the darkness (it was almost like it was thinking, "Not this crap again!"). The modern AN/PVS-14 night vision devices work well, but the green glow that illuminates the night for you can make you feel disoriented and claustrophobic. I eventually found the strength to get up with all the weight. I stumbled around, making my way towards the dirt path that ran along the power plant walls. As I walked, I encountered a soldier laying in the field. He resembled a turtle, stuck on his back by the weight of his pack. I helped him to his feet. A few minutes later, once again on dry land, we reorganized. Then the "fun" began.

My section had to secure a main entryway into the compound. After landing, we were to search the homes in the immediate area. It was dark, of course, the only illumination coming from a few bulbs casting an ominous glow around some of the doorways. Once the helicopters left, there was nothing but silence—no barking dogs, no sounds from inside the houses. No doubt, the local residents had heard the incoming helicopters but were smart enough to stay inside. Once we consolidated ourselves and caught our breath, we moved down the dirt path that ran along the cement walls. The construction of these walls was typical third world. Large gaps ran between each section, which allowed us to easily slip underneath the wall and into the compound. But before we could take over one of the main entry points into the power plant, another section of soldiers had to complete their assignment by clearing the homes around the compound. While this went on, we stopped to rest against the wall. A contingent of the Iraqi army joined us, and we waited while the engineers and other units swept through the power plant to eliminate any insurgents and search for weapons caches. While we waited, PVT. Gilley and I lay down in a small hole and stuck our heads under the wall for a good view. We saw nothing exciting, just the inside of an abandoned power plant. However, we heard explosions, indicating the engineers were blowing open doors and holes in the walls of buildings to gain entrance. Gilley and I stayed in the hole for at least half an hour.

As I sat in the hole, I noticed SGT. Moore and a few others walking toward a nearby house. Gilley and I stood up. I asked a remaining member of my section where they were going. That's when an Iraqi soldier only a few feet away stood and raised his weapon directly at me, ready to fire. Afraid that the Iraqi soldier might shoot, Gilley ducked back into the hole. Fearing any sudden movement, I just stood there, staring at the Iraqi soldier one second away from putting a bullet in me.

Once he recognized I was American, he lowered his weapon.

This incident wasn't really the Iraqi soldier's fault. Not knowing I was in the hole a few feet away, he reacted with alarm when I suddenly popped up. He had every right to jump up and point his weapon, believing I'd snuck under the wall to surprise him. Nevertheless, the incident was disconcerting. The sun had yet to rise, and there would be death before lunch.

Once the sun came up and the engineers had finished looking for weapons caches, we set up a road block at one of the main entrances, preventing entry into and out of the compound. But we had no means of blocking the road, so we had to improvise. In addition to needing something to block the road in case a suicide bomber drove up to our makeshift checkpoint, my chain of command decided we needed vehicles to haul our packs and gear around. The duty of "borrowing" cars for these tasks from the local Iraqis fell on me. I was the only soldier in our section who understood a few words of Arabic, so I was elected to be the interpreter. I guess I was the most logical choice. Both Janes and Moore knew I liked interacting with the locals, so if someone were going to die acquiring car keys, it might as well be SGT. Kendel.

Resigning myself to the task and armed with my Arabic language guidebook, I walked over to the nearest house a few yards away, accompanied by PVT. Gilley and the (as usual) hyper-nervous SGT. T. As I approached, the man of the house greeted me. He politely invited me into his home. I think he knew the drill by now, as most Iraqis did. His wife and children stepped aside while I made a cursory search of his house. It had been searched earlier, and I knew there wasn't a threat. I tried to be as pleasant as I could, but when it came time to ask the man for the keys to his car so I could "borrow" it, he looked at me strangely, as well he should have. How would you like to have a bunch of American soldiers land by helicopter in your front yard in the middle of the night and then show up in the morning demanding the use of your car? I'm sure there's something in the Geneva Convention against such actions, but what were these poor bastards to do? Have their lawyer file a complaint with the U.S. government? After a tortuous period of attempting to explain to this man in Arabic that we needed his car, he finally got the point. I held out my hand and asked for the keys. He looked around and saw nothing but armed American soldiers. He really had no choice. With obvious apprehension, he reached into his pocket. I tried to reassure him that we would return his car, but he didn't look very convinced. I didn't blame him.

Taking his keys, I hopped into the car, a nice blue sedan, reasonably new, better than most in Iraq. I took off my helmet, started the engine, and got the a/c going. I didn't want my friends to think I was a suicide bomber, so I radioed them at the check point a short distance away. I told

CPL. Gibbs that I'd be driving up to the checkpoint shortly in a blue car and requested he tell the others not to shoot me. He acknowledged my request. With my helmet off, I cranked up the radio, blaring "Hajji" tunes, and drove toward the checkpoint, assuming they knew I was coming.

They didn't.

Apparently when CPL. Gibbs said, *"Don't shoot the blue car,"* my two friends in the road heard, *"Shoot the blue car."* Not good. Anyway, there I was, driving a little too fast, radio blaring, making a joke of the situation, when I saw PVT. Baker begin to raise his weapon at me and yelled something to CPL. Gibbs.

Something was wrong. I stopped the car abruptly. Baker was a hair's breadth away from putting a dozen bullets in my chest. SPC. Fleming, who manned our makeshift foxhole, had turned the machine gun toward me ready to unleash a barrage of bullets. At the last second before firing, they recognized me, with my uniform and digital grey bandana on my head. That would be the last time I would get in a Hajji car and drive up to a checkpoint. At least now I know what it feels like to be a tomato farmer driving up to an American checkpoint.

By maybe ten o'clock in the morning, not long after nearly being shot by my own friends, I would be asked to knock on another door and "borrow"—basically *steal*—another car for our use. This fairly well-off family had three cars from which to choose. At the end of negotiations, I had another set of keys placed in my hand. The owner, fearing what he was quite right to fear, said in broken English, *"No bombs?"* He made hand gestures indicating his minivan being blown up. I smiled and told him no, we would not let that happen. His words were almost prophetic.

It was just about lunch time, and I'd almost been killed twice by then. In spite of it all, I was getting a little hungry. With one of the "borrowed" cars blocking the road, a makeshift fighting position, and a poncho to block the sun, I settled in with SPC. Fleming. After the engineers had finished their job, word had reached us that they'd found no insurgents or weapons caches. As I lay in the dirt, sweating profusely, I began to realize that this whole mission was a joke, a complete waste of time. Unfortunately, I started to relax. There are a number of signs all over Iraq stating, *"Complacency Kills,"* and they're right. Lying there in the hot sun under that poncho, I found myself drifting off to sleep behind the M240 machine gun. Fleming was already knocked out next to me. I wanted the helicopters to return so we could get the hell out of this place. About an hour had passed filled only with heat and perspiration with nothing noteworthy going on.

Then I heard something odd, a sudden whirring *"zzzzzz"* sound. I never saw the rocket, though I heard it go over the compound wall. It had flown right over our heads. I figured someone was firing inside the power plant arbitrarily, hoping to hit either American or Iraqi soldiers inside. No big deal, I thought, and I relaxed a little. Then a second rocket hit right in front of the house where I'd been standing when I "borrowed" the keys from the first man. No big deal, I thought again. That one must have fallen short. A couple of seconds passed. *Zzzzzzz.* A third rocket landed across the dirt road where SGT. T, SPC. Felix (the dog killer), and CPL. Gibbs manned positions behind some dirt piles.

Oh shit, I thought. They're not firing into the compound, they're firing at *us!* I looked behind me and saw my friend SPC. Petty on his hands and knees, doing everything he could to find cover under the minivan I'd promised nothing would happen to. He yelled into the radio for the Viper element to provide us with cover. Once again, in their infinite wisdom, the "higher ups" in the 48th Brigade didn't have the Viper element on call in the immediate area. They would have to redirect their mission from the airport and fly south to aid us. After the third rocket, the guys on the other side of the dirt road got up and ran for their lives behind the compound walls. As SGT. T hustled by, I asked if he wanted me and Fleming to stay behind the gun. He paid no attention—he was saving his ass.

At this point, Fleming and I had our heads down in the dirt as far as they'd go. Petty ran behind the walls once they got his message for the Viper element. I suddenly remembered my promise to the man whose mini-van we had "borrowed." *"No bombs?"* he had asked, *pleaded*. Karma can be a real bitch, I thought, as I pictured a rocket landing directly on top of his mini-van. Then I heard the distinctive *zzzzz* sound of another rocket. This one landed less than thirty feet to the left of us. I felt a sudden gratitude for the muck I'd cussed earlier; the soft, damp earth absorbed most of the impact. When the rocket exploded, I looked at Fleming and said, "You grab the gun and I'll get the ammo! Let's get the fuck out of here!" We ran as fast as we could up the road and behind the compound wall, jumping into a hole along with everyone else. I looked at CPL. Gibbs.

"Thanks for taking off on us," I joked. He just stared at me.

It was lunch time. I had yet to eat, and I'd nearly been killed three times. The afternoon wasn't looking too promising.

* * * * *

Fortunately, none of our group were killed. The first rocket that flew over the wall hit a shed where one of our Iraqi interpreters and some Iraqi soldiers were sitting to avoid the sun. It blew Nelson, the interpreter, to pieces, and wounded two or three Iraqi soldiers. Later, the raid on the power plant became known as *Operation Just Because*—just because that's exactly what it was. We had mounted a huge air assault on a defunct power plant simply to make it look like we were doing something.

The 48th Brigade brass would dismiss the fact that we discovered no insurgents or weapons caches. "The operation was a success because we confirmed that this facility is secure and that no insurgent activity is being conducted here," stated LTC. Steve McCorkel, commander of the 2nd Battalion. But we had to wonder, *since the United States military possesses satel-*

lite technology and sophisticated aircraft with night vision, why couldn't we tell if two hundred armed insurgents were actually operating within the power plant? Therefore, we launched a massive operation and risked sending ourselves home in body bags to prove that something that might be there wasn't there—one step closer to total victory in the global war on terror.

We didn't leave the power plant that afternoon; in fact, we were forced to sit around the compound until the following afternoon. We dug fox holes along the banks of the Euphrates River and spent the night, waiting for word on the choppers. That evening along the Euphrates was a surreal experience. We could only dig maybe two feet down into the hard ground with our entrenching tools, leaving ourselves silhouetted from the other side of the river. We had little choice though, because we needed a position in which to cover the power plant from the river's edge. The foxhole accommodated me, Gibbs, Felix, and Ross. We'd brought enough ammo and explosives to take on an army, but had failed to bring certain necessities like sufficient food and water. One of the biggest mistakes was not bringing one of the most essential items in a war zone— toilet paper. That night, lying on the ground near the foxhole, I awoke to the strangest feeling: cold. At first I had no idea what the sensation was; it must have come from the river, but it felt odd to suddenly feel something other than heat. Periodically throughout the night, another unit popped red flares over the river to illuminate the area and scan for insurgents trying to sneak up on us. It reminded me of the scene from *Apocalypse Now* where red flares streak over the water while the patrol boat makes its way up north toward mad Colonel Kurtz and the unknown.

I'm not a morning person, so I'm generally not a big fan of sunrises. However, watching the sunrise along the banks of the Euphrates that day was worthwhile. Of course, I was only here due to another typical intelligence blunder, similar to the raid on the funeral home. Nevertheless, that morning on the river, *Operation Just Because* provided an opportunity to see the lives of Iraqis unfold. With my binoculars I looked out over the river at a small house nestled in a lush green palm grove a short distance from the water. I thought the scene must have been very much the same as it had been thousands of years ago when the prophet Abraham walked the land, with dogs barking, cows and goats moving about, and a woman walking down to the river with a bucket to collect water for tea. For me, this commonplace Iraqi scene was a memorable experience.

Digging fox holes and securing the back side of a powerplant located along the Euphrates River, in this commonplace Iraqi scene, was a memorable experience for me. —Photo by Scott Ross.

For whatever reason, Iraqi insurgents are not "morning terrorists" any more than I am a morning person. Though around ten or eleven, the mortar rounds began. We evacuated our foxholes and ran to the only part of the power plant that offered overhead protection. Huddling inside a long unfinished cement tunnel, we sat out the mortar attack. Their impacts shook the ground. Some fell so close that dirt and shrapnel landed less than a hundred meters away. This went on for about an hour and then suddenly stopped. During these attacks, I tried to sleep. If I was going to get blown up, I would just as soon be asleep when it happened.

After the hour of periodic shelling, we returned to our foxholes. We had no reason to stick around. We'd found no insurgents, no weapons caches, *nothing*. Our net gain was a cool ride in a Black Hawk helicopter and the witnessing of a lovely Euphrates sunrise. Our net losses included a fiasco of a landing, one dead Iraqi interpreter, and a number of wounded Iraqi soldiers. That my friends and I came very close to being statistics by nearly getting killed fit into neither category.

Later that afternoon, we received word that we'd be returning to Baghdad International Airport by evening. As we marched through the power plant to exit the compound, I saw the "threat" that the power plant had possessed: about twelve bored-looking Iraqi men, sitting on the ground, arms tied behind their backs—apparently the skeleton crew who maintained the plant. A few months later these poor individuals would have to go through the same nightmare again when our replacements, the 101st Airborne Division, conducted the exact same mission on the same power plant. I'm sure those soldiers were told, as were we, about the two hundred insurgents and dozens of weapons caches. Unfortunately, 101st Airborne wouldn't be able to laugh over the incident. Some of their men would die.

CHAPTER ELEVEN

WHEN EGO PREVAILS

*Military glory—that attractive rainbow that rises in
showers of blood—that serpent's eye that charms to destroy.*
Abraham Lincoln

Insurgents in Iraq had various reasons for wanting to kill American soldiers: religion, removing an occupying power, and of course, money. These motivations dominated, but like Americans, insurgents also succumb to the charms of glory and ego. Buddhism regards ego as the major impediment toward enlightenment. In his book, *Good Life, Good Death*, Tibetan lama Gehlek Rinpoche teaches that "the maker of trouble, the source of all our suffering, the destroyer of our joy, and the destroyer of our virtue is inside. It is Ego."

After one particular daytime IED attack, the man responsible could have easily vanished. However, his own ego led to his capture. LT. Donaldson, our platoon leader, decided to stop the patrol one day in a lush palm grove to take a break from the afternoon heat. LT. Donaldson's section relaxed, leaving the gunners awake and vigilant, standing in the turret of each humvee and scanning the area while the rest of the patrol either slept or stood near the vehicles. After an hour or two, everyone exited the palm grove, making the mistake of leaving the same way they'd come in. Near the edge of the grove, SPC. Vaughn, Donaldson's driver, spotted something odd directly in front of the vehicle. Stopping the humvee abruptly, he said, "What's that buried in the dirt?"

LT. Donaldson and Sam Bopp got out to investigate. Not wanting to walk right up on the mysterious object, Donaldson ordered Bopp to shoot at it. Taking cover behind the vehicle, Bopp fired three shots that ricocheted off metal with attached wires. Meanwhile, another member of the section noticed a small white Toyota pickup truck inching slowly down a dirt road about a hundred meters away. The man stared at them as if waiting for something to happen. He looked so suspicious that Lt. Donaldson ordered one of the humvees to drive around the suspected IED and intercept the suspicious truck.

Donaldson detained the driver and interrogated him. The man insisted he hadn't buried it, so Donaldson—who was in no mood for games—ordered him to walk over and stand on top of the object. The man's eyes bulged. He panicked when he realized the American was serious and suddenly changed his story. He admitted he had planted it, but said someone else had made it. Now, if the detainee had simply driven off instead of inching suspiciously down the road, he would've gotten away. But his own ego prevailed. He wanted to watch the destruction of a humvee and, in all likelihood, the resulting American deaths.

For the average person who hasn't served in the military, the desire to get a "kill" seems insane. But in war, when you've trained hard to meet the enemy and imagined exterminating him, you may live for the "kill." For example, the film *Jarhead* is a true story about a group of young Marines during the first Gulf War in 1991. The Marines are confused

WALKING THE TIGER'S PATH
PAUL M. KENDEL

and angry when the war ends after only four days. No one has killed any enemy or even fired a weapon. Near the end of the film, all the men fire their weapons into the air to release their pent up aggression. In the Vietnam War film *Full Metal Jacket*, the lead character, Joker, declares, "I wanted to see exotic Vietnam, the jewel of Southeast Asia. I wanted to meet interesting and stimulating people of an ancient culture and kill them. I wanted to be the first kid on my block to get a confirmed kill." His statement is in jest, but it is also a criticism of those around him who possessed that desire. While at Camp Stryker, we had plenty of opportunities to fire our weapons. Some soldiers killed, but most did not. Some guys even saw getting a "kill" purely as an opportunity for vivid story-telling to their buddies back home in the local bar. Serving in Iraq gave an ordinary American soldier—someone who worked in a dull, monotonous factory or government job—*power*.

The majority of soldiers in my unit went to Iraq with the purpose of serving with honor and distinction. Our training had established how we were expected to conduct ourselves in a war zone. Our mission's purpose was to protect and stabilize the area, not just as a military objective, but for the sake of the civilians and, by extension, the Iraqi government. However, maintaining the mission's integrity required that the integrity of individual soldiers remain intact.

One evening we received word that a family living in one of the ubiquitous broken down buildings around the Safe House had information about a rival family that had supposedly threatened to attack the Safe House. We stopped our patrol a short distance from the informants' house in the late evening. SGT. T told us we weren't going into this house with guns blazing, but only to talk to them about the rival family who'd reportedly threatened them as well as us.

We were to walk up to the house, knock on the door, and allow our interpreter to speak to the family. An almost full moon cast an ominous glow over the area. We moved out from the humvees using night vision and made our way down a short dirt path through some small trees in an effort to come up on the house unnoticed. The upper level was unoccupied, and I could see that parts of the walls were missing. The family resided on the bottom level. Lights shone from the main room near the entrance. We moved quietly up to the back of the building and encountered an old man resting up against it. We had the interpreter talk to him and ask him what was happening in the house. Following this brief conversation, which I didn't hear, SPC. Petty and I were instructed to stay at the back of the building to provide rear security while the rest of the section went to the front of the house to speak to the family. Less than a minute had passed when I heard a loud bang as the front door was kicked open, followed by two rapidly fired shots, *pop, pop* from an American weapon. *What the hell happened?* I thought. This was supposed to be simple: walk up to the house, knock on the door, and ask a few questions. There wasn't supposed to be any *shooting*.

I told SPC. Petty to stay put while I went around to the front of the house. What I found was utter confusion: women and children screaming as they came outside onto the steps. Calling out "friendly coming in" to announce my presence, I entered the building. Inside was a small foyer, directly ahead was the kitchen, and to the left was the main living room. From the living room floor, two men handcuffed with plastic ties around their wrists stared at me. At the end of the room in the corner, a shirtless Iraqi man slumped in the middle of a pool of blood that was spreading into the rest of the room. SGT. Moore stood over him. The scene reminded me of pictures I'd seen of Ernest Hemingway standing proudly and triumphantly over a lion he'd hunted and shot on an African safari. In that instant I remembered what Moore had said to me earlier that morning, something I'd found disturbing but quickly dismissed. "I can't go home on leave without a kill!" he declared as we got dressed. He was due to return home for two weeks within a day or two. "I've been in Iraq for five months! How can I go home and drink beers with my friends without telling them I shot anyone?" he lamented.

I left the house and called to SPC. Petty to come and assist me. At the entrance to the building, a young boy, who I recognized from the Safe House, said, "Why did you do this? We like America." Without knowing the details of the incident but realizing that something had gone terribly wrong, I thought to myself, *Not anymore you don't*. My gaze shifted to a young woman, no more than 19 or 20 years old, holding a brand new baby in her arms. Her stare seemed to place the blame for what had happened inside the building on *me*. I soon discovered that it was her husband lying in a pool of blood on the floor.

Once SPC. Petty arrived, we went inside to clear the rest of the building. We had no idea what was going on. After nearly slipping and falling in water on the kitchen floor, we made it up the stairs to the upper level. With the roof and most of the walls missing, we quickly cleared the upper level for potential danger and returned to the living room. Moore still stood over the body of the wounded Iraqi. I moved toward him and placed my weapon on the couch. I helped him pull the man away from the corner of the room and into the middle where we could lay him out on his back. We attempted to provide medical care. SGT. Moore prepared an I.V., while I tried to hold the man down, who kept squirming on the tile floor in a half-conscious state. The pool of blood continued growing; I kept slipping in it while trying to hold the man down. One of the bullets had clearly hit a main artery because the blood was coagulated and dark. The wounds were below the waist, so we had to remove his pants. He wore no underwear.

We looked at his wounds. One bullet had penetrated his left leg; a second bullet had grazed his scrotum. The skin was hanging open, exposing the shiny, white testicle within. I'd never expected to be this close to an Iraqi, especially a naked one shot in the balls. While SGT. Moore placed a bandage around the man's leg and prepared the I.V., I asked him what happened. He told me when he entered the living room, along with SGT. T and PVT. Gilley, the man was sitting on the couch and reached behind it for what he thought was a weapon. He put two bullets in him. It turned out to be a metal pipe, not a gun. But SGT. Moore could not have known this. He had a split second to react. Why he busted the door down and went in with guns blazing, only he knows. We were just supposed to knock on the door and use our interpreter to speak to the family. But in Iraq things can change quickly. One minute you're walking up to a house with no expectations of violence, and then suddenly you're compelled to break the door in, and you end up shooting a man in his living room surrounded by his family, including his wife and newborn child.

Fifteen minutes later, a medic from the Safe House arrived. We got the I.V. in the man and stabilized him for the moment. I looked around the room. The two other men had been removed. An Arabic language game show of some type blared from the television. I paused for a moment, caught up in the surreal scene. This man was bleeding to death on his own living room floor with his family outside, weeping for him; and I was suddenly transfixed by a game show on T.V. Outside, SGT. T had called in the incident to Animal X-Ray, our tactical operations center. When SGT. T had followed SGT. Moore into the room, he got smacked in the arm by a boy with a small shovel. SGT. T pushed the boy away, but panicked by the blow, he backed out of the room, nearly knocking over PVT. Gilley in his haste. He would not return.

The wounded man was obviously close to death after losing so much blood. We requested a medivac helicopter, but got denied. A wounded Iraqi didn't warrant immediate evacuation. We were to drive him back in one of the humvees to a medical facility at Camp Stryker, so we put him on a stretcher and carried him out.

No one other than me and the medic from the Safe House seemed concerned that we get the man to a medical facility before he died. He'd lost an enormous amount of blood but was still breathing and would move about occasionally. We attempted to lay the stretcher across the back of the humvee, but it was too long—we couldn't close the doors.

WALKING THE TIGER'S PATH
PAUL M. KENDEL

We fumbled around a bit, and then I decided we had to do something—quickly! The medic and I pulled him off the stretcher and laid him out over the back seats and the metal plate where the gunner stands. Not the most comfortable position in which to transport a wounded man, but we had little choice. In the course of getting him inside, his testicles caught on a metal ammo can, ripping the skin even more. Still semi-conscious, he continued bleeding, but nothing like the flow in the first few minutes. We covered him up, moved the patrol out, and headed back to Camp Stryker. It only took ten minutes to arrive at the base, but once inside, another ten or fifteen minutes went by before reaching the medical facility near the airport.

Once he was receiving medical attention, the urgency to save the man's life didn't seem to exist. Everyone in the medical facility, including the nurses, were more occupied with their amusement over his having been shot in the balls than they were with trying to keep him from bleeding to death. I didn't linger. I returned to my tent to change uniforms because the one I wore was caked with dried blood. That night's patrol had only begun, and we would soon have to go back outside the relative safety of the wire into the darkness, where the possibility of death always waited. I had left the medical facility believing the wounded Iraqi would live. I was wrong. He died a day later, and SGT. Moore received his "kill."

The photos we took documenting the scene—blood splattered walls, the naked man on his back in a puddle of his blood, his ripped open testicles—proved a source of entertainment as SGT. Moore proudly displayed them on his laptop to various members of our company who came around to see them.

As for me, I will never forget the look on the face of the man's wife while she held their brand new baby in her arms. In her mind it was *me* who'd killed her husband. To her, all American soldiers were the same.

CHAPTER TWELVE

PRAISE: A TWO-EDGED SWORD

Regret is a sign that we have acted without discernment... The point is to learn as much as possible from the feeling of regret.

—Sakyong Mipham,
Ruling Your World

I should've known better, but I was angry. On this particular day, I was not myself. Normally, I wouldn't exchange an opportunity to lie around for a chance to get myself and others killed. Weeks earlier, I'd become a T.C. (truck commander) of a humvee with my own crew. I was in charge of the patrol, not technically the head person, but I was leading the patrol that day. SGT. Moore was on leave.

The temperature had soared to 120 degrees. We splayed out lethargically in the shade at the Safe House. In my mind, I kept replaying a recent phone conversation I'd had with my wife. As usual, she'd been disengaged, disinterested, and cold. She'd go through the motions, giving perfunctory responses about her day and the kids, but never did she ask how I was coping with Iraq or how she might help me deal with being away from them and in the throes of war. She showed no interest whatsoever in what was happening to me. I grew more and more irritated with her behavior: the mishandling of our money, not paying off our bills, and her refusal to search for a home for us. When I challenged her actions, the lack of them, or her tone, she found excuses. When I pushed any of the issues, she'd spin the blame back on me. What I really wanted more than anything was for her to wait patiently for my return so we could work through our issues. Instead, she focused incessantly on problems between us. I shoved these concerns into the back of my mind to the best of my ability, but they kept returning with a vengeance.

Unable to bear the disturbing thoughts in my mind any longer, I sprang to my feet and announced, "Let's go drive around and blow something up!" Everyone gawked at me in bewilderment. CPL. Gibbs didn't look pleased with my sudden enthusiasm. At that moment, I was thinking about finding a field and firing some rounds or high explosive grenades at a dirt mound or something, not at human beings. In the past, I had been proud of my patience and self-restraint in difficult situations. Margot had praised these attributes, stating in one letter that I have a "profound ability to maintain [my] seat in the midst of ridiculously terrible storms, [and] that is a quality that can't help but be of benefit to everyone around you."

On this day, however, all that would change.

Our patrol consisted of three humvees. While driving around, we got a call to stop and investigate a large hanger off Route Aeros, the main road connecting with the primary supply route called Tampa that went from Kuwait all the way up to northern Iraq. It was one of those assignments we'd get in order to make it appear that we weren't just driving around, wasting gas. Our TOC (tactical operations center) needed something to put down in their logs. Across from Aeros, near the hanger, was the small town of Al- Salaam, where my cigar buddy Daylon Brown and his section had discovered an unwanted body and had dumped it at the doorstep of an unfortunate police officer at two in the morning. After searching the hangers and finding nothing of relevance, I decided to take our patrol into Al-Salaam. The town did not have a great reputation for being friendly to American forces and IED's had been discovered nearby, but there had been no serious problems.

Unfortunately, my emotions had clouded my reasoning, and my decision to take the men into a questionable area proved my weakness. I was angry with my wife, disgruntled with my life, and I didn't care what happened to me. I think I was looking for some kind of fight.

Previously in Al-Salaam, the local children swarmed our humvees, literally preventing us from doing our job. They would beg, saying, "Pepsi, my friend, Pepsi?" We'd throw handfuls of candy away from the vehicle to make them go after it just so we could get away. If you think Ultimate Fighting (a Martial Arts competition) is brutal, you haven't seen ten Iraqi kids going at it over a few pieces of candy. Usually there'd be one kid, bloodied and beaten, who'd emerge from the pile with most of the candy in his hand.

Al-Salaam appeared deserted. Most of the children were in school, but usually some kids and young adults would be milling around in the streets. Not on this day. I drove toward the center and stopped right in front of the elaborately constructed mosque. The minaret stood like a sentinel over the town. I got out of the humvee and walked behind the vehicle. Ross scanned the nearby rooftops with his M240 machine gun. Gilley got out of the driver's seat and began to urinate next to the vehicle.

CPL. Gibbs was the TC for the second humvee. As I walked up to him behind the vehicle, he asked what we were doing here. I informed him that we would set up an OP here for a bit. Gibbs looked at me unhappily. Under his breath, he muttered something like, "Fucking SGT. Kendel!" A few seconds later I heard machine gun fire from behind me. I turned and I saw Ross firing his M240 machine gun toward a nearby

Scott Ross behind the M240 machine gun scanning our sector for insurgent activity.

rooftop. I immediately jumped back into the humvee, got on the radio, reported that we were moving out of the town, and told Gilley to go. As we headed down a street leading out of the town, I looked up. Ross raked the entire rooftop with bullets, reminding me of scenes from *Black Hawk Down*. In fact, we have a tape of the incident. SPC. Felix placed his digital camera on the dash of his humvee as he was driving and captured the action. On the tape, the voice of CPL. Gibbs' is clear as he yells, "Put the fucking camera away and drive!"

At the edge of town, I had a choice to go left or right. Left would take us back toward the center of town, so I told Gilley to go right. We turned, and after about a block, a long street appeared on the right that led back toward the mosque. As we passed, Ross and the others fired down the street. According to PVT. Baker, he shot and killed a man at the end of the street, using his M240 machine gun. We moved on to the edge of town, but a ditch prevented us from continuing forward. I ordered Gilley to turn around, but the other two vehicles were backed up behind us. Since I didn't want to return to the center of town, I told SFC. Janes to lead us out to the right of the ditch, where we could make our way around it. I followed in behind him, and all three humvees drove down a dirt road just outside the town before we stopped and requested back up. During a routine patrol, other elements were part of our AO. We also had a QRF (quick reaction force) on call to support any element in need, and we had the Viper element—the Apache helicopters flying above. Fortunately for us, we had extra ammunition at the Safe House, too. When we reported our situation to our TOC, they immediately notified all available units to assist us.

After setting up our patrol a short distance outside the town, the gunners of all three vehicles continued to lay down suppressive fire toward the rooftops of the town. Reinforcements soon arrived. Not that we really needed that much help—we thought we only had to worry about three or four guys at best, but we never knew for sure. Like flies drawn to crap, a chance to actually engage and shoot the enemy would bring almost everyone to Al-Salaam except my former squad leader, SGT. T, whose humvee crew was off during this particular patrol because he was too scared to come out even though he was part of my section.

SGT. T was sometimes so frightened during patrols that when we set up an OP somewhere, he would hang his ass off the side of the humvee while still inside it and take a crap instead of walking a short distance from the vehicle to relieve himself. During a routine TCP, he actually shot at an old man on a donkey cart because the guy was moving up to us at one mile an hour, and I guess he thought it was a DBIED (donkey borne IED). Before we left Camp Stryker and moved down south, a friend drew a picture of a Combat Cowards Badge on the wall of the Safe House. He was referring to SGT. T, who, when leading regular night patrols, found excuses to stay and lay around the Safe House rather than go out and patrol our sector as required. His favorite excuse was, "I just ain't feelin' it, dog," to justify not doing his job. We all understood and felt his fear. It wasn't like any of us wanted to go out and get killed, but if you didn't patrol, you couldn't prevent someone from planting an IED, and that meant the next section might get hit by an IED because someone was too afraid to do his job.

Once our reinforcements arrived, we fired at everything: clothes drying on lines, air-conditioning units, even satellite dishes. Jason Royal nearly fired on a civilian standing on a rooftop. A woman whose head was covered in black appeared like an image in an arcade—her head rose up and just as quickly went back down, apparently when she realized the threat to her safety. The scene seemed so strange that Royal thought he was imagining things.

A large fuel drum sat at the edge of town, and I suddenly got the bright idea to put an HE round into my grenade launcher and fire at it. I hoped this round wouldn't be off the mark. I had a brief moment of dread based on my previous grenade firing experience. To my shock and delight, it actually landed right where I aimed. The loud boom sent dirt and debris flying next to the fuel drum and drew the attention of SFC. Janes, who shouted, "Who the hell fired that?" I shrugged my shoulders and said innocently, "*What?*"

Other guys started to load grenades into their launchers, too, until SFC. Janes ordered them to stop. It seemed that one gratuitous grenade explosion was sufficient.

Our shootout continued for some time. After months of driving around waiting to be blown up without a chance to shoot back at anyone, Al-Salaam gave us a chance to blow off some steam like the Marines at the end of *Jarhead*. While all this firing into the town was going on, the citizens of Al-Salaam went about their ordinary business relatively unfazed, like the tomato farmer we shot up on our first night who casually munched on a cucumber after nearly getting killed. One woman walked down the street holding the hand of her young daughter as if everything was perfectly normal. Young men milled about in the street. Shops remained open for business.

The initial enemy rifle fire had come from the rooftops close to the mosque. We needed to move into that area before the men who fired at us could slip back into the general population. Since neither our company commander nor our battalion commander had arrived, I suggested we move two of the Bradleys pulling security at the edge of town and replace them with humvees. We could then put a squad of soldiers in the back of each Bradley and drive back into town to the area where we'd taken fire, dismount from the vehicles, and conduct a door to door search. SFC. Janes, as well as the senior NCO in charge of the Bradleys, agreed with my plan. When SGT. Jones, a squad leader from Third Platoon gave his approval, everyone backed my plan. I would lead one squad of three other soldiers that included CPL. Gibbs (who was quickly becoming even less pleased with my decision to set up an OP in Al-Salaam), Petty, and Gilley. I stuffed extra HE rounds for my grenade launcher in my pockets, as well as ammo magazines. The other guys took as much ammo as they could carry. We had no idea how long we might be operating away from the rest of the sections or how much contact with the enemy there might be.

We climbed into the back of one of the two Bradleys. I looked at the guys with me. This was about to become serious. Once the ramp came down and we headed to clear the first building, anything was possible. We would be out in the middle of the street where snipers on the rooftops could pick us off. We had the gunner of the Bradley for support, so we definitely had superior firepower and the advantage. Gibbs, Petty, and Gilley looked ready to go. It was an auspicious day for Gilley—his birthday.

And that's when the whole plan got cancelled. The Battalion Commander got involved and ordered us to stand down. He wanted the Iraqi Army to be the ones to sweep the town. Our adrenaline was pumping, and we were ready to take the fight to the bad guys, but we'd now lose the advantage as we waited for the Iraqi Army. CPL. Gibbs and I would not get to break down any doors, but the action at Al-Salaam was far from over.

By this time we had encircled the entire town, and the Viper element was flying above. According to one of the Apache helicopter pilots, they had spotted a muzzle flash from the top of the mosque's minaret, the tall needle-like structure where speakers at the top announce the Muslim call to prayer. Our company commander, CPT. Marc Belscamper, had arrived at the scene and received authorization to return fire at the minaret. Once the order to fire was given, it became a true real-world video game. I gave the go-ahead to fire to my gunner, PVT. Ross; he elevated his M240 machine gun and began raking the minaret from top to bottom. PVT. Baker, gunner on another humvee, started tearing into the minaret as well. Their bursts of fire crisscrossed each other as they riddled the structure with bullets, pounding the speakers at the top. With our

rifles, we began popping off shots at the building. It felt good to be actually shooting at something, even if it was nothing but an inanimate object. This barrage of gunfire went on for a minute or two before someone began calling a cease-fire.

It took about two hours for the Iraqi Army to arrive and organize themselves. At one point we thought we were taking fire again from inside the town, but it was a group of Iraqi soldiers firing their weapons from the backs of their trucks. Unfortunately, they shot from behind us, their bullets going right over our heads. None

Mosque and minaret at Al-Salaam.

of us trusted their marksmanship, and we didn't want to get shot in the back. We told them to stop firing, but at least they seemed motivated. With their arrival, my section with our three humvees drove around to the backside of town to set up security positions while the Iraqi soldiers began to sweep through. I watched young men wander up and down the street. About two to three hundred meters away stood three young men. From this distance I couldn't tell if they were armed or not.

I gave my binoculars to SPC. Youngblood, a gunner on one of the other humvees who had a better view from the turret. He told me one of the young men had an AK47. Youngblood's lack of attention was questionable at times, and I should have been more patient. He once left his M16 rifle behind at the Safe House by accident; I made him do pushups in the dirt for fifteen minutes as a consequence for his forgetfulness. I yelled to SFC. Janes that a man in the street had a weapon. He told me to shoot him. Yet even if he was armed, he wasn't shooting at us, so there was no immediate threat.

Coming to Iraq, I had no problem defending myself or my friends if threatened. Maybe it was the shock of the moment—the hostile fire, the adrenaline rush in the back of the Bradley, waiting to roll into town to knock down doors—that caused me to abandon my normal caution. From a military standpoint, shooting was justified, but since the man appeared to pose no threat, I would've normally waited to make sure he really did have a weapon. Caught up in the situation, I leaned across the humvee's hood, steadied my M4, looked through the sight, placed the small red dot on the center of the man's chest, and fired. I felt like I was going through the motions, outside my body, and someone else was pulling the trigger. The round missed the man's head by only a few inches. He stood in the street, stunned for a moment. I took better aim and fired a second round. This one missed by less than an inch. Realizing someone was shooting at him, he darted across the street and sprinted for cover as quickly as the dog SGT. Moore had tried to gun down. I'd assumed he'd been holding an AK47 pointed at the ground by his leg, but when I saw him running, I realized he didn't have any weapon at all. I had shot at an innocent man who was just standing in the street.

Suddenly, my senses returned. I was overwhelmed by a wave of guilt at what I'd done and a sense of relief that I'd missed. At least I wouldn't have to explain why I'd shot an unarmed civilian. After all my efforts at being level-headed and objective, after all of Margot's praise, I'd fallen blindly into an act of aggression like so many others who didn't seem to care who or what they killed. Maybe because the man was so far away it was like a video game, like he wasn't really a human being. I had held his life in my hands and chosen to end it as casually as you would change the channel on your television. I had played God.

The sun started to set. The Iraqi army began their door to door sweep of the town, but the snipers had had ample time to blend back into the general population. No suspected insurgents were caught.

When I reflected back on what happened at Al-Salaam, I saw that the whole violent sequence was caused by suppressed energy and anger that suddenly exploded. The Buddhist teachings talk about the karmic chain of events. Once the ball of anger gets rolling, you feed it and it grows. Catch it initially, and you can prevent it from going to the next level. However, my rage had hooked me, gained momentum, and progressed into a dangerous situation. If I hadn't run away from my pain about my wife, if I had faced my fears and anger directly, Al-Salaam might not have happened.

I wasn't the only soldier who felt the desire to expend his emotions. The unit also needed to expel the pent up energy of sitting around in the heat, remembering that we had eight dead friends still un-avenged. Even though we'd supposedly captured the men responsible for their deaths, we hadn't been able to extract *blood*. Not even one of us was experiencing the kind of war we expected, and no one was having a good time. This created a collective need for some kind of large-scale event—for everyone.

Later on, back at the base, Bopp and Gilley were sitting on their cots, talking. I came up as Bopp said, "I never saw anyone shooting at us."

Gilley replied, "Ross said he saw three guys on the rooftop, and they fired at him."

I sat down next to Gilley, interjecting, "To be honest, I didn't actually see anyone shoot at us at all."

Bopp threw up his hands. "Thank you!" He went on: "I'm not saying no one fired a shot at Ross, but it wasn't this coordinated attack on the patrol. Maybe one bored guy popped a shot off for kicks, but it wasn't a big ambush with a whole force."

Everyone had a different perspective on what happened and what the Iraqi shooters were doing. But did any of us actually see anything?

The whole conflict was a massive figment of everyone's imaginations. We shot at walls and air conditioners, but finally, we were shooting at *something!* When the other units showed up, they reinforced this—everyone wanted to get some action. This became obvious when the Apache helicopter reported seeing someone in the mosque's minaret. Everyone opened fire on it, from every possible direction, eager to find an opening—any opening—for the expression of their rage. Our imaginations completely riddled that minaret with real bullets.

When SSG. Howard had searched the minaret on a sweep of the town with some Iraqi soldiers, they found no shell casings or blood stains—no evidence at all of a sniper. PFC. Baker's claim that he'd literally cut an enemy fighter in half with his machine gun fire looked dubious when they went through the streets without finding any evidence of blood or bodies.

After the incident, an elderly Iraqi woman came up to us and said that no one had shot at us; it was just a guy celebrating a birthday in his backyard, firing a few rounds in exuberance.

Within our minds, we can create and perceive anything we want. That day in Al-Salaam, we created a projection of our frustration, a delusion to satisfy some inner restlessness. We created an enemy that simply wasn't there.

When I wrote to Margot about the event, she sent me teachings on Right Thought and Right Action, part of the Buddha's Eight-Fold

Path—how to think clearly and act appropriately. I reflected deeply on them and recognized that, especially when shooting at the man with the imaginary gun, I didn't think—I just acted. I had no actual reason to react; even if he'd had a weapon, he hadn't been shooting at us. I resolved that if I was ever in a situation like that again, I would take a step back and look at the bigger picture. I would recognize that I was aiming at a human being, possibly with a wife, a family, a job, a *life*. I would recognize that I am in his country, there to protect the peace rather than to kill at any opportunity.

I thought of the compliments Margot had given me. I was not worthy of them. The following was from my first email to Margot in over a month:

> Dear Margot,
>   In your past letters you praised me for having unique insight and compassion that is rare here, but I discovered that I'm really no different than anyone else. I've been embarrassed to write because of some of the flattering things you said about me. I don't think they are really true.

And then I wrote this:

> Most people in my unit wouldn't have given this incident a second thought, except for the bad marksmanship. For days I thought about what the Buddha taught. RIGHT ACTION, RIGHT THOUGHT. Even though I didn't kill that man, and I'm thankful I didn't, at the time I WANTED TO. I spoke before about the man who had sat in the dark and waited to blow me up, and I became just like him. I may have regretted it later, but that doesn't negate the fact that my intention was to kill, just like his was. Iraq opened a door for me; it showed me that I'm just as capable of violence and ugliness as the people we fight. I'm not sure what this realization means for me, but I know I hope I never have to be in another situation like it. And if I do, I hope my actions will be different. I'm sure I've disappointed you in many ways, but I have truly appreciated your help.

She wrote back:

Praise and blame are funny things, aren't they? They can really demonstrate that nothing is quite solid, and that things can flip very quickly, making one feel that praise has somehow manifested as a criticism but that was only in your thoughts.

I've been thinking about your latest adventure, and I had some immediate thoughts about it, but I wanted to be sure that my response was appropriate and helpful for you. Therefore I consulted my colleague, Lodrö Gyatso, who is an ordained monk and works with us here at the office. He confirmed my own feelings about it, and he was able to articulate things quite well. He said that there are four aspects of an act that must be present in order for it to be a negative karma-producing event:

1. Intention
2. Execution
3. Desired result is achieved
4. Satisfaction in having performed the action.

If any of these four elements are not present, then the karmic act is not completed. You expressed a lot of regret, which is a great purifier in this case. Regret is clearly the opposite of feeling satisfaction in having accomplished the action. As Gyatso said, this isn't a doctrinal loophole for avoiding negative karma, but it's actually a reflection of the karmic process itself. Karma is completely intertwined with and inseparable from our habitual patterns and our habitual states of mind. So I guess you were correct to worry that you could strengthen the habit of anger and aggression which would of course spawn future anger and aggression, ad infinitum. But the mental state of regret undercuts and weakens our habitual formations and habitual tendencies. Gyatso pointed out that regret is sort of like a computer virus. The computer is programmed to do certain things reliably again and again. However, a computer virus interrupts the programming.

You made the statement, "I discovered that I'm really no different than anyone else." ...Yes, none of us are really different from anyone else, but so few of us actually ever discover that. We are the same in that we are all in this samsaric boat together. We are subjected to passion, aggression and ignorance (or ignoring.) We are habitually programmed to respond to our world with these self-preservation tricks, some of us more blindly than others, but it is inevitable that we will fall victim to our own programmed (notice I <u>did not</u> say inherent) responses from time to time. The fact that you actually saw what was going on is a very bright beam of light that illuminates a lot of darkness.

So no, you have not disappointed me, by any means, but you continue to demonstrate a greater vision, even at times when hell wraps its tentacles around you. You have to take into account the fact that you are in a sort of super-charged samsara there in Iraq, and even your home and family failed to offer much respite. In the normal peaceful world, an intense psychological moment of being slammed against a wall does not contain the same capacity for dramatic reaction as it does when you are exposed to gun fire, constantly feeling danger and death, and walking around with a rifle in your hands for protection. The fact that you were able to have the insight you did should be very encouraging to you.

Please take good care of yourself Paul. Write soon.

Your friend,

Margot

Margot's letter reassured me deeply. Realizing the bigger picture included understanding what a difficult situation I was in and forgiving myself for reacting to my circumstances. But in the months remaining in my tour of duty—and even after I returned home—I would need constant reminders of this sense of gentleness toward myself because I was continually pushed to the brink.

CHAPTER THIRTEEN

HIGHWAY WAR

*We cannot well do without our sins; they are the high-
way of our virtue.*

—Henry David Thoreau

After five months at Camp Stryker, we turned our sector over to
members of the 101st Airborne Division. When we were relieved of duty
there, they began a systematic refurbishing of the Safe House: providing
more sandbags and security, and painting over our graffiti decorating
the building. They took over with arrogance and swagger, dismissing
my advice to help the local families by employing their children. I'd had
enough of that kind of mentality, witnessing its effects first hand. Para-
chuting behind enemy lines with egotistical bravado to defeat the evils
of Nazism was one thing, but bringing that mentality to a situation that
required sensitivity and understanding was a recipe for disaster. On my
last day outside the wire at the Safe House, I watched the lower-ranking

soldiers sweating profusely as they filled the sandbags. I tried to tell their Platoon Sergeant that he should use the local kids to do this. "Just pay them a few bucks," I said, "and they'll happily do the job." The locals valued the work because it helped feed their families, with the additional benefit of creating good will towards the Americans. I wanted to tell him that keeping the Iraqis employed would make them less inclined to blow us up. His snide response: "That's what we have Privates for."

In 1990, the 48th Brigade of the Georgia National Guard had gone through months of training for a deployment to participate in the liberation of Kuwait, but the unit never deployed. At that time, the active duty military didn't trust the National Guard to join them in a "real war." In 2005, the active duty units we replaced were more than happy to have us take over—times had changed.

But very few of the 101st listened to our advice, even though we'd been operating in our sector for five months and knew what we were doing. They were the mighty 101st Airborne, the famous division from the *Band of Brothers* mini-series. They had great equipment, but their leadership failed to understand the nature of our mission. They went in thinking they'd be engaging "the enemy" every day. When they drove around, they'd park off to the side of the road. I don't know what training the 101st received about IEDs, but they are usually planted on the side of the road in the dirt. We always stopped our vehicles on the road itself if possible. During the transfer of our sector, Derek Mack, who'd informed us of the deaths of Fuller, Kinlow, Brunson, and Thomas, rode along in an attempt to advise members of the 101st of the danger. When their lieutenant ordered the vehicles off the paved road, he yelled at him, "Keep those vehicles on the road! If you want to endanger yourself and your men in such a stupid way, I'm going to leave the vehicle and wait for another convoy!" After a time the lieutenant backed down and moved the vehicles back onto the paved road. A sad joke among my unit was that the entire training for the 101st and their subsequent deployment entailed watching *Band of Brothers* over and over.

The most fear I felt in Iraq came during the ride along with the 101st Airborne while showing their men around our sector. I didn't want to get killed a few days before moving south, and I didn't trust their leadership. On my last night outside the wire with a section from the 101st, we only made it about a mile outside Camp Stryker when their driver rolled a vehicle into a ditch. They must have received even less training with night vision than we did. The next day, when we finally left the Safe House and our sector, I paused and looked at some of the young soldiers who acted as drivers and gunners. I knew many of them would die.

They did. The 101st, upon assuming command of the sectors belonging to the 48th Brigade, lost more men in the first few weeks than the 48th Brigade did in five months.

My Company left out of Baghdad International Airport and flew south to a former Iraqi airbase known as Tallil, also called Camp Adder by the U.S. military. Here I would have the opportunity to accomplish something I'd hoped for when I arrived in Iraq: visiting some of the rich archaeological heritage of the country. Just outside the base, only a five

A rare opportunity to accomplish something I'd hoped for when I arrived in Iraq, to sit on the steps of the Ziggurat of Ur. —Photo by Scott Courdin.

minute drive away by humvee, stood the famous Sumerian city of Ur with its restored Ziggurat, a stepped pyramid-like structure. The Ziggurat made an impressive backdrop to the base, which was otherwise unremarkable. During the Iran/Iraq War (1980-88), Saddam Hussein had built the airbase near the ruins of Ur on purpose, hoping the important historical site would prevent Iranian aircraft from bombing the base. He applied the same theory when he staged fighter aircraft at Tallil during the first Gulf War in 1990-91, hoping to impede American bombing as well.

At Tallil we spent the first month living in a large tent similar to the one at Camp Stryker. We'd arrived early to replace the unit conducting convoy missions, so we did nothing but wake up in the morning, have roll call, and then go back to sleep. It made us lethargic after five active months in Baghdad. Eventually, we moved into two-man trailers with cable television. Though small, for many of us the trailers beat living in a tent with fifteen other guys. My roommate was SSG. Crane, a few years older than I was and definitely a high-mileage unit who'd clearly done way too many drugs in his youth. Out of the army for over a decade, he decided to come back into the National Guard. His timing was not fortuitous. After such a long break, he suddenly found himself on the fast track to Iraq with the rest of us. We got along fine, although he did have a habit of cursing his ex-wife in his sleep and periodically snoring.

When we moved to the south of Iraq, which was safer, I assumed our mission would become easier and less dangerous overall. However, it entailed driving right back up to the same areas we'd patrolled while stationed at Camp Stryker. In fact, now our escort details would take us north of Baghdad and out into the dangerous and extremely volatile Al-Anbar province. Though we slept in real beds in nice air-conditioned trailers with cable television, our mission in Iraq hadn't necessarily improved. After a time, some of us began to wish we'd stayed at Camp Stryker for the rest of our tour.

Personally, I wished SGT. Moore had stayed on leave for the rest of the deployment. During the short time he was back in the States, I'd begun

When we moved from Baghdad to the south of Iraq, we brought our paranoia about suicide bombers with us, even though the south was regarded as a safer area. The gunner on the lead humvee would shoot at a car that didn't pull over to the side of the road fast enough. Firing at or near cars was sometimes an interesting experience. It was fun to pop off a few rounds at cars at times, though such games could get bloody. During a routine convoy mission, SPC. Russell Felix, the infamous dog killer, acted as gunner; I drove; CPL. Gibbs was TC. A lot of construction stretched along Route Tampa near Tallil. We'd passed the Italians who manned the checkpoints along the road nearest the base and headed north. Very few civilian cars drove up and down the main highway with American and Iraqi convoys, although more individual cars clustered the road near towns. On this day, a lone car came toward our convoy and failed to pull all the way over to the side of the road.

In Baghdad the locals had been well-trained to pull over the moment they saw an American patrol coming down the road, but not the locals in the south. When the approaching car failed to get over far enough, Felix shot a burst from his M240 machine gun to its left. When he fired, I happened to look to my left. About a hundred yards away I saw his rounds kicking up dirt around an Iraqi construction crew. He hadn't seen the three or four construction workers sitting off to the side of the road. Watching them jump off and dive for cover was both hilarious and disturbing. People can certainly move fast when bullets are flying—scattering just like cockroaches. As temporarily amusing as the moment was, I had to tell Felix that he'd unknowingly nearly gunned down three or four innocent Iraqis. He laughed and apologized. I told him to watch what he was doing next time.

Our convoy missions took us to various parts of Iraq. The longest, and sometimes the most dangerous, involved a trip to Al-Taqaddum Air Base, about 90 kilometers west of Baghdad. Called simply T.Q. by most Marines and soldiers, it was a very remote base that lacked many of the amenities found at other forward operating bases such as Anaconda or

Camp Victory. Barring frequent stops due to suspected IEDs, it would take a good eight hours to reach the base. Usually, we would break the trip up by stopping at FOB Duke before continuing on to T.Q. in the morning. Parts of the drive reminded me of Ft. Irwin, California, with wide open flat desert in every direction. A convoy mission to T.Q. allowed us to experience more of the country and its diverse landscape. We would pass salt lakes, where families, as in Biblical times, lived in reed huts. We had to avoid large IED craters on the precarious route. The road to Al-Taqaddum, only partially paved, provided perfect opportunities to place an IED.

One day we passed the remnants of a humvee belonging to a Marine patrol recently devastated by an IED. As we passed the spot of the attack, just before crossing a bridge over a small river, evidence of the explosion remained. Pieces of metal were scattered in every direction. A ubiquitous orange cooler, one of thousands distributed by the army and Marines, sat a few feet from the depression in the road made by the blast.

In a video I made on the way to T.Q., I lamented the poor state of protection on the humvees we rode in. A couple of chains and a bit of nylon rope held a metal door on. Far from being "up armored," these older humvees were all we had to work with at times. The makeshift door didn't fit right, thus leaving a large gap that would have allowed shrapnel to enter if we'd been hit. The humvee Sam Bopp often rode in had a hole in the floor; he could watch the ground pass him by as he drove along.

When insurgents first began their attacks, IEDs were truly roadside bombs, meaning they exploded off the side of the road. Once the army realized these dangers, they began "up armoring" our humvees. Unfortunately, this didn't include armor on the humvee bottom, soon identified by insurgents as a vulnerable spot to hit a vehicle. They adapted and began to place their bombs under the road whenever they could instead of off to the side. This improvisation sadly led to the deaths of the eight soldiers from Alpha Company at Camp Stryker.

One night, I was acting as gunner on the lead vehicle as we left T.Q. From a distance I noticed a car and truck in the road, lights off. As the convoy drew closer, they didn't move, prompting me to fire in rapid succession three red tracer warning rounds off to the side of the vehicles but close enough to get their attention. Suddenly, bright flashing lights appeared on the top of the vehicles. As we came closer, I realized I'd fired at an Iraqi Police patrol. Oops, my bad! Once the rounds landed near them, they moved with lightning speed to get their vehicles off the road and hit their police lights. I'm happy to say, they took the whole incident in stride. As we drove by, I said to one policeman, "Assif," which means "sorry" in Arabic. He smiled at me and repeated the statement. Another officer raised his hand to his chest as if he had been shot, making fun of the fact I'd nearly killed him. I smiled at him as we drove on. One had to love Iraq—just when things seemed humdrum, they could get exciting, and amusing, in an instant, though often at someone else's expense.

Riding in the gunners' hatch in such a cavalier manner attracted the ire of SFC. Janes. After arriving at FOB Anaconda one evening, he berated me for standing up too high in the gunners' hatch during convoy missions. Not that I was overly reckless, but it provided Janes with an opportunity to make me look bad. Other gunners who acted the same way I did were considered "aggressive." After we parked the vehicles, we had a meeting where we stood in a circle. SFC. Janes said, "I don't like to single anyone out, but, SGT. Kendel, your methods of gunning are just plain stupid. You're taking unnecessary risks." He said this in front of privates and others below my rank. I was taken aback. He stared at me with a look he hoped would embarrass me in front of the men.

But having my usual sarcastic comeback at the ready, I said, "That's okay. I'm not really worried about dying. I have God on my side." Knowing that I didn't take organized religion seriously, he just stared at me, shook his head, and walked away.

CPL. Gibbs turned to me, shaking his head, and said, "Damn, man. You just can't win."

But SFC. Janes and I had a history that went back to Al-Salaam. My quick decision in the heat of battle to form two squads to go into the town in Bradleys and search for those who'd fired at us was hardly recognized. I'd formulated a plan while Janes waited for orders to come from above. Later, Janes found an opportunity to confront me about the incident.

"You know," he said, sounding guilty, "if you had gone into Al-Salaam, all of you would probably have been killed."

I just looked at him. In retrospect, I can say that the Al-Salaam firefight proved illusory, but on the spot, with bullets supposedly flying, I'd made a decision in a critical situation. We had Bradleys and Apaches and a clear advantage. Janes' assessment was an attempt to mask his own ineffectiveness as a senior leader. In fact, three years later, in 2009, when the 48th Brigade was mobilized for a deployment to Afghanistan, he would be fired as 1st Sergeant from his infantry company for incompetency.

During convoy missions we'd drive as fast as possible on major highways such as Route Tampa, but slowed at the periodic checkpoints, manned and unmanned, designed to allow for random vehicle inspections. To drive through these checkpoints, we had to wind our way through cement barriers and other impediments. Insurgents would bury IEDs among the dirt piles and other debris scattered around them, often planted with the cooperation of the Iraqis manning the checkpoints. SGT. T had an IED go off near his humvee one night while driving back from FOB Anaconda, an hour north of Baghdad. The standard procedure when reacting to an IED is to push through the blast, but when driving behind large fuel trucks this strategy may not be the wisest course. An IED creates a large amount of dust and debris, obscuring your view. A truck driven by a TCN in front of you will often stop when an IED goes off because he's shocked by the explosion, and his natural reaction is to hit the brakes. A humvee pushing through a blast under these conditions can create an unfortunate incident. SGT. T ordered his driver to push through the cloud of dirt and debris. When they came out of it, they found that the KBR truck driving in front of them had

WALKING THE TIGER'S PATH
PAUL M. KENDEL

stopped because of the IED explosion that went off nearby him. Their humvee slammed into the back of the KBR truck, wounding everyone in the vehicle. None were seriously hurt, but SGT. T and his gunner PVT. Baker suffered knee and ligament damage. PVT. Thompson, driving next to SGT. T, escaped physically unscathed. However, a pointed extension of the truck's bumper instantly pierced the bullet-proof windshield, halting inches from his face, leaving him staring at the point aimed right between his eyes. This near death experience brought him intimately close with his own mortality. Upon returning to the States, he left the infantry and became a chaplain's assistant.

Our company would endure a number of near fatal attacks such as this. SGT. Jones, the one who'd backed my plan to go into Al-Salaam, was nearly killed one night in an attack of that nature. An IED blew up directly in front of his humvee, causing flames to shoot through the dashboard. The humvee stalled and died, but he and his entire crew had time to escape before the vehicle went up in flames. Jones told me that after the humvee had rolled off into a ditch on the side of the road, he, his driver, and his gunner stood on the shoulder waiting for help.

At the front of the convoy when they got hit, the rest of the trucks continued to drive by them following standard operating procedure. So, as SGT. Jones stood there with his humvee burning a short distance away, the first humvee passed by and stopped, acknowledged Jones, then abruptly drove on without offering assistance. And then the next humvee drove past without stopping. What the hell? he thought. Can't they see my burning humvee on the side of the road? We could use a lift here, for Christ sake! SGT. Jones assumed they would come back, but when he saw the rear humvee, the last one that could give them a ride, he began to get nervous. This vehicle slowed down and seemed to realize their plight, but then it too began to drive off. Fearing he and his men would be left stranded, he quickly took off his Kevlar helmet and threw it at the humvee, getting the gunner's attention.

The vehicle stopped. SGT. Jones screamed at them, telling them what happened and that they needed a ride. Apparently, they hadn't recognized him. Since Jones and his humvee had been temporarily attached to a different company pulling a convoy mission that night, none of the other men in the convoy knew Jones or his men. When they drove by, they thought he and his men belonged to a patrol operating in the area and didn't realize they were part of their own convoy.

That incident was just one more interesting example of miscommunication and confusion. Fortunately, Jones survived the incident and returned home to his family and its newest member, a baby girl. Like me, he'd gotten his wife pregnant while home on pass just before leaving for Iraq. Thankfully for him and his wife, they conceived a beautiful, healthy baby girl, the same thing my wife and I had hoped for—and lost.

In an email to Margot, I reflected on the six months I'd been in Iraq:

> The karmic consequences of my actions over the last six months have really been bothering me. I knew coming over here that I wasn't going to make a real difference in the greater scheme of things because I'm just a soldier, but I had hoped to help people in some small way. Instead, much of what I have been personally involved in has led to nothing but death, pain, and sorrow...[my] involvement in certain incidents will affect me adversely. Your letter and its explanation of the four acts necessary for "negative" karma were helpful. But there is much I have been involved with... incidents that will haunt me for the rest of my life.

Chapter Fourteen

Hope at the End of a Machine Gun Barrel

You must not lose faith in humanity. Humanity is an ocean; if a few drops of the ocean are dirty, the ocean does not become dirty.
—Mahatma Gandhi

"Car! Car approaching! Three o'clock!" Gibbs screamed suddenly from below. I'd been looking nervously up at the passing apartment complexes —a perfect place for snipers. Heart pounding, I spun the turret around as fast as I could, finger on the trigger, ready to blast away—and saw the last thing in the world I'd want to pull the trigger on.

A pair of piercingly dark eyes.

She was an incredibly beautiful little girl with thick black hair, maybe four or five years old. I will never forget those eyes—eyes completely at odds with the face of an enemy.

If that lovely little girl had been in a car seat strapped into the back like a child would have been in the United States, I would never have looked past the sight and down the barrel of my M240 machine gun into her eyes. But there she was, leaning on the dashboard of her father's car, gazing directly up at me. I paused for a moment and just stared back at her. Suddenly, her father smiled and waved at me and told his little girl to do the same. It seemed so utterly incongruous. With my machine gun pointed at this little girl's head, she calmly waved at me. I waved back and smiled.

The day had begun as a routine convoy mission through the city of Diwaniya, a predominately Shiite city about fifty kilometers east of Najaf. In southwest Baghdad, suicide bombers created a real threat. In the predominately Shiite south, they did not. However, some of us found the transition difficult. For example, when we first went through the city of Diwaniya, it was complete chaos: cars all around us, pulling out of side streets and homes, driving right up on us. Soldiers freaked out—a lot of them thought every automobile was a suicide bomber.

When a military unit deploys to hostile environments such as Iraq and Afghanistan, the military gives soldiers rules of engagement (ROEs) designed (at least in theory) to instruct them on when they can engage the enemy. In Iraq, especially at Camp Stryker, our ROEs were more like loose guidelines. If we felt threatened in any way, we were expected to shoot. Fighting an enemy we rarely saw made our job extremely difficult. When any car or person could suddenly blow up and kill us, we had to make split second decisions. At Camp Stryker our sector was mostly rural, and this environment allowed more room to fire warning shots at cars or to react if a car came too close. When we moved to the south of Iraq and assumed our duties escorting fuel trucks around the country, many of us carried the same mentality from Camp Stryker. If a car got too close, we fired warning shots; if we felt threatened, we shot at it.

Sometimes the Iraqis had no idea how close they came to their untimely demise. Jason Royal, acting as gunner, once shot at a car along Route Aeros to encourage it to move over. He watched his round bounce off the pavement in front of the car, but to his alarm, an Iraqi man happened to be standing alongside the road smoking a cigarette. Royal watched as the round ricocheted between the man's legs. The Iraqi man casually continued smoking, oblivious to his hair-thin encounter with death.

Once I was the gunner, and Gibbs was T.C. in the lead vehicle, which of course is the first one to encounter traffic. Accustomed to wider spaces in which to gauge the threat ahead of time, we seemed to be surrounded by threatening cars. Off to the left, I saw a white Peugeot come out of a garage behind some trees. Gibbs, who saw it appear abruptly out of the trees, screamed, "Car to your left! Shoot the fucking car!"

Knowing clearly it wasn't a suicide bomber, I didn't shoot.

Gibbs shouted, "What the hell are you doing? Why didn't you shoot that fucking car?"

I dropped lower down into the hatch so I could look at him: "It's okay. I saw him pull out from his garage. He wasn't a threat."

Generally a level-headed person, Gibbs accepted my explanation and left it at that. I guess he trusted my judgment, far different from Moore who berated me for not shooting at that car even though innocent children may have been killed in the process.

As I mentioned before, on occasion I had to act aggressively out of fear—not from a physical threat, but a fear that those around me wouldn't trust me if I didn't act in an expected way. I would fire at cars, purposely avoiding the driver by putting bullets into a tire or underneath the car. Once I got a taste of what it feels like to be a NASCAR driver when I slammed the humvee into the side of a car, forcing it out of the middle of the road in order to get it to move out of the way of our approaching convoy. As long as it looked like I was making an aggressive attempt, everything seemed to be fine. I wasn't scared; I just knew when a threat was a threat and when it wasn't. But I had to put on a show, so I pretended to shoot at humans so my fellow soldiers would trust me.

Once in Diwaniya, a car with four elderly men wearing traditional black and white kaffiyas on their heads pulled up close to us. They were grey bearded, well-groomed men who were simply driving onto the main road through town, probably not expecting any problems. I was acting as gunner and CPL. Gibbs as TC. He yelled that a car was approaching too closely on our right side. If it had been a suicide bomber, we would've been dead already, but to respond, I popped up out of the turret with my M4 rifle and looked into the faces of the four elderly men, their heads turned back at our humvee, staring up at me. I quickly realized that the car and the men were no threat. Not a lot of suicide bombers kill themselves accompanied by friends, especially elderly men. Still I fired three bullets into the trunk to make it seem like I was being aggressive. I'll never forget the looks on the faces of those men: utter bafflement. They must have thought, What the hell did we do? We're just driving through town! Why are the Americans shooting at our car? It would've been amusing to witness the driver explaining to his wife why he came home with three bullet holes in their car trunk.

However, not every gunner evaluated potential threats as I did. One night, during another early convoy mission through Diwaniya, PVT. Baker panicked and opened up on civilian vehicles converging on the main road, shooting at every one he could see. Women and children rode in some of those cars, though no one knows whether they were killed or wounded; the convoy just rolled on. He repeated the same overzealousness once along Route Tampa when he fired on a car causing it to burst in flames, possibly killing the innocent family within; such was life in Iraq and our mission to expunge terrorism from the world.

The mind of the tiger—the mind of discernment, Sakyong Mipham explains—creates a little gap that gives us an intimate look at our choices in life, preventing us from blindly reacting to what happens around us. We can stop and think and make a decision based on wisdom and compassion, rather than on hate and fear.

One moment of too much adrenalin, or too little, could be devastating. We held people's lives in our hands—the lives of our friends and the lives of Iraqis and their children. We were all just trying to get through another day. In Iraq, when the people do something as simple as drive to the market, they have to deal with the fact that American soldiers might shoot at them if they come too close.

As I explained to Margot:

When I pivoted that gun around at that car, if I had been more aggressive, acted out of more fear, or maybe hate, I could have killed that little girl as well as her father. And do you want to know the really frightening thing? The convoy and my vehicle would have driven on as if nothing had happened. The Army never taught me how to play God. My experience with the teachings of the Sakyong that I have read have helped keep me grounded during my time here in Iraq...without your personal guidance over the last six months my life here in the "Charnel Ground"...would have been extremely difficult. I have written much about the darker side of life here, but that is because I have been stationed in one of the more dangerous areas of the country. But the fact is, not everything is negative here; I can see hope in people's faces. I have tried to look at the people here not as enemies, as many of my friends have, but as human beings dealing with a most difficult situation. Being a participant in a military occupation of a people is not a pleasant thing. And being on the receiving end is certainly even less pleasant.

We take a lot of things for granted in the United States. I don't think the average American would deal well with having machine guns pointed at them on their way to the gym to work out. My experience [in Iraq] has made me think about how the Tibetan people have dealt with living under a military occupation. They have not sacrificed their integrity, their belief in basic human goodness and compassion, even in the face of near-total destruction. And in the face of that little Iraqi girl, I saw hope, even when the world around her would seem to be in total chaos.

The military can train a soldier to shoot, to drive a tank, or fly a helicopter, but they can't train you for the unexpected. You can't be programmed like a machine to react to all circumstances in a way that conforms to what the military would like. Human emotion plays an important role in a time of war, even if military leaders would like to think otherwise. The President of the United States might send a young man to war, and his leaders might instruct him in his assigned duties, but at a critical moment such as a decision to kill another human being, that decision is the soldier's, and his alone. He has to live with the consequences of his actions. For me, I could have easily killed the little girl and her father that day. Thankfully, I didn't.

Instead, for a brief moment, I saw something positive. I found it in that little girl's eyes. Hope. She didn't look frightened when I stared at her past the barrel of my machine gun. What I saw was acceptance. She had adapted to her world, one of violence and hate. Her youth and naiveté were a gift, something that will most likely change in coming years. Like the tomato farmer, her father, too, seemed to have accepted the nature of their life. He had managed to take the absurdities of existence in Iraq in stride and not let it affect him or his young daughter. He could still smile and have his little girl wave at an American soldier when, seconds before and under different circumstances, both might have died in a hail of machine gun bullets. As we drove away, I couldn't help but think that the next day or the next week, another convoy mission, another humvee, might drive through the same town, stopping at the same bridge with a gunner who was less restrained than I was, resulting in the death of that young girl or another child in a similar situation. The Iraqis are resilient people—they have to be. Iraq might be on the verge of a civil war, but as long as there is hope and belief in resiliency and patience, a little girl with beautiful dark eyes might one day play an important role in her country's future. It is said that the eyes are a window to the soul; in hers I saw the spark of something better.

CHAPTER FIFTEEN

FIRED AND FIRED UPON

The sweet way to corrupt a youth is to instruct him to hold in higher esteem those that think alike than those who think differently.
—Friedrich Nietzsche

When I began this deployment, I'd expected most of the soldiers around me to suffer some degree of arrogance and overall ignorance of the war in Iraq, Islam, and Middle-Eastern culture—like the man who yelled, "Kick some ass!" as we stood on the parade ground, about to depart for Iraq. But that's just typical blind patriotism, a force used for centuries to motivate people to kill others. Americans are not known for their historical and cultural understandings of those who look, think, and act differently than they do. Our own government went into the war with Iraq without a greater understanding of the consequences of invasion and the sectarian conflicts that would arrive, so how can one expect a common soldier to grasp their complexity? I had tried to express my sentiments on these subjects, but my opinions were dismissed. Men like

Moore, Bopp, and others who believed in their superiority disregarded my knowledge of Islam and the Middle East, seeing it as threat. I'd accepted the nature of my situation but had begun to lose tolerance for the attitudes of some of the men in our platoon, especially SGT. Moore. And after months of separation from my kids, my wife's complete lack of support, the grinding stress of fourteen-hour convoy missions, and disillusionment with what we'd accomplished in Iraq, I began to unravel. I was going through the motions to pass the time, without hope or inspiration about the mission, just waiting for it to end so I could go home.

January 23, 2006
Dear Margot,

You asked me once if I thought I was a "moderating" influence on my friends here. I never answered you before, but the answer is "no." One of my friends who I have been through a lot with over here asked once, "Why are you nice to these people?" There was really no point in answering him if he had to ask a question like that.

My interest in the people and lack of hatred and anger towards them has often been seen as suspicious. In the army you're trained to hate your enemy, and compassion and kindness are for the weak. Our current political climate in the United States is one of pride and nationalism in our country and an often ignorant and blind fear and hatred for others who don't look or think like us. I have been constantly singled out here and laughed at for my so called "liberal views."

If not wanting to hate other people and trying to see the basic goodness in people in a time of difficulty is liberal, then I guess I'm "liberal." It has been very reassuring to speak with you over the last six months...[you've taught me that] there's nothing wrong with showing compassion to others and wanting to resist anger, even when you're surrounded by people that may dislike you or even want to kill you. I understand the fear exhibited by some of my friends. And even some of the anger, especially towards those that may have killed our friends...but sadly, I have not seen the compassion and kindness from some that I thought I would.

Following the deaths of our friends from the two massive IED blasts, many of the soldiers around me, including my squad leader, SGT. Moore, instinctively reached for their Bibles for comfort. This was a natural reaction, of course, because their next patrol might be their last. The deaths of friends brought the war home, made it real, intimate. But their readings and their prayers were for themselves and friends, not for those beyond "the wire." We were brought to Iraq, we were told, for one reason—to help the Iraqi people. But when the war hit home with the deaths of friends, that no longer mattered.

Shortly after arriving in Iraq, SGT. Moore made a point of visiting an Iraqi family living near the Safe House to bring some medical supplies to aid a little girl, maybe five years old, with badly burned legs. Our Iraqi interpreter told us the child may have been burned on purpose, a retaliatory act by the father against the mother for a particular offense she might have committed. He said that he was familiar with other cases where an enraged husband would take his frustrations out on a female member of the family, often the child. We didn't know if this was the case with the girl living near the Safe House, but SGT. Moore left bandages and medical ointments with the father and mother. They seemed pleased and appreciated his efforts. A reason for SGT. Moore's altruism might have been that he had a daughter on the way and sympathized with the child's plight. Nevertheless, such acts of kindness and compassion would wane once our own people began to die. The general consensus was, "Fuck the Iraqis. What matters is going home alive."

A clear example of this was our relationship with the Iraqi children. At first many of us saw the Iraqi kids as cute, while with time this view would change. Instead of handing a cold Pepsi to an Iraqi kid after cries of "Mista! Mista! Pepsi?" he'd get a plastic Gatorade bottle filled with warm urine from a humvees's gunner. Some would pass candy we knew to be sour and unappealing to unwitting children, who spit it out with the obligatory look of revulsion to rounds of laughter. Others played tricks on them, like tying a candy bar to a piece of fishing wire and throwing it out to children begging on the side of the road for a Pepsi or candy. When the children ran toward the candy bar, the wire would be yanked away, making them scamper after elusive bait. These acts brought a lot of laughs and helped pass the time, but they certainly didn't help us win any "hearts and minds." The Iraqi children weren't perfect either. Children throwing rocks at our humvee when we passed through a town reduced our level of kindness toward the general population.

But it wasn't just the children; they were on the periphery. The indifference and lack of desire to save the Iraqi man shot in front of his family by Moore exemplified our relationship with the Iraqis. "We" mattered; an innocent Iraqi didn't warrant the cost of fuel for a medivac helicopter, nor did he justify a concerted effort to get him to a medical facility. No, he became a source of amusement. A "kill" in Iraq, the death of a human being, whether he's "the enemy" or an innocent man, is sadly often considered nothing but a statistic, an opportunity to gloat, something to be admired like the number of home runs a player hit during his career.

But a human being is not a statistic. SGT. Moore had a wife waiting for him at home and a room being decorated to welcome the arrival of their unborn daughter, while the night Moore shot that Iraqi man, an innocent child had a father taken away forever. There was nothing "statistical" or amusing about the Iraqi man's death; it was a sad loss, a common one that afflicts the Iraqi people every day. Whether an American soldier did the killing or a fellow Iraqi, the tragedy is the same.

I concluded this email to Margot:

> So no, I have not become a "moderating" influence; my views are usually laughed at and dismissed, so I have just tried to survive and make it through each day. And that's what I will continue to do.

In Chapter Fourteen of *Ruling Your World*, "The Confidence of Delight in Helping Others," Sakyong Mipham teaches that "all of us can embody...generosity throughout the day. We can bring someone a cup of coffee, let our friend read the newspaper in silence, give our spouse another napkin when hers has fallen on the floor. We can help push the car when it's stuck in the snow...The sun shines, whether it is day or night, and so should our concern for others." When I read this, it reminded me of an incident that occurred in 2002 while deployed to the Kingdom of Saudi Arabia with the California National Guard.

It was a simple trip into Riyadh to see a few sites and return to the base, though things didn't quite work out that way. After narrowly avoiding a large dirt mound and barbed wire, the Chevy Suburban I was driving, along with five of my friends in it, slammed hard over a rock, impaling the vehicle. We were attempting to push the car off the rock without success when a young Saudi man, dressed in his finest suit, arrived in a brand new BMW and offered to help. After another twenty minutes of fruitless effort, we all gave up. A second Saudi man in a truck stopped, pulled out a cable, and offered to pull our vehicle off the rock. He was an old man with a friendly, accommodating face—one that said, "I don't care if you're an American infidel, you're a human being in need, and I'm going to stop and help you out." He used his truck and tow line, enabling us to drive back to the base (albeit four hours late). We thanked him, and he was clearly happy to have helped. It never ceases to amaze me how lack of understanding and acceptance, or perhaps openness about religious beliefs other than one's own interferes with seeing people as simply human. No matter what the color of one's skin or the nature of one's religious beliefs, everyone on earth appreciates help with a disabled car.

In late November 2005, the quarterly newsletter of Shambhala International, *The Dot*, published a number of my first emails to Margot under the title "Contemplating Anger and Compassion in Iraq." It pleased me that my emails had been published for the Shambhala community, but I showed the article to no one. I wanted to share it but was afraid no one would understand what I was trying to say. I was afraid I would come off as a typical bleeding heart liberal who didn't understand the realities of the world—someone who lacked "common sense." And so, fearing ridicule, I kept *The Dot* to myself. Later I wrote to Margot:

> January 25, 2006
> Dear Margot,
>
> I don't think I'll be passing around copies of *The Dot* to the rest of my friends (I wish they could appreciate the Sakyong's teachings the way I do—they could definitely use the help; they just don't know it!)...I just hope the anger that many of them have developed will recede with time once they are out of this hostile environment. Most of them are truly good people, but they are HUMAN, and like most of us, susceptible to the evils of pride and ego. Many came over here looking for personal glory, or to "fight terrorism" and those who "threaten freedom," common buzz words we hear every day. But the reality for most has been quite different. We have rarely seen any "terrorists" to actually fight, and instead of "glory," we have only seen many of our friends blown to pieces. And in frustration, many have directed their anger towards the general population—even though only a small percentage are even a threat to us at all.
>
> The "anger" toward the Iraqis I'm talking about is not physical (it has occurred, however), but a personal anger that they will probably bring home with them. Maybe it's just a defensive mechanism—a blanket hatred toward a people is far easier than trying to understand them and what the real problems are.

But I was not completely alone. I had "The Sheets" and my cigar buddy, Daylon Brown, for support. The song "The End" by The Doors will forever be connected to the movie *Apocalypse Now*, but it is an odd song to use to motivate yourself before going outside the wire where you may be killed. However, The Sheets is an odd individual. He stands six feet tall, weighs at least 240 pounds, is extremely pale, and has a shaved head. He looks like a neo-Nazi. He's far from a racist, but he does have a strange affinity for the history of Nazi Germany. One day at a checkpoint, while a convoy of vehicles went past carrying Iraqi soldiers, The Sheets stood and gave each vehicle the Nazi salute. The first few vehicles passed with no reaction, but then one Iraqi soldier, most likely an officer, looked at The Sheets and returned the salute with a "Heil Hitler"—according to The Sheets, one of his most memorable moments. He did feel bad later when he realized the coalition soldiers manning the checkpoint were from Poland. Anyone who knows their WWII history knows the Germans didn't exactly treat the Polish with hugs and kisses.

Men such as The Sheets and I were considered "idiots" because we thought differently than many around us. I've encountered on numerous occasions those without an education mocking those who do as lacking in "common sense." This is often a face-saving strategy for those who feel self-consciously uneducated.

The Sheets.

While based at Tallil in the south of Iraq, many of us frequented an authentically Italian pizza place. The pizza was greasy and usually disgusting. Nevertheless, they had unrestricted Internet access and a good cup of cappuccino. Daylon Brown, The Sheets, and I would often hang out there and smoke cigars.

Early one evening out in front of the pizza place, I told the Sheets, "I thought Bopp and Moore had a real attitude today when they were talking to you about me."

The Sheets hesitated. "Well," he volunteered after a brief pause, "they think you're an idiot. But if it makes you feel any better, they think I'm an idiot, too."

"Why do they think that?" I asked, surprised.

"I don't think they were referring to your actual intelligence, Sergeant, but to your religious and political views. Your criticism of the way they think. You kind of make them look stupid. You challenge their beliefs, and you don't hide the fact that you think they're hypocrites. I think they're hypocritical, too."

"Why do they think you're an idiot?" I asked

"I don't think they trust me. They purposely excluded me from some of the more critical missions and raids out of Camp Stryker."

It offended me at first, but then I thought about all the conversations I'd overheard in which someone else had been criticized. The Sheets and I weren't being singled out—everyone had a negative opinion about someone in our platoon—but The Sheets and I had made ourselves susceptible to closer scrutiny. At least in my case, I knew I'd caused it. Getting into political and religious debates with people who think differently and are less opened-minded will invariably lead to a backlash of some sort.

One night during a patrol near Camp Stryker, we had set up an OP near an agricultural field not far from some small homes. It was late at night, and we were all bored. I began a conversation with The Sheets about the origins of Christianity. I told him how much of the Christian religion was derived from Persian cults, primarily that of Mithras. In fact, much of what we think is uniquely Christian has actually been borrowed from earlier religions. I mentioned how some scholars of the Bible and St. Paul believe that the saint had been exposed to Persian cults while living in Syria, especially the city of Damascus, as a youth. He most likely took much of what he was exposed to and incorporated it into his early formation of the Christian church. Above us, in the gunners' hatch of the humvee, sat Pvt. Baker. Baker considered himself a devout Christian. Listening to our conversation, he began to take offense. He clearly disagreed with my views.

Leaning over the edge of the humvee's turret, he said, "You're a fucking moron! Damascus was part of ancient Israel!"

I looked up at him and shot back, "Damascus is the capital of Syria. It was never part of ancient Israel. Get your history and geography right. And if you want to call me a moron, why don't you come down here and say it to my face?"

I told The Sheets to get up in the turret to replace Baker when he began to climb down. We were clearly poised to start brawling in the middle of a combat zone. Not really the smartest thing to do. Before things got to that point, SFC. Janes came over and stopped the situation from getting physical. I'd been involved in religious debates before, but only this encounter had gotten out of control. It was my own fault. I knew how Baker thought and purposely carried on the conversation with The Sheets where he could listen in.

The following day I ran into Baker near the port-o-potties. I walked up to him and said, "Look, I want to apologize about the other night. I had no right to offend you the way I did."

Baker looked relieved and replied, "I'm sorry, too, Sergeant. I should never have called you a moron."

"It's okay."

"It's just that Christianity is dear to my heart," he continued. I found myself thinking that his tendency to shoot at cars without regard to the lives of women and children made his Christian love a little suspicious. But I kept my views to myself and instead extended my hand to him. We shook hands and continued on our way. Following this event, I tried to tone down any discussions of religion among my fellow soldiers.

Knowing others perceived The Sheets as an "idiot" certainly helped assuage my discomfort at being singled out because The Sheets was one of the most competent drivers in our company and knew the convoy routes better than anyone. If I had to be the first man going into a hostile building, I'd want The Sheets to be the man covering my back. He was regarded as different because he thought for himself and didn't subscribe to any particular belief system; he had an open mind willing to consider views "out of the norm." When The Sheets and I started hanging out together after we moved to Tallil, Moore and Bopp warned him to stay away from me because my views, both religious and political, were considered atypical and a threat. The Sheets, to his credit, told them that he preferred to create his own opinion of people, not based on what others had to say. He didn't agree with me on everything, but he valued hearing about things from a different perspective.

With a sinking feeling, I contemplated my military career. After nearly twenty years in the Army and National Guard, I had not exactly experienced a meteoric rise to the top of the leadership ladder. And it had been mostly my own fault for various reasons. I spent the majority of my time in the Guard just hanging out with friends on a drill weekend, drinking beers. I never really wanted to take it that seriously. The invasion of Iraq changed things. However, various circumstances, such as my strained relationship with my wife, distracted me, reducing my ability to perform at a leadership level the way my chain of command expected. I was just trying to survive the deployment. I did my job, of course, but without the initiative expected of me. I just didn't have it in me.

As described earlier, my relationship with SGT. Moore had deteriorated greatly. I was simply going through the motions because I was spent. During one convoy mission to T.Q. out in the Anbar province, my ability to function as an NCO, at least the way my chain of command expected me to, reached a climax. A problem with my vehicle's radio started it. After an hour of effort with SGT. Moore attempting to make it work, we couldn't get the radio functioning correctly before moving on to T.Q. We couldn't simply plug in the radios in our humvees and be ready to go; they had to have the timing set specifically so every T.C. in each vehicle could hear one another. As a TC, I had never bothered with the radios because it was the driver's job to have the vehicles up and running before a patrol. Electronics has never been my strong suit, but as an NCO, I should have cultivated a better understanding of how to set them up. I'd become complacent. When we moved south and I began to operate as a driver because of the long hours, it became my responsibility to have the radio ready, and I was unprepared. Normally, this would have been easy to rectify, but at this point I couldn't always rouse myself to do more than necessary.

When our convoy pulled into the staging area at T.Q., I needed to go to the bathroom badly. I was the TC, and I got out of the vehicle, promptly beginning to relieve myself near the back of the humvee, an area with nothing but sand and a small building where you sign in and receive departure paperwork. Most everyone did the same around the humvee the minute we stopped a convoy or arrived somewhere. While I was urinating in the sand next to the vehicle, SGT. Moore, an ex-Marine, walked up. T.Q. is primarily a Marine base, so I guess he didn't like my peeing on ground that belonged to the U.S. Marine Corp. He flipped out.

"What are you doing?" he asked me. "Tell me you're not pissing on the ground?"

I held my dick in my hand and said, "Yeah, I'm taking a piss."

"Are you a fucking idiot? There's a porto-john right..." He looked around for a moment, confused, and then spotted one a considerable distance away. "Right there," he said, pointing at a building.

"Yeah, I'm an idiot," I told him, tired of his pompous tirades.

"When we get back to Tallil, you're going to learn how to put a radio in a vehicle and set it up," he told me condescendingly, smiling at me like I was retarded. "But you'll probably just forget how to do it anyway," he added, turning his back on me.

Nonchalantly, I responded, "Yeah, probably," just to be a jerk. And I've always been good at being a jerk when so inclined.

Then he turned and flipped out again. "That's it. You're fired! You're fucking fired!"

I wasn't exactly sure what I was being "fired" from; I was in Iraq, and I was pretty sure he couldn't "fire" me from the war. He was "firing" me from my T.C. position, which meant now I could only serve as gunner or driver.

Sadly, CPL. Gibbs, who'd been my driver, suddenly found himself promoted to T.C. Not that he wasn't fully competent, but the sudden turn of events threw him. He didn't want to see this kind of conflict, though at this point he was used to me messing with his life. I didn't really care in what capacity I functioned. My life sucked, so what did it matter? And now, I only blame myself. Moore may have acted belligerently sometimes, but he wasn't wrong. I should have taken the time to better familiarize myself with the radios. On the road with a convoy of fuel trucks, communication was vital to the safety of the entire mission. He was a competent leader, and I had no problem deferring to his superior tactical knowledge, but that didn't mean he knew everything. Following his "firing" me, my situation in Iraq began to deteriorate even more, and my need for the comfort of the dharma grew.

Reading *Turning the Mind into an Ally*, I'd learned to use contemplation as a way to steady myself. "The words are the gateway to the meaning," Sakyong Mipham wrote. "As you continue to place your mind on them, eventually the words fall away and their meaning or the experience to which they refer will arise." His emphasis on "keeping your seat," meaning to maintain a stable, positive mind that wasn't overcome with emotional reactions, that could stay grounded and appreciative of life, was something I thought about a lot, especially while in the solitude of the gunner's hatch.

I wrote to Margot about one of these experiences:

> I just got back this morning from a convoy escort mission and found out we'll be heading out again tomorrow afternoon. Not a lot of time to rest. It looks like I'll be spending Christmas on the road, dodging IED craters. The only positive thing is that we're going to a base called Taji, a little north of Baghdad, that has Iraq's only Taco Bell. I guess a Burrito Supreme for Christmas dinner beats a can of cold Vienna sausages and a bag of Doritos any day.[1] I tried an unusual form of meditation last night while we were driving back to our base in the south of Iraq. I was riding in the gunner's hatch of our humvee, sitting on a plastic cooler we use as a seat behind the machine gun, listening to The Who, my favorite rock band. I have been feeling a little stressed out lately—the job here, being away from my family for the holidays.
>
> I focused on my breathing and looked up at the moon. It was really a beautiful night, with clouds in the sky that helped give the moon an eerie glow. I thought about what the Sakyong wrote in his book about keeping a positive attitude. I focused on my breathing and tried to relax. Sure, I may be in Iraq and there was a chance that we might be hit by a roadside bomb that could have blown me into a thousand unrecognizable pieces, just like what had happened to some of my friends. But I was alive and I have a lot of wonderful things in my life: my wife, children, good friends. And now I have a spiritual friend in you to help me as well.

---

1. My Thanksgiving dinner.

WALKING THE TIGER'S PATH

PAUL M. KENDEL

CHAPTER SIXTEEN

PRESCRIPTIONS
FOR A MODERN WAR

It is easy to get a thousand prescriptions, but hard to get one single remedy.

—Chinese Proverb

In Iraq everyone did what they had to do to get through each day, though not all these "methods" were broadly admired. You can watch almost any Vietnam War film and see the decadence attributed to the soldiers. Iraq has its own scandals: Abu Ghraib, alleged civilian massacres, and rape. Stress, anger, and just pure hate have driven soldiers to commit all kinds of heinous crimes since the beginning of modern warfare. There's no apologizing for their actions, but this is simply a part of war. Most old WWII films have portrayed the American soldier in a universally positive light—a heroic, honorable, and courageous figure. Generally, it wasn't until Stephen Spielberg's *Saving Private Ryan* and Terrence Malick with *The Thin Red Line* that Hollywood presented the

American soldier during WWII in a more realistic light. The events of 9/11 and our current "war on terrorism" have elevated the position of the American soldier, marine, or airman, placing them on a pedestal much like the American military figure of the late 1940s and 50s.

During Vietnam, especially near the end of the war, many soldiers turned to such drugs as marijuana and heroin to get them through the day. Bars on base as well as in town made alcohol readily available. Massage parlors and whorehouses also catered to the needs of the lonely soldier. The current wars in Iraq and Afghanistan have been a little different. Whorehouses were unavailable, hash was around but took a little work to acquire, and there were no massage parlors and strip clubs. I take that back, you could get a manicure and pedicure as well as a massage in beauty salons. The girls from the Philippines who worked there were very nice, but they didn't give a "happy ending" after your massage, no matter the price. In fact, within a few weeks of opening, the military banned us from going into the beauty salons because some guys from a different company tried to receive a "happy ending" but were denied. I ignored this restriction, however, and went in for periodic pedicures. I actually talked The Sheets into going in with me one day. At this point in time, I don't think he had trimmed his toes in years. The pedicure included a soothing bath and foot massage. In the end The Sheets was pleased, especially since I paid for it. He became even more pleased a couple of months later when his toenails grew back pointed and looked like "raptor toes."

Today's wars are waged in the most uptight, non-alcoholic, and just downright un-fun places on earth. You get sent to some godforsaken place like Iraq or Afghanistan, expected to sacrifice your life for God and country, and you can't drink a beer after a day of putting your life on the line. What the hell has war become? Why can't it be like in M*A*S*H where Hawkeye has his own still in his tent and a bar nearby? But soldiers in adverse situations find ways to overcome most restrictions.

"Mista, mista, whiskey?" the Iraqi boys would ask. At first they sold you alcohol secretly, but once the realization dawned on them that the

American soldier had to have his liquor and was willing to pay for it, the Iraqis would openly yell out that they had whiskey for sale. At first each can—Five Kings (40% proof), imported from the United Kingdom—sold for five dollars. But like any good, greedy capitalist knows, it's supply and demand that matters. The price quickly hiked up to ten dollars because they knew we'd pay it.

It didn't matter what time of day, even at two in the morning, they'd suddenly be standing there, appearing out of the dark when we arrived at Cedar II (the drop off point near Tallil) with our empty fuel trucks. These "street" hawkers lived in Bedouin-type tents out in the desert, a short distance from the road. They could see our convoy coming, allowing the parents to wake up their ten- or twelve-year-old sons to go out and sell cans of that evil substance banned by Islam. Of course, we'd see beer and whiskey cans scattered along the roads wherever we went—hypocrisy transcends all religions and borders.

Fortunately, modern medicine has learned to assist today's soldier with mental and physical issues, or at least suppress them. The army, in its infinite wisdom, has realized the best way to make soldiers function and be willing to get themselves killed is to medicate them. Modern American culture: when in doubt, prescribe a pill. In Iraq, the medical staff, as well as the therapists, found ways to help you get through each day. For those serving in a combat zone, many regularly were prescribed such drugs as Xanax, Prozac, Ambien, and other happy pills. While deployed to Saudi Arabia in 2002, I took Prozac to help deal with some of the immediate idiocy I encountered. I tried the same tack before I left for Iraq. The Prozac seemed to work well for the first few months. At one point, when I ran out, I felt I didn't need any more. But when we moved to the south of Iraq and the bullshit grew, I began to feel anxiety and stress, accompanied by chest pains. Of course, this moment in time happened to coincide with the deterioration of my relationship with my wife.

During one convoy mission to FOB Anaconda, we spent the night near Camp Stryker, our old stomping grounds. Before I went to sleep on my cot that night, I finished reading the chapter from Ruling Your World concerning the tiger's path and how to make the right decision. "Upon arising, have a positive and open attitude," Sakyong Mipham says. "Look at the lay of the land before deciding what to say and not to say, what to do and not to do." As soon as I awoke, I remembered these words. I took a long breath. I was in a war zone but alive, and I had a new day before me. I could worry about what might come, what I was missing at home, my relationship with my wife—but all these were simply distractions. I couldn't change my current situation, but I could shape my mind to have a positive, open attitude, even in a hostile place like Iraq. I took another deep breath and felt better about my circumstances; the rest of the day passed without chest pains. However, this didn't solve the long-term problem.

This was in winter 2006, a few months before I would return home. I'd given up on expecting my wife to be there for me. Over the holidays I received a Christmas card from her five days after Christmas! The late arrival had nothing to do with the mail; it was postmarked a couple of days before December 25th. Shortly after the holidays, she informed me that she wanted me to get my own place when I came back from Iraq.

Dear Paul,

I have been meaning to write you for a very long time and just could not bring myself to do it. I am not sure what I want to say to you but feel that you need to understand why I am breaking up our family. I feel that I am not getting what I need from our marriage...We have had so many challenges in our marriage, and all this time I have had alone has made me do a lot of thinking about what **I** want and what will make **me** happiest. Right now I just can't be in a marriage that I feel that I am putting in my 100% and not getting it in return. I am exhausted and have completely lost who I am in doing so. I want a marriage that revolves around the family first and not our individual needs. We have gone so far from that in the past couple years that I just can't stand it anymore. I am not at all saying it is completely your fault because it is not ... I need to be by myself right now and discover again what **I** want and need. I know this sounds completely selfish on my part, but it is just what I need to do. Paul, I do love you with all my heart; you are a wonderful man with such a beautiful heart and mind... please don't ever forget that... I do know that we do have a strong bond with each other and no matter what, that will never change.

Love, Robin

I was shocked, but in the past my wife had made rash decisions at a moment's notice (usually prompted by advice from her mother or friends) while in an emotional state. I assumed that she was going through another period where she needed "to find herself," or something similar. Plus, her letter seemed contradictory, and I didn't understand exactly what she was saying. But through the Sakyong, I did understand her motivation.

"Fixating on how we want the world to be and trying to make it stay goes against the natural grain," he explains in *Ruling Your World*. "That tightness and the sense of claustrophobia it creates is 'me.' Our negativity gives us something to hold on to. We think that if we hold on tight enough, we can manipulate the world to make 'me' happy." My wife was clearly feeling negative, both about me and what her life was expected to be.

In Iraq I had created my own defense mechanism for survival. I tossed the letter onto the bed, went to take a shower, and tried to put what she said out of my mind. I didn't have the energy to deal with it—I was just trying to make it through each day by staying alive.

Following the deaths of our friends while at Camp Stryker, the survivors involved in each incident depended on the army's "combat stress" unit to help them cope. Its counselors, trained to work with soldiers who've experienced traumatic events, also dealt with more mundane combat zone issues such as anxiety, stress, and lack of sleep. Knowing this, I made an important decision one night to visit the unit.

We'd just returned from a two-day convoy mission. Tired and stressed out, I'd just laid down on my bunk to watch a movie under the assumption that we'd have at least a day or two off before the next mission. Word arrived, however, that we were expected to go out the following morning to T.Q., which entailed at least a three-day mission. "Be ready in the morning," I was told. Something in me snapped. I just couldn't do it. I got up, put my uniform on, and went over to the combat stress unit.

At this point, I had continual chest pains. I'd put off seeking medical attention in hope that they would pass, but they hadn't. Knowing it was most likely not a physical condition because this issue had occurred before, I needed more medicine such as Prozac, which I was taking when we arrived in Iraq. But it wasn't just a need for medicine. I'd had enough—enough of the people around me; of Moore's pompous Marine attitude; of phone conversations with my cold, indifferent wife; of struggling to stay awake for twelve hours on brutally monotonous convoy missions that left me with too much time to think. I needed a break.

I'd avoided going before because, like many soldiers, I felt that asking for help with combat stress and speaking about my problems made me feel weak. How many soldiers had fought in WWII and Vietnam and survived without going to such a facility for assistance and drugs? In Iraq we rode around in air-conditioned humvees, lived with air-conditioning, and ate regular hot meals that often included steak and lobster. The war in Iraq was a little different. And then again, maybe it wasn't.

Entering the combat stress facility, which was part of a renovated building belonging to the Iraqi army during the Saddam years, I found the people to be very nice. The officer on duty, a Major Masterson, sat me down and we talked. I told him about the chest pains and anxiety and about the lack of support from my wife. He was very caring and helpful. I told him how I'd taken Prozac in the past. At the end of our meeting, he prescribed me both Prozac and Xanax to help with the anxiety and chest pains.

The Xanax worked wonders, but it was situational. By February 2006, when I called my wife, she had little sympathy in her voice. I had to beg her to send something from my boys, like art work from school or pictures. She seemed chilly and distant. I eventually accepted it along with everything else. While I'd been away, my wife had adapted by creating a temporary new life for herself, one in which I played a marginal role. At this point in my tour in Iraq, I really needed her support. It would never come. So I relied on pills to get me through each day. But it wasn't only pills that helped.

Reading Pema Chödrön's book, *When Things Fall Apart*, inspired me to keep working on my attitude. This book really resonated with me at a time when I was feeling down. (In fact I sent a copy to my wife, which she left unread—like she did the letters published in *The Dot*.) As Pema suggests, "Practicing loving-kindness toward ourselves seems as good a way as any to start illuminating the darkness of difficult times."

For me, however, the difficult times had only begun. As I had done while at Camp Stryker, I went out on convoy missions with my copy of *Awakening Loving-Kindness*. Before departing for a mission one day while acting as a gunner, I sat up in the turret reading. A friend walked up and asked what I was reading. I showed him the book: *Awakening Loving-Kindness*. He looked at me a little funny and walked away. He thought it odd, I guess, to be reading such a book before a mission where I might have to shoot and kill someone. But I didn't see it as odd, just inspirational. Some men carried a Bible and a cross or crucifix with them for comfort. I carried cigars and Pema's book.

One day my former squad leader, SGT. T, took me aside and asked some personal questions. "Is everything going well at home?"

I said, "No, not really."

He then asked if I would like to talk about it.

I said, "No, not really."

He told me it appeared that I "didn't seem to care about anything," referring to my recent actions. Apparently, another soldier had complained to him that, while out on a convoy mission, I didn't seem to care if I was blown up or not. To placate him, I told him I would tighten things up and then walked away. The truth was I really didn't care. I really wasn't that concerned with being killed. I didn't put any of my fellow soldiers in danger, of course, but my apparent indifference toward death alarmed a few of those around me. Xanax and Prozac made a wonderful combination: they relaxed me so much that I was honestly not that concerned whether or not I got hit by an IED. At night on the road, driving as fast as possible, I could do very little to prevent it. There was no point in worrying about taking a hit from an IED. Xanax took the worry away.

Of course, not all of us were experiencing family issues or other stresses. For the lucky ones, their wives or girlfriends sent regular letters of support, as well as boxes of items to help them survive. In my case, my mother would come through, being the truly loyal person that she was. She'd send me alcohol disguised as fruit juice. I told her that they might x-ray the packages, as they'd done in Saudi Arabia, so I instructed her to pour the Vodka or Captain Morgan into empty juice or water bottles. Not that her involvement concerned her that much, but she put "Aunt Lizzie" on the return address. Aunt Lizzie, a friend of the family, knew nothing about my mother's nefarious postal engagements.

Not long after being fired as TC by SGT. Moore, I was transferred away from him to work under SGT. T in a different section, where I resumed duties as a TC when necessary. However, SGT. T did not appreciate my attitude and sarcasm, nor did our young platoon leader, 2LT. Tafil, who'd joined us at Camp Stryker shortly before we moved south. Both men received less than respect as senior leaders of our section. I've already highlighted SGT. T's leadership skills. Before beginning a convoy mission, SGT. T would stand in front of his humvee and give a briefing: whether the roads were clear, what to look out for, and such. On a mission to T.Q. one night, SGT. T had been spooked by a number of things.

Over the radio, he said, "What was that?" in an excited voice.

"Just some lights coming on at a few houses, nothing to worry about," I responded. Lights had a habit of coming on and off spontaneously in Iraq, due to irregular power outages.

A short time later, I heard his voice again over the radio, and it sounded agitated. "What was that? Did you see that streak?" he asked. Everyone could hear the panic in his voice and recognized his paranoia over the radio.

"It was a shooting star," I explained, shaking my head.

SGT. T said nothing.

During the safety briefing before our next convoy mission, with the 1st Sergeant present, I interjected, "Don't forget to watch out for those spontaneous lights that come off and on and be careful of shooting stars—they can be dangerous," letting my comments hang in the air. SGT. T just stood there without looking at me. The other members of my section who knew SGT. T tried not to laugh or simply turned away to avoid any embarrassment.

I've just never been good at keeping my mouth shut. Sarcastic comments come as natural to me as passing gas and help explain my less-than-meteoric rise through the army's ranks.

During one meeting I suggested we should call ourselves "Tafil's Turds" because our section got little admiration, due directly to our leadership.

2LT. Tafil said, "Why can't we be called Animal Turds?" ("Animals" being our company nickname).

I responded, "Because, sir, without you, we wouldn't be the turds that we are."

Needless to say, my tenure with SGT. T and 2LT. Tafil ended soon after these incidents.

One of the biggest challenges during our convoy security missions was staying awake. The army provided free energy drinks like Red Bull and Rip It to help us keep alert. Some guys became addicted to them, but I could only consume so many energy drinks. Today, I feel ill just looking at a can of Red Bull (except when it's mixed as a Jaeger Bomb).

While the energy drinks helped, I also smoked cigars to keep me awake. A few times I looked over at my driver and saw him beginning to nod off and had to tell him to wake up. Without problems, such as the

Author taking a break during a routine convoy mission north of Baghdad.

roads turning "red" due to the discovery of an IED, it would take seven or eight hours to get to FOB Anaconda, north of Baghdad. On most evenings, we'd have to sit and wait for the roads to clear. Sometimes we'd sit in the middle of Tampa, the main supply route, for hours, just waiting to hear that we could continue. In the relatively safe area of southern Iraq, we never encountered an IED, but once we got north of a base called Scania, about three hours' drive from Tallil, the game was on.

The army issued us combat ear plugs meant to protect our ears against hearing loss in case an IED went off, though the real world of Iraq usually conflicted with army safety. If we used the ear plugs, we struggled to hear the TC give commands; and it was hard for the T.C. to listen to the radio. But what really made it impossible to wear the ear plugs was needing to listen to your iPOD or CD player while driving. I listened to music with one earphone in my left ear while the other remained open to hear the TC

For me, music helped the most when it came to staying awake while driving all over Iraq. But for some, basic human error could lead to disaster.

Once, while returning from Anaconda, an hour north of Baghdad, to Tallil, our convoy drove through an Iraqi checkpoint, and my driver nearly killed me. We must have been going about 50 miles an hour, and he didn't see a cement barrier directly in front of our humvee. Other vehicles had already passed through, kicking up dust. I screamed at him, "Left! Left!" at the last second. I very rarely scream like that, and it must have shocked him out of his complacency. He turned the wheel hard to the left, dodging the barrier directly in front of us but lurching toward another cement wall. To avoid this wall, he whipped the wheel back to the right. The vehicle swerved hard—back toward the wall we had barely missed. For a moment I thought we would miss it, but the right rear tire caught the very end of the barrier, ripping it to shreds and damaging the back of the truck.

Thanks to the Xanax and my overall disposition, I calmly called up to the lead vehicle in front of the convoy and informed him that we had collided with a cement barrier. At first I thought we were okay, but after a few minutes, the smell of burning rubber indicated that we had to pull over. The lead vehicle acknowledged our situation and began to stop the convoy. Stopping a twenty vehicle KBR convoy isn't normally a problem when out on a long stretch of desolate highway. However, we were now in Baghdad. Breaking down on the side of the road in Baghdad was not a good thing.

I soon discovered that there's nothing more fun than standing on the side of the road in Baghdad, waiting to get shot while you change a tire. Fortunately, each convoy had two trucks called "bobtails" that were designed to assist other trucks and humvees in case of a breakdown. The rear bobtail pulled up to us and the repairman, an American, got out. He had power tools to remove the shredded tire and put on our spare. While I stood there looking at the lights of Baghdad, SGT. T showed up. His humvee was driving in the middle of the convoy where it was safest. He got out and began to berate my driver for nearly killing me—not that he cared that much for my safety. After a few seconds of screaming, he stopped and looked around, like he suddenly realized, *Oh shit, I'm on the side of the road in Baghdad; people might like to kill me.* Recognizing the life-threatening nature of his predicament, he jumped back into his humvee and drove off, leaving me, my driver, and the American truck driver to take care of the tire. Without SGT. T's vehicle I now only had my gunner for protection. I didn't feel especially scared; I was on Xanax, so life was good. I found the whole incident quite amusing, actually. According to CPL. Hernandez, in charge of the lead vehicle (and the only Mexican-American in our entire company), I was laughing when I told him over the radio how we'd collided with a barrier.

If we'd hit that barrier straight on, I'd either have ended up dead or in a hospital in Germany. The 48th Brigade had already lost three soldiers in a humvee accident when the driver fell asleep at the wheel and ran into the side of a bridge. While going through the checkpoint, I had my helmet off, which I sometimes removed for a short time because it got uncomfortable on long trips. If we'd hit that barrier, my head would have slammed into the bullet-proof window. And to think I was worried about roadside bombs.

The American driving the bobtail quickly changed our tire, and the convoy continued on its way. Before I got back into the humvee, I took one last look out across Baghdad, where most of its citizens were fast asleep. A city of six million, its lights glowed in the sweltering evening. Once again, I'd come close to death or serious injury. Some moments in time are unforgettable. One of those moments took place when I called my wife to tell her that she narrowly missed receiving half a million dollars by collecting my death benefits. She dismissed me and my description of another incident that nearly cost me my life. A few months earlier, after the deaths of the last four soldiers by a five hundred pound bomb, I'd stopped explaining to her anything that happened to me in Iraq; it had become obvious that she no longer cared, and I'd just have to deal with it.

CHAPTER SEVENTEEN

A CHARNEL GROUND WITHOUT GUNS

Watching a peaceful death of a human being reminds us of a falling star; one of a million lights in a vast sky that flares up for a brief moment only to disappear into the endless night forever.
—Elisabeth Kübler-Ross

After ten months in Iraq, I could safely say, I've had enough—of the war and of a lot of the people around me. I was ready to go home. As it turned out, I would be forced to leave Iraq a few weeks early due to unexpected circumstances.

I usually called my mother every two or three days, depending on when I was out on patrol. During one call, I knew something was wrong when my uncle answered the phone. He informed me she'd been in the hospital for the last two days with stomach tumors.

Alarmed, I called the hospital and spoke with her. Her mouth was so dry she could hardly talk. Because she was being tested, she was not allowed to have water. She was tired, so our conversation was brief. I immediately spoke with the hospital representative in charge of Red Cross messages, asking her to send it to my unit in Iraq. When the first Red Cross message arrived, the nature and severity of my mother's illness was still undiagnosed.

Military bureaucracy prevented me from reaching my mother's bedside for almost a week. My higher chain of command apparently believed my attempt to leave Iraq was, in fact, a lie. Earlier, two other soldiers had returned home due to their mothers' deaths. When I informed my superiors of my own mother's condition, they apparently believed I was trying to jump on the dying-mom bandwagon.

When I told my wife about my mother's condition, she was sympathetic and offered to move from my mother-in-law's house into an apartment when I came home to try to make things work. I felt relieved by her words and quickly wrote off her attitude over the last few months as another attempt to "find herself." I needed support and was happy to have her on my side again.

Finally, after three more Red Cross messages urging me to come to her hospital, and an appeal to Senator Martinez' office in Florida, I managed to navigate the deliberate foot-dragging of the army bureaucracy and receive permission to go to my mother. After ten months in Iraq, I walked unceremoniously to the airfield, accompanied by The Sheets and Daylon Brown. After we reached the airfield, my friends stayed with me for a while. Daylon and I smoked a couple of Cohibas, and then they left. Less than an hour later, I walked with a few other soldiers out onto the airfield, up the ramp of a military cargo plane, and sat down in the back; minutes later, we lifted off on our way to Kuwait. The 48th Brigade would be out of Iraq in a few weeks; I wouldn't have to return, but I'd soon find a new charnel ground waiting for me at home.

I spent the night in Kuwait and then flew to California through Dallas. In a phone conversation from Kuwait, a representative of the hospital told me that my mother had been placed on life support and couldn't speak. Arriving at the airport, I'd expected someone to be waiting to pick me up. My wife had said one of her friends would be there to drive me to the hospital. Standing in the baggage claim area for about ten minutes, I realized she had not followed through on her promise, and resigned to the situation, I went outside and hailed a cab. Before reaching the hospital, I swallowed two Xanax pills, believing it would help with the reality of seeing my mother in whatever condition she was in. It was six in the morning when I arrived at the hospital, dragging my duffel bag behind me. I must have looked pretty haggard, not having showered or shaved since Kuwait. The hospital staff had been expecting me for days, and the nurses were very friendly and helpful. They told me she could no longer see, but if I got close enough and spoke into her ear, she could hear me and would respond by fluttering her eyelids.

When I walked into her room, I saw that her skin had become wrinkled, and had a yellowish tint. She appeared drained of all energy and life. My wife used to remark about the youthful look of my mother's skin. That probably explained why she looked at least ten years younger than she really was. My mother had always been so vibrant, so alive. Seeing her there on a hospital bed with tubes in her nose seemed unreal. Blood had collected heavily over the last few days to bloat her stomach.

I held her hand and spoke into her ear. "Mom," I said. "It's me, Paul. You got me home from Iraq safe."

Her eyes fluttered briefly, apparently acknowledging my voice.

"I love you," I told her.

I couldn't think of more to say. She was going to die—we both knew it. What could I say? Give her words of encouragement? Tell her everything was going to be okay, that she would live? I must have said more to her after telling her that I loved her, but I can't remember now. It was such an unreal moment. I felt numb, detached from everything around me. This just couldn't be my mother lying there on that bed. Iraq and now this? I'd expected her to be greeting me with a big smile when I returned home.

Shortly thereafter, her eyes stopped fluttering when we spoke to her. The nurses had told her I was on my way. Her eye movements were the first and last time I received any kind of acknowledgement from my mother. I continued to hold her hand and talk into her ear, but without response. I think she held on as long as she did just for me, and once she knew I was out of Iraq and home safely, she could let herself go. I like to

Author with his mother at Ft. Irwin, CA. shortly before his deployment to Iraq.

think that by getting sick and ultimately dying, she somehow saved my life. If she had never gotten sick, I may have come home with everyone else, perfectly safe. But I like to think of her death as auspicious—that by helping me leave Iraq early, she saved my life.

Later that afternoon, I spoke with the doctor. "Your mother's cancer is like a salt shaker," he explained to me when I questioned him about her condition. "There are tumors spread everywhere. We would have to literally remove her entire stomach to stop the cancer."

I nodded my head. "I understand," I replied quietly.

"She agreed right away to try chemotherapy," the doctor continued, "but the cancer was too far gone and she was too weak. She deteriorated rapidly after the chemo treatment. There is virtually no chance of recovery."

As I absorbed the finality of the prognosis, I recalled my phone conversation with her in Iraq when she was still cognizant. "I got a Red Cross message, and I'll be leaving soon. You're getting me out of Iraq."

A sigh of relief was obvious in her dry, rasping voice. "I'm so glad…so glad, good." She was too weak to continue our conversation.

"Goodbye, Mom," I had said, trying to ignore the sense of premonition. I'd had enough of death. I didn't want to think of my mother as its next victim.

"You don't have to make any decisions about your mother right now," the doctor told me.

I knew I would have to turn the life support off, but I wasn't ready for my mother to die. I was numb and confused. I felt as though I were having an out-of-body experience, like I was robotically going through the motions—as though I were a spectator. I nodded. "Yes, doctor, I understand. Thank you." Then I added, "I would like to wait another day."

"That's fine," he responded kindly as he left the room.

I stood and stared at my mother lying there, blind, speechless, bloated with her own blood, a sad caricature of her normal, vibrant self. So it's real, I thought to myself. She really is going to die. I began to think about how much death I'd experienced over the last ten months—friends, an unborn child, Iraqis, some innocent, some not. A young woman left alone to raise her baby because the child's father had been shot and killed on what should have been an ordinary evening around the television with friends and family, killed by the very people she'd assumed were there to help.

Later that evening, I went out and got drunk. I bought beer to take with me and smuggled it into my mother's room. At some point I passed out in my seat. The next thing I remember was a nurse waking me up at about three in the morning. A different shift had come on duty, and the nurses weren't so kind.

I remember the not-so-nice night nurse asking me in a surly tone, "Who's in charge of you?"

I said, "Donald Rumsfeld." Apparently, even in an extreme state of intoxication, I still managed to maintain a level of sarcasm. She left to call my cousin Susan, who'd flown in from Dallas to help her father, my uncle Leroy, while I was dealing with my mother's condition. I must have fallen asleep again because my only memory from that point on was Susan shaking me gently.

"Paul," she asked, "are you okay?" (According to the day nurse, the night staff feared I was suffering from PTSD or something rather than a mass consumption of alcohol mixed with Xanax).

I woke up with some confusion. I looked at the floor and saw two strangely misplaced bottles of beer, one opened and one not, next to the chair.

"The nurse says you can't stay here. She called me to come get you."

I said nothing and started to get up out of my chair. Susan helped steady me as I stood. The surly night nurse glared at me. We left the room, and that's all I can remember until the following morning.

When I returned to the hospital, the nurse who'd been caring so gently for my mother through her illness was shocked to see me up so early and feeling reasonably well. With a small smile on her face, she informed me that my actions of the night before were not well received. "But I found your comment about Donald Rumsfeld amusing," she said.

Oh God, I thought. The events of the previous evening began to come back to me. "I guess I should make some apologies for last night," I told her.

She said, "Forget it." She understood my situation well. I got the feeling that the night nurse wasn't well liked by her peers. Having made funeral arrangements earlier in the day, I spent the afternoon with my mom. That experience proved to be as unreal as everything else. Again, I was going through the motions, signing papers for my mother's cremation, and continuing to feel like I was on the outside, watching everything unfold behind glass.

When it came time to turn off the life support, my cousin Susan and my elderly cousin Trudy arrived at the hospital. My uncle Leroy chose not to come. They told me later that he'd sat in a chair and cried when he learned his sister's condition was terminal. I guess he just couldn't handle being there when they turned off the life support. Before the nurse began to remove the tubes keeping my mother alive, she warned me that what could come next might be bad.

"I've seen worse," I replied.

She said, "Yes, but this is your mother."

She was right, of course. That was my mother lying there on the bed. Even at this critical moment—seconds away from ending her life—I still felt oddly detached. Maybe it was the Xanax, or just the suddenness of the situation, but I couldn't bring myself to cry—that would come later. I walked over to the side of the bed and leaned down close to her ear.

"Goodbye, Mom. I love you."

I kissed her on her forehead and walked back to the foot of the bed. I told the nurse she could begin to turn the machines off.

We heard her body gurgle. Saliva bubbled on her lips. She gasped slightly, and that was it. She passed easily, painlessly. And I must be thankful for that; she did not have to endure the humiliation of a rest home and a long, painful wait to die. She went out with class, with complete control of her faculties, the way she would have wanted.

Within minutes of my mother's passing, a man from the funeral home appeared to collect her body. He was quick and clinically efficient. The nurse began to voice her objections to the man's sudden arrival, but it wasn't his fault. He was only doing his job.

With the machine turned off and my mother gone, there was no point in lingering. I told the nurse not to be upset with the funeral home guy; I'd go downstairs while he removed the body and return a little later to retrieve my things. Outside on the hospital patio, I smoked a cigar and thought about my mother, about Iraq, and the homecoming with my wife and children.

When I returned, the nurse had my things packed. "Thank you for all your help," I told her.

She smiled. "You're welcome. Your mother was a very kind lady. I enjoyed being with her."

"Yes," I said. "She was very kind."

The nurse sighed and hugged me, and I left as I had come in—dragging my duffel bag.

* * * * *

That evening we held a makeshift memorial service for my mother at my cousin Trudy's home. During the service, Susan related a phone conversation she'd had with my mother while I was still in Iraq. She conveyed to me that my mother had resigned herself to the fact that I might die. I found this an odd way for her to think. My mother was very religious (at least most of the time), and I know she placed my name on at least half a dozen prayer lists. In my phone conversations with her while in Iraq, I never detected anything in her voice or words to make me think she held that fear.

Going through my mom's effects was an illuminating experience. I found a diary in which she kept meticulous daily notes while I was deployed, describing the immediate cause of death (i.e., roadside bombs, small arms fire) of every National Guard soldier killed in Iraq. For a usually optimistic person, she seemed to have had a rather bleak view of my chances of survival. Yet, she never expressed those doubts in any of our phone conversations or when I saw her on leave.

After going through her personal items, I had the sad feeling that my own life had changed dramatically. I'd imagined that my mother would be at Ft. Stewart with the other families when I returned with my unit from Iraq. The graphic memories of violence and death still hung over me, but I pushed them aside. I saw a much better future ahead. It was at last time to return home to my family.

CHAPTER EIGHTEEN

WELCOME HOME, SGT. KENDEL

When things fall apart and we're on the verge of we know not what, the test of each of us is to stay on the brink and not concretize. The spiritual journey is not about heaven and finally getting to a place that's really swell.

—Pema Chödrön,
When Things Fall Apart

I felt so relieved to finally be coming home. After ten months in Iraq, the deaths of friends, and my own mother's death, I wanted to be with my wife and kids. I'd have a weekend with them before having to report to Ft. Stewart for the remaining weeks of my active duty. My flight into Jacksonville airport and the emotional meeting with my family mirrored my previous return, six months earlier. My boys ran to me, and I hugged and kissed them. My wife and I embraced, kissed, and held hands. My father and his wife waited for us downstairs. They met me with a big white banner proclaiming, "Welcome Home, Sgt. Kendel."

Returning to the airport in Jacksonville, the author's two sons, Alex and Sean greet their dad.

We had a pleasant dinner and spent the first night in a hotel. It was a Friday and I had to report to Ft. Stewart on Monday, leaving me little time to settle in. We stopped at my mother-in-law's so that my wife could pack a few things. While she packed, I joined my boys in their room. On a table sat a school project. I asked Alex, the oldest, what it was.

"It's a robot," he told me. "Momma and David made it for me." He then looked embarrassed, as though he'd given away a secret. You can always trust a seven-year-old to spill the beans.

"Who is David?" I asked.

"I'm not supposed to talk about David," he replied, his eyes leaving my face.

Really, I thought. After pressing the issue, he told me that "David" was Momma's "friend." I suddenly felt sick to my stomach. It couldn't be true, I kept telling myself. My wife wouldn't do something like that to me. I knew we had some problems, but she wouldn't do that. Not to me.

She could never hurt me that way, not after all I'd been through. Maybe "David" was just a friend; my wife had had male friends and roommates in the past, I thought to myself as we left for the hotel. Maybe I was reading too much into things, but the nagging thoughts stayed with me until we reached the hotel. After putting the kids to bed, I went outside to smoke a cigar. I walked to a local gas station to buy a beer and then

WALKING THE TIGER'S PATH
PAUL M. KENDEL

retreated to a dark, quiet place to smoke and to think. Over the course of the next hour, I began to believe that my wife had, in fact, betrayed me.

I finished my cigar and beer and returned to the hotel room. The boys slept in one bed, while my wife lay half-awake in the other. I crawled into bed with my boys.

"What are you doing?" she exclaimed in surprise.

"I want to be with my boys," I replied, too tired and just not in the mood to deal with it. She wasn't happy with my sleeping arrangements.

In the morning she arose early to drive to work. While she showered and dressed, I moved into the other bed. About to leave the room, she turned and said, "This isn't going to work, is it?"

I sat up in bed. "Why don't you tell me who 'David' is?"

Sighing, she lowered her eyes. "He's just a friend."

"Did you sleep with him?"

She looked at me, took a deep breath—and lied. "No," she said. Then she turned and started out of the room with the attitude that I'd transgressed upon her integrity. Choosing to believe her, I got up, hugged and kissed her, and apologized for my erroneous belief. We made up, and she left the room happy. Later that afternoon, I sent her flowers, apologizing once again for having suspected her of infidelity.

Over the weekend my wife and I bought a brand new minivan and found a suburban townhome and created some semblance of family bliss. But she walked around with an attitude. I tried placating her by apologizing for past mistakes that I was sure she resented, believing that if I assumed the majority of blame for past conflicts, she would be happy. This was a Buddhist teaching called "Drive all blames into one," meaning you should take all the blame in a situation yourself, even if you don't deserve it all. Absorbing the aggression, you create space for the other person to be less irritable and defensive. "When we take the blame," Trungpa Rinpoche has said, "we absorb the poison, so then the rest of the situation becomes medicine." I made an attempt to absorb the poison.

"I know I should have done some things differently," I told her.

"Yeah, yeah," she said, taking in every self-deprecating word as a means to validate her affair. After about ten minutes, I'd expected her to interject with something like, "It hasn't been all your fault, Paul. I've made mistakes, too," but that never came.

Finally, I felt compelled to say, "Well, you know, Robin, you haven't exactly been perfect. When it comes to finances…"

She cut me off. "Wait a minute," she said loudly with resentment. "But you just said it was all your fault!"

My shoulders sank, and I said, "Of course I don't think it's all my fault. I was trying to be nice…"

She turned and walked out of the room. I sat on the bottom bunk of my children's bed. I guess I hadn't really taken all the blame after all.…

On Monday morning I awoke early to depart for Ft. Stewart; the sun was just beginning to rise. My wife was still sleeping as I got up and looked out the window of our bedroom: brand new town homes; manicured lawns; our shiny, freshly purchased minivan; people walking their dogs. The perfect suburban fantasy, I thought. A few days earlier, I'd been watching the nurse turn off my mother's life support. A few days before that, I was dragging my bags through soupy Iraqi mud. I laughed to myself, thinking of the dream-like cacophony of turns my life had taken. I realized I had a damn good life—a beautiful wife, two near-perfect young boys. As I walked away from the window, I also knew none of it was meant to last.

After two days of performing rear detachment duty at Ft. Stewart, my wife once again expressed her need to "find herself," suddenly informing me that she'd found a roommate to live with her in my now ex-townhome. Even after I'd been kicked out and went on to finish the last few weeks of my active duty service, I still refused to believe my wife had cheated on me.

Once the 48th Brigade returned to Georgia, we began the demobilization process—turning in equipment and follow-up medical evaluations. Because I'd left Iraq a few weeks earlier, I didn't attend the triumphant return ceremonies of Alpha Company and the rest of the 48th Brigade.

Instead, I was doing paperwork at a desk. When Alpha Company arrived at the barracks after having been honored for their service and joyously greeted by their families, I was there to meet them. It was my anti-climatic job to sign them out.

SFC. Janes walked in and said, "How's your mom?" Considering his lack of assistance in my efforts to leave Iraq to see my mother before she died, he'd most likely subscribed to the "dying mother conspiracy."

"She's dead," I said flatly.

"I'm sorry," he mumbled, avoiding my eyes.

Ross approached a short time later with his consolations. "I and the rest of the guys thought the way they treated you was really fucked up." I thanked him. It was nice to know how my departure had been received.

Anxious to rejoin their friends and family, my unit quickly dispersed for the day, leaving me to return alone to my hotel room. My wife had most likely reacquainted herself with "David" in the interim period while I was at Ft. Stewart. In retrospect, not long after I'd left for training at Ft. Stewart, her behavior had changed. The signs were there. She'd most likely started an affair shortly after I left and months before I deployed to Iraq. There had been someone before "David"; I just refused to believe it.

In an effort to justify her affair, she told me later that she had "met someone else and moved on." In a few words she dismissed our marriage vows, our last ten years of life together, and the raising of our two young children.

Following my sudden eviction from home and the termination of my active duty service, I had no idea where I was going to live. My father and his wife offered no support, not even a night or two at their condo on Amelia Island until I could get myself together. But this is where my karma finally took an upturn. Margot happened to be staying at her house in New Smyrna Beach, Florida. She invited me to come down and stay with her and her husband. Their beautiful beach house had a wide wooden deck with a palapa and a swing right on the beach, a short distance from the water. On a flag pole at the end of the deck, a Shambhala flag waved majestically in the wind.

Friends of Margot and her husband came over to visit and generously offered their condo down the road, close to the beach, for me to stay in rent-free for a while. The condo in New Smyrna Beach provided a perfect two-month refuge for me in a time of need. Once the realization set in that my wife had cheated on me, I was not a happy man. I didn't sleep well, and I drank too much. I was lost and struggled to regain my balance.

Through their generosity, Margot's friends gave me an opportunity to begin the healing process in a tranquil environment that provided the emotional space to begin the book I'd decided to write. The more I looked at the emails I'd written in Iraq, the more I began to realize that they went beyond vivid descriptions of the horrors and pain of war; they described in detail what I'd learned from my time in Iraq—about myself, my friends, and humanity in general. After my letters appeared in *The Dot*, the Sakyong's executive secretary had even encouraged me to write a book. I realized that what I had to write was not simply a description of some terrible events or places in a time of war; it would be about my own spiritual journey along the Tiger's path: keeping my seat in the face of confusion, discriminating right action from wrong, seeing the world with an open mind.

I spent quality time with my boys at the beach, the pool, and in the jacuzzi. The condo became our own little world, a place where we could escape from reality. But when the boys left and I was alone, I fell back into the whirlpool of my thoughts.

I still had the naked pictures of my wife that I asked her to send me when I was in Iraq. There were fleeting periods during my tour where she seemed supportive. I often looked at the photos when I was alone at the condo. I still felt very attracted to her and wanted her. I had a card she'd sent me in which she'd told me how much she loved me and wanted to grow old with me. One night after returning from Moe's, a local dive bar across from the condo, I began working on a bottle of wine. I'd had entirely too much to drink and was extremely emotional. I picked up the photos and decided to burn them. I didn't have a match or a lighter, so in my drunken state, I decided to burn them in a pan on the stove. This method managed to scorch the edges of a few pictures, but mostly filled the condo with smoke, and the fire alarm went off. I opened the door and tried to clear out the smoke, then sat down on the couch, defeated. Damn, I thought, I can't even burn her goddamn pictures!

Fortunately, my boys, though too young to fully understand what was going on, did recognize that I wasn't happy and offered what support they could. Alex would tell me, "Daddy, you need to meet a hot chick, one that won't cheat on you when you go to the Army."

I was already living in a beach paradise in New Smyrna, but I still wanted to get away—away to familiar places and friends. I'd spent the last decade or more traveling to a tranquil beach town called Playa del Carmen in Mexico, south of Cancun. This ultimate party place was more low-key than Cancun, and I had a good friend I'd known for years who lived there with his own bar. I easily coerced The Sheets, Daylon Brown, Jason Royal, and Derrick Mack—all friends from Iraq—into joining me for a week long alcohol-induced haze, mostly attributed to Captain and Coke, but it was something we all needed after Iraq. When we returned, The Sheets stayed with me at the condo for a few days before heading back to Covington, Georgia.

One night, we got extremely drunk at Moe's. The Sheets still had his thing for Captain and Coke. When we returned home, he was acting a little odd, silent and distant—he seemed to want to talk about something important. As we sat out on the balcony, he soon became very emotional.

Trying to hold back tears, he said, "I can't believe we lost all those guys in Iraq, man. All those guys, dead! I was doing alright, having a good time until that woman said those things."

"What things?" I asked him.

"You were playing pool. This woman sat next to me. The bitch started going off about how stupid it was for us to be in Iraq. If she had just kept it political it would have been okay, but she said the problem with Iraq was not just the politicians, but the soldiers who were fighting the war. She acted as though we, and the guys who died in Iraq with us, were to blame for what was happening there."

He broke down right in front of me, tears streaming down his face. I was shocked. The Sheets was a pretty reserved kind of guy, but I guess it was time for him to release the emotions surrounding the deaths of friends. I listened and offered as much comfort as I could.

After about fifteen minutes, he regained his composure. "I'm glad you were here, man. I don't know what I would have done if I'd been alone."

"I'm glad I was here, too," I returned, trying to reassure him.

"Please don't tell anyone about this; I can't believe I lost it."

"I won't tell anyone," I said.

Having survived the trauma of the previous evening, The Sheets took his leave the following day. I'm telling the story now with his approval.

Soon after, my wife called to tell me she had some mail for me that had been sent to her home. In a bizarre and fortuitous occurrence, a package had arrived from my deceased mother, the last package she'd sent right before she went into the hospital. It contained the usual letter and newspaper clippings she'd been sending to me the entire time I was in Iraq. When I received the package from my wife, the day and its significance eluded me. I opened it and read the letter:

> Sunday, March 5, 2006
> Dear Paul,
>
> I plan to mail one more big envelope to you, after I get next week's Time Magazine. Then, that will be the end of your mail! The 10th is this coming Friday. Oh, I am so happy and excited that you are finally coming home! That has been a very long and painful time in Iraq. I will keep on praying for your safety until you are home!
>
> Lots of love + God's Blessings!
> Mom

WALKING THE TIGER'S PATH
PAUL M. KENDEL

I called Margot the following day to inform her that I'd received a package from my mother. "You received the package yesterday?" she asked.

"Yes," I said.

"Yesterday was Mother's Day."

I sat stunned with the phone in my hand. I've never been good at remembering dates and birthdays. Yesterday was Mother's Day? What were the odds of receiving a package mailed to Iraq from your now deceased mother on a day like Mother's Day? I looked at the calendar for 2006. On the day of her last letter to me (Sunday, March 5th) she had written:

> Can't sleep at night—very uncomfortable. (Cousin) Bill will take me to Fountain Valley Hospital walk-in clinic at 3:00. I want to go into the hospital!

Though sick and wanting to go into the hospital, she had still found time to write to me. Now, even after her death, my mother found a way to assist me and provide support. Other than her kindness, the post-Iraq support from all other members of my family seemed non-existent.

Veterans returning from service face a common experience, according to *Time* magazine. An unknown soldier etched his indictment onto the wall of a sentry box in Gibraltar. You imagine him there, many wars ago, keeping watch and weighing his prospects for a normal life:

> *God and the soldier, all men adore,*
> *In time of danger and not before.*
> *When the danger is past, and all things righted,*
> *God is forgotten and the soldier slighted.*

My father's pride in my service to God and country vanished quickly, replaced by a desire for normalcy, as if I'd never been in Iraq at all. "Why don't you just go back to work? You have responsibilities as a father," he told me. Of course I understood that I had responsibilities, and I did everything I could at the time, but I simply couldn't transition back into an old life that was no longer there.

After my wife kicked me out, I thought I'd get some degree of support from my father and his wife. That never occurred. Robin had outlined for them my transgressions in an email in order to justify her affair, essentially creating a "story-line" to explain her actions. But we can all recreate events of the past—exaggerate, falsify, and spin them around—and with time we can begin to believe that they're actually true. Through my long months of training and deployment to Iraq, she had ample time to recreate the past, making her fiction a truth to them. Whether they actually believed her explanations or not, they took her side. Of course, I hadn't been perfect, but they should have understood that there were two sides to every story; I'd been away, unable to defend myself in the face of her angry mother and new-found friends who'd never even met me. But none of that mattered. Her story worked—or they were just happy to believe it.

One day, we took the boys to a water park and were generally enjoying the day—until my father's wife turned to me and said, gesturing at the boys, "At least that's something you haven't screwed up." I hardly believed what I'd heard. Any other time I would have questioned her, but I was already so disheartened, so beat up by my life and the people around me, that I was struck dumb.

My father and his wife ignored my difficulties completely—refusing even to listen to stories from Iraq. On the first night of my return, I sat in my father's living room, drinking beer. They asked me what being in Iraq was like, and to their horror, I began to tell them with all the colorful language of a soldier. After a couple of minutes, my father and his wife just got up and left the room. I paused, mid-sentence, wondering what had happened. It turned out that they took offense to the language I was using but didn't bother to tell me. Instead, I felt stranded in the middle of my own story.

Wanting to guarantee the security of their continued visits with their grandchildren, my father's wife sent a sympathetic card to my wife, telling her to cheer up and hang in there—you're going to get through this... as though it were my wife who'd been betrayed! I wanted to know where my sympathy card was. But I had become a liability. Any show of support for me would be considered detrimental to the continued acceptance of my wife. I felt completely alone; the grandchildren mattered, and that was all. I was now a threat. One minute, it appeared I had a happy home and family; the next minute it was gone. As it turned out, I wasn't really lost and alone. I had good friends, and of course I had Margot. I would soon discover that I had the Shambhala community, or sangha, for support, as well. As Trungpa Rinpoche explains, "Without that sangha, we have no reference point; we are thrown back into the big samsaric soup, and we have no idea who or what we are. We are lost... the sangha is made up of thousands of people who are alone together, working together with their own loneliness, their own aloneness."

Long months ago, the Sakyong had written to me: "Human beings through their actions bind themselves to seemingly intractable and convoluted situations. It's not brain-power alone, but rather the weight of genuine compassion that will resolve this." With time I'd begun to forgive my father and his wife for their lack of support, as well as those who I believed had wronged me in Iraq. The only answer for me was to feel genuine compassion. Forgiving my wife for her actions was a different and more difficult story, confirming the Sakyong's statement: "We all have our list of people we exempt. But if we want to generate peace in the world, we cannot make exceptions. The way to extend compassion to all is to keep growing peace in our own mind."

These descriptions of my wife's affair and disregard for my well being may paint a negative picture of her as a person. But over the last few years I've accepted the truth that regardless of the way she treated me while in Iraq, she's a very kind and caring person. Most importantly, she's a good mother. I have to accept, without bitterness and regret, that our ways have parted; we are simply on different paths now. If it was not for her I wouldn't have two beautiful boys, and with time maybe we could even become friends. The Tiger's Path of discernment had led me safely through a hostile and painful environment in Iraq and an equally hostile and painful homecoming, threading its way through many charnel grounds. It's also shown me a new path, a path toward forgiveness.

Chapter Nineteen

The Warmth of the Great Eastern Sun

The way of the Great Eastern Sun is based on seeing that there is a natural source of radiance and brilliance in this world which is the innate wakefulness of human beings.
—Chogyam Trungpa Rinpoche
Shambhala: The Sacred Path of the Warrior

I should have better explained my reasons for traveling to Colorado and attending the Sakyong's talks to my father and his wife. I purposely avoided the issue because I was afraid they wouldn't understand my interest in Shambhala, as well as my relationship with Margot and her non-profit work. It was July 2006. During dinner in St. Augustine, Florida, a couple of days before I left for Colorado, they asked me about the talks and what exactly I was attending at the Shambhala Mountain Center. My father's wife asked me if this was some kind of cult. I tried not to laugh and told her it was not a cult and that the Sakyong was not Jim Jones; there was no danger of my drinking cyanide-laced Kool Aid. The more I thought about it, I couldn't really blame her for thinking I had slipped into some strange Charles Manson world. I was very vague when it came to explaining how I had become friends with Margot, how I was offered a rent free condo to stay in while I was in New Smyrna Beach, Florida, and why I was traveling to Colorado. With everything I'd been through, I saw how they might think I'd lost my mind. And to be honest, without the Dharma and Margot's help, I might actually have lost my mind. But I maintained my seat, as Margot had said, in the face of adversity.

The flight to Colorado included a four-hour layover in Atlanta. I figured I would find a good place to sit down and drink a few beers while I worked on my book. I got onto the tram to the concourse. The doors closed and that robotic-sounding voice came over the loudspeaker: "Next stop, concourse B as in Bravo." We zipped along. "Next stop, concourse C as in Charlie." Great, I thought, they're using military letters for each stop. We zipped along. The robotic voice: "Next stop, concourse D as in David." What the hell, I thought, the nightmare just follows me wherever I go—I simply can't escape. As annoying as the voice on the tram was, it wasn't nearly as painful as hearing my children confuse the name "Daddy" with "David." When I'd pick them up for the weekend, my boys would spend the first few hours of our visit addressing me as, "David, I mean Dav...I mean Daddy."

My wife took my trip to Colorado as an opportunity to quietly slip divorce papers into my luggage the evening before I left—a nice parting gift. I tried unsuccessfully to keep it from bothering me. In a phone conversation with her, I agreed to most of the terms outlined in the papers, but I asked her to think things over while I was in Colorado. I would deal with the realities of my marriage when I returned home; for now, I felt happy and relaxed and looked forward to the talks by the Sakyong.

Shambhala Mountain Center sits high in the Rockies on 600 acres in northern Colorado. Fortunately for me and my sanity, cell phones don't work at this elevation. Here I finally found some semblance of peace. Trungpa Rinpoche, who founded SMC, had an unquestionable belief in human goodness and dedicated his life to creating an enlightened society. The land was donated to Trungpa Rinpoche, and when he saw it for the first time, he said it reminded him of Tibet. It was perfect. In 1971, he invited a dozen or so hippies to move onto the land. They could stay as long as they liked if they built cabins for themselves. Called the "Pygmies," they became the first community of what was then called Rocky Mountain Dharma Center. Since that time, the center has offered hundreds of programs on Buddhist meditation, yoga, and other diverse contemplative disciplines. Now known as Shambhala Mountain Center, named after the legend of the enlightened kingdom, it is both an introductory and in-depth center for students studying the Shambhala Buddhist teachings. With the construction of two new lodges, a sacred studies hall, children's center, gift shop, and dining and housing space, Shambhala Mountain Center can now accommodate over 500 people in the summertime.

The Center's most stunning feature is a sacred landmark known as "The Great Stupa of Dharmakaya Which Liberates Upon Seeing" representing the Buddha seated in meditation posture. Thousands of people from all over the world come to visit this structure, the largest, most elaborate example of Buddhist monuments in North America. Opened in 2001 after 14 years of construction, the Great Stupa, dedicated to Chogyam Trungpa Rinpoche and housing his cremated remains as well as other relics, is an important symbol for not only the survival of Tibetan Buddhism, but also its influence in the West.

The location of the Stupa and other structures at SMC is not arbitrary; there's an energy there that can only be experienced by walking the grounds. Orange, white, red, and blue prayer flags flutter in the wind along paths connecting the various parts of the center. Deer wander peacefully throughout the land. The mountains rise majestically behind the stupa, creating a magnificent backdrop. Whether it's snowing or the

The Great Stupa of Dharmakaya.
Photo taken by author during a winter retreat in 2008.

bright sun is shining down upon you, you can't help but feel comfortable and completely at home. Only a few places in the world have made me feel so welcome and peaceful.

The July weather at Shambhala Mountain Center got exceedingly hot, but after Iraq, hot weather didn't bother me so much. The Sakyong's talks, meditation, and yoga exercises were held in a large white event tent erected in the summer for big programs. When I arrived at the center, Margot told me that I might be honored with a private interview with the Sakyong. If I did meet him, I had no idea what I would say or how to act under such circumstances. Once again, Margot helped me along as she had while I was in Iraq.

Seeing the Sakyong for the first time was an unforgettable experience. As he entered the meditation tent, accompanied by a retinue of teachers and attendants, most of those in the tent held their hands in *anjali* (the hands pressed together at the heart in a gesture of respect) and bowed. He returned our bows respectfully. Meticulously dressed in robes of rich brocades and silk—the traditional gold, yellow, and maroon of Tibetan lineage holders and monastics—he presented himself in a way that exuded royalty. An avid runner and weight-lifter, at forty-six, the Sakyong appeared to be in excellent physical shape. Recently married to a beautiful Tibetan princess, he epitomizes much of what the typical American or European imagines a re-incarnated Tibetan lama to be. But he is much more. His incredibly soothing voice made me feel comfortable and accepted. His most striking characteristics are his sense of humor and his smile. His overall presence, his energy, his basic goodness, it is all infectious.

About two months before I left Iraq, I began wearing a bracelet with the names of four of "the eight" who'd been killed. I had two bracelets, each with the names of four of our dead friends, but I only wore one, with the names of Fuller, Kinlow, Brunson, and Thomas. They had died first. When I heard I would receive a private interview with the Sakyong, I made an important decision. It came during his talks and subsequent meditation sessions. I had worn the bracelet long enough. It was time to let my friends go. Wearing the bracelet led to strangers asking if I had been in Iraq, and that only led to more painful memories. It was important to honor them, but it was equally important to let them go, not from my heart or my memory, but I had to move on. And that was when I decided that I would offer the bracelet with the names of my friends as a gift to the Sakyong.

The Ruling Your World program divided into small groups in order to meet the Sakyong in his private office. My group included Margot and her husband Cliff, the last to meet with the Sakyong that day, with dinner scheduled shortly after. I certainly felt a little nervous to be meeting him. I was sweating profusely from the heat and feeling a little dizzy from not having eaten much that day. The room was small, but large enough to accommodate our group. In one corner stood a shrine, and on the walls hung traditional Tibetan thangka paintings. A number of cushions sat on the floor, with one placed right next to the Sakyong. About three people walked in before me, all avoiding the cushion closest to the Sakyong's chair. When I walked in I went straight to the cushion next to him and sat down. Not only did I want to sit as close as possible, but he had a small fan running on the floor next to his chair to ventilate the room. The moving air helped me recover slightly. Once the rest of the group filed in, each person had a minute or so to ask him a question.

The Sakyong again wore the traditional robes of bright gold, yellow, and maroon, creating an imposing figure. When it came my time to speak, I simply said, "I'm just happy to be here and not in Iraq." The Sakyong smiled and nodded. Everyone else in the room agreed. Once the rest of the group departed and the door closed behind them, I walked to the center of the room and stood before him. I bowed, holding a *kata* (a traditional Tibetan offering scarf) out to him with my head down. He put it around his shoulders and then replaced it around mine. He gestured toward the cushion I'd been sitting on. Looking down at me from his chair, he smiled and said, "It's very good to see you."

Sakyong Mipham Rinpoche in Boulder, CO, 2005 —Photo by Gary Allen.

I smiled back and said, "It's very good to see you, too." He extended his arm, and we shook hands. After having my kata returned to me, it is sometimes customary to offer the kata in return. However I wanted it. I asked the Sakyong if I could keep it. He smiled and said that was fine. I said, "I want to trade you something for it."

I removed the bracelet from my right wrist. "The teachings say that in order to free oneself, one should give away his greatest possessions," I said, explaining that I'd worn this bracelet in Iraq and that it bore the names of four friends who'd been killed.

"I want you to have it," I said, handing it to him. "It's time to let them go."

He took the bracelet and thanked me. He asked, "Are things getting any better in Iraq?"

"No, things are not getting any better."

"Did you have a chance to meditate while you were over there?"

"No," I said. "But driving around in a humvee, waiting to get blown up, offers a unique opportunity for contemplation. Living in an environment like Iraq, with so much hate and pain, makes you appreciate the importance of living in the now. Everything around you takes on a greater significance when you don't know if you'll live to see another day." (The following day the Sakyong spoke briefly about what I said to him to his audience in the shrine tent).

I thanked him again for the personal email he sent to me while in Iraq and re-iterated how much it had helped, how it had aided me in controlling my anger and aggression.

"You're very welcome," he said. "How are things going at home now that you're back from Iraq?"

I quietly laughed to myself. I knew he would ask this question.

"Not so good," I began. "My wife had an affair while I was in Iraq, and I had to leave a few weeks early because my mother died…"

The Sakyong looked down at me while I paused, his face showed genuine concern and sympathy for what I'd just told him—and sadness.

"I still love my wife," I continued.

"Of course," he said.

"I'm still holding out hope that she might come around, but our marriage is most likely over."

"I'm very sorry to hear this."

"Thank you," I told him.

After a brief pause he changed the subject away from these painful events. "Do you think you will have to go back to Iraq?" he asked.

"No," I said. "But we might be going to Afghanistan soon. Don't worry—if I do, I promise to send you a postcard."

The Sakyong smiled at this. It had been a long and eventful day, and I knew he was a busy man. I thanked him again and rose from my seat.

Pema Chödrön teaches that it is rare to connect with the right teacher and be willing to reveal all your intimate feelings and fears. The Sakyong had made me feel incredibly comfortable, more than willing to discuss such sensitive issues as my friends' deaths and my wife's affair. He radiated kindness and compassion. Until now, I'd relied on Margot for advice, but as she'd told me before, she wasn't qualified to be a true spiritual teacher. During those long months in Iraq, she'd filled that role. Now having met the Sakyong in person, I understood that her role had its limitations. As she laughed, she told me that she would become my true spiritual teacher after she becomes enlightened, though that might take a little while. She will always be an advisor and a very good friend, but when I left the Sakyong's office, I understood what she'd meant by the importance of connecting with the right person—the one qualified to take you to the next level of your spiritual journey.

> Warriors-in-training need someone to guide them: a master warrior, a teacher, a spiritual friend, someone who knows the territory well and can help them find their way...This kind of relationship is valuable for many. It is rare that students initially feel ready for a more unconditional commitment with a teacher, working very intimately on where they are holding back...Either the relationship with a teacher evolves to a place of unconditional trust and love, or it doesn't. We have to trust the process. In either case the relationship with a teacher encourages us to trust our basic wisdom. It teaches us to be steadfast with ourselves.[1]

Before I left the room, I bowed before the Sakyong. He didn't look up; he sat there, staring at the names on the bracelet. Without raising his head he said, "I will pray for your dead friends."

---

1. *From The Places That Scare You* (2001), Pema Chödrön

I would later learn that the Sakyong would place the bracelet with the names of Fuller, Kinlow, Brunson, and Thomas on his personal shrine at his home in Boulder.

I thanked him. As I left the room with the Sakyong holding the bracelet, I knew I'd found my teacher—and a new family—the Shambhala sangha, a place filled with kind and compassionate people.

CHAPTER TWENTY

DIVORCES AND PLAYGROUNDS

There are times to cultivate and create, when you nurture your world and give birth to new ideas and ventures. There are times of flourishing and abundance, when life feels like in full bloom, energized and expanding. And there are times of fruition, when things come to an end. They have reached their climax and must be harvested before they begin to fade. And finally, of course, there are times that are cold and cutting and empty, times when the spring of new beginnings seems like a distant dream. Those rhythms in life are natural events. They weave into one another as day follows night, bringing, not messages of hope and fear, but messages of how things are.

—Chogyam Trungpa Rinpoche

My return to Jacksonville from Colorado after such an incredible experience at Shambhala Mountain Center quickly brought back memories of my two previous airport scenes: my wife and kids at the end of the hallway and my boys running to greet me. Both times were extremely emotional. But this return home was far different—no loving wife and children, just a long, sad hallway and a shuttle to take me to my car. Before landing, the captain of the plane made an announcement. Apparently, Delta Airlines is trying new tactics, like Southwest, by incorporating humor into their flights to make the trip more comfortable. The captain told the passengers that the turnaround in Jacksonville would be quick, and he'd appreciate all passengers disposing of their trash into the bags being brought down the aisles by the flight attendants. He said, obviously joking, "Please discard all newspapers, magazines, and any unwanted love letters into the trash bags." I have some unwanted divorce papers I'd like to throw away, I thought as he finished his message.

No longer in Colorado—my temporary refuge within the Shambhala community over for the moment—I'd have to return to life as usual, like it or not. But I didn't feel as alone as I did when I first returned from Iraq; I was now a member of the sangha. When life becomes difficult, as Chogyam Trungpa Rinpoche said, "we take refuge in the sangha as companionship...Your friends in the sangha provide a continual reference point, which creates a continual learning process. They act as mirror reflections to remind you or warn you in living situations. That is the kind of companionship that is meant by sangha. We are all in the same boat; we share a sense of trust and a sense of larger-scale, organic friendship." This reference point would aid me greatly in the months to come.

A key point expressed by Sakyong Mipham in *Ruling Your World* is that you may not always be able to control your external world, but you can control your response to it. In Iraq I couldn't control my wife's actions, but I could control my response to them. In the months following my return from Iraq, I tried everything I thought possible to reconcile with my wife. I was willing to forgive her completely. I tried appeasing her; when that didn't work, I tried to make her feel guilty. Maybe that would make her change her mind and realize her mistake. Eventually, when all else failed, I berated her, calling her every name in the book. In the end, it came down to divorce.

A few weeks after coming back from Colorado, I attended my first National Guard weekend since leaving Iraq. Returning to my unit after nearly three months was odd. Seeing the people I'd served with in Iraq brought back a lot of memories, some good, some painful. At the entrance to the armory, two memorial posters hung on the wall with pictures of the eight soldiers killed from Alpha Company. I stared at the photos of Fuller, Kinlow, Brunson, Thomas, Anderson, Jones, Shelley, and Haggin. When we had these "death photos" taken before we deployed, no one took them that seriously. It was just something the military required. But there was a reason for them. In a glass showcase across from the posters hung a photo of the first memorial service showing SFC. Anderson and SSG. Jones standing in honor of our fallen comrades. The date read 28 July, 2005. Both Anderson and Jones would be dead two days later. In the back room of the armory, I found something unsettling: the bags and personal items belonging to some of those killed. Anderson's green camouflage patrol cap sat on a table beside a military training manual with Kinlow's name on it. These items had been sent home to a different armory following their deaths and eventually got forwarded to Alpha Company.

There were a few men I'd served with in Iraq with whom I still had issues. I was cordial; I'd moved on and had more important things to deal with. A day after I returned from the National Guard, I met my wife in the lobby of her office building to sign the divorce papers. I brought my boys with me because I'd picked them up from school. The whole experience was so casual: meet with the notary, exchange pleasantries, and sign the papers ending our marriage. After ten years together, six years of marriage, and two beautiful boys, this was it. I wish things had turned out otherwise, but my wife and I are on different paths now, and I have to accept that. After ten months in Iraq, the deaths of friends, as well as my own mother's death and my wife's affair, I think I've learned a hell of a lot—about myself, about the character of those I trust, who my friends really are, and about love, which comes in many different forms. I'm on a new path now, and I have a long way to go. As the Sakyong says, "Moving through our life with the steady vigilance of a tiger, we no longer feel the need to prove ourselves, because we know the truth of our own peace."

My interest in dharma continued to move forward. In September 2006, I traveled to California and worked a temporary job for the Anaheim Union High School District, testing youths and adults in their English language skills. It was only a six week job, but it gave me time to sort through my mother's effects and get the rest of her things in order. It was almost like having some quiet personal time with her that I didn't have before she died. I sat in her room, exactly as it was before her death, and sorted through the drawers of her dresser. I discovered things, little trinkets and personal heirlooms, that helped me bond with her even though she was dead.

While in California, thanks to a friend of Margot's who gave me his ticket, I flew back to Colorado to the "Compassion in the Rockies" program at Shambhala Mountain Center. On the day of my birthday, September 17th, a snowstorm cleared out, leaving a chilly morning and a blue sky for the Dalai Lama's arrival by helicopter. He came to bless the Great Stupa of Dharmakaya and receive an award for peace. I joked with the hundred people waiting in line at the port'o-potties that he'd come to celebrate my birthday. Thanks to Margot, I was able to sit in a section close to the edge of the stupa, where I had an excellent view of the Dalai Lama. The experience was unforgettable, another unexpected event that now seemed to be a natural part of my spiritual journey.

My wife had the boys for Thanksgiving, and then I was told she was taking them to visit "David's" family at Christmas. I lost my mother, my wife, and in a sense, my sons since returning from a war—my first major family holiday after returning from Iraq. In order to avoid being alone, I found myself fantasizing about getting away. One day, during the student testing, I started thinking about where in the world I could go. I had money; a death benefit from my mother left me six thousand dollars, and I had money left over from Iraq when I'd re-enlisted. It was all I now had because my wife had spent everything else. I could go anywhere. Bora Bora, India…For reasons I didn't understand at the time, I chose Spain. It would take a few years, but I finally realized it was the place where my wife and I had been the most happy before we were married. We took a three-week trip to Spain and Morocco. On our first night in Madrid, we broke the cheap bed in our hotel while making love. We traveled to Córdoba on New Years' Eve, where my wife danced with a little Spanish girl in a romantic cobblestone square; we explored the Alhambra palace in Granada, and we got drunk on sangria in Seville. Spain had been a dream. I could have flown anywhere, but I didn't. I wanted something familiar—someplace where I had made good memories. So I returned to Spain.

I spent a week in the ancient city of Toledo. It was interesting, but every morning I felt lost and alone. I was alone, and I discovered that I couldn't recreate the past. I never made it back to Córdoba or Granada; in fact, I left a few days early. I fibbed to the woman at the airline ticket counter, telling her that I needed to return home early because my mother had died; she had died, only it occurred about five months earlier. It was not quite a lie, but it got me out of the two hundred dollar fee to change my ticket.

Once I returned from Spain, Christmas reared its ugly head. I needed another escape from a family that was no longer there, so I decided to sign up for a week of the winter *dathun*, a month-long meditation retreat at the Shambhala Mountain Center with Sakyong Mipham. While at dathun, I met the president of Shambhala, Richard Reoch. When I was introduced to him, I bowed; he returned the bow. Then to my surprise he gave me a hug as if we were old friends. I was a little shocked, but he told me he was familiar with my letters published in *The Dot*. He could only talk briefly but assured me we would talk soon.

The next day, I went to the Sacred Studies Hall for the Sakyong's talk. Outside the sun was shining on the snow. Near some small pine trees sat a grey statue of a seated Buddha. Snow covered his crossed legs and was piled in a small clump on his head. Inside the shrine room, a bright yellow meditation cushion belonging to President Reoch had been placed directly in front of the elevated sitting platform reserved for the Sakyong. An assistant to President Reoch told me that he'd reserved a place for me. I sat down on the blue meditation cushion next to his gold one, feeling distinctly out of place in the important people's seating.

When the talk concluded, one of President Reoch's aides invited me to have tea with the President the following day. Arriving ten minutes early, I came to the beautifully embroidered yellow and orange hanging that covered the doorway of his suite and knocked. With only my feet showing beneath the hanging, he said, "Paul, please come in."

I said, "Could you tell it was me by my feet?" I heard him laugh and walked inside.

With subdued elegance and a kind, gentle face, he appears unassuming. Born in Toronto in 1948, he became a Buddhist at age six. After working for Amnesty International for a number of years, he was appointed to head the organization's senior management in 1978. He left his post in 1993 and has since continued his efforts as a consultant to human rights and peace groups in Sri Lanka and on both sides of the Irish border. He's the author of *To Die Well*, a book on holistic care for the dying. The Sakyong appointed him President of Shambhala in 2002. He looks a bit like a Caucasian monk with glasses and close-cropped hair. He was dressed casually in a white dress shirt, black pants, no tie, and a vest with Shambhala pins over the left breast. A string of mala prayer beads was wrapped around his left wrist. After I sat down he said, "How have things been since you returned from Iraq?"

As I had with the Sakyong, I smiled and said, "Not so good. I had to leave Iraq a few weeks early because my mother died. And shortly after coming home I discovered my wife had had an affair, and we're now divorced." Probably not what he'd expected to hear, but with time I would learn he had heard stories far worse than mine.

"I'm sorry to hear that," he said with genuine sympathy. I then presented him with a collection of some of the best chapters from my book. He seemed pleased to receive them. We discussed the emails I wrote to Margot while I was in Iraq, specifically the one's printed in *The Dot*. To my amazement, President Reoch informed me that he'd used my emails on more than one occasion as subject material for some of his talks. In Boston, he titled one talk that involved the issue of peace and war, "Contemplating Sgt. Kendel." When he told me this, I was a little surprised. Margot knew nothing about it. During a visit to Alaska, he was informed that he'd have to give an impromptu talk at the university in Juneau, also on war and the issue of peace. Needing material at the last minute, he went to his computer and retrieved the emails I'd written. He was able to use these in his discussion and said they were well received.

Over tea I told him I couldn't wait for 2006 to be over. He then told me a strange thing. He said that maybe the last year had actually been the best year of my life. I looked at him doubtfully, thinking that maybe he'd been inhaling too much incense. He explained to me how he came to be president of Shambhala.

When he was thirty-five years old, he was in excellent health until he suffered a slipped disk. After months of excruciating pain, he began practicing *t'ai chi* (an "internal" form of martial arts movements). This proved therapeutic, and his back pain disappeared. As a consequence of his back pain and his yoga practice, he was exposed to the more secular Shambhala teachings. He told me how Chogyam Trungpa's book *Shambhala: The Sacred Path of the Warrior* changed his life. It had had a similar impact on me in Iraq. He would eventually become president of Shambhala due to his year of pain.

The hour and a half I spent in President Reoch's suite confirmed a lot about what was important in my life. He told me that the first step to getting my life back together was showing loving-kindness toward myself. I had to be kind to me first before I could do more for others. To be a better father, a better person, I had to realize that I have been a good father and a good person. I needed to stop letting others make me think otherwise. My wife's affair was not my fault. Everyone makes his own decisions in life, and I guess she thought she was making the best one for herself; everyone has his or her own path to take. Sitting across from President Reoch, I was struck by his profound calm. He seemed to radiate equanimity, contentment—compassion. His interest in my welfare was genuine. He wasn't selling something or looking out for his own interests. I was envious. He had found a place in his life where he fit, where he was meant to be. Maybe for some of us, it takes a slipped disk or a tour in Iraq to be placed on the journey. He may be right—perhaps 2006 will prove to have been the best year of my life.

* * * *

Author with President Reoch, after a retreat. Shambhala Center, Boulder, Colorado.

Early one morning, a couple of months later, when I was back in Jacksonville, Florida, under-employed, teaching a couple of adjunct history classes at Florida State College at Jacksonville and crashing at my friend Ric's house, I received a surprise visit from none other than the venerable Chögyam Trungpa Rinpoche himself. I wrote an email to Richard Reoch, describing it:

Dear Richard,

I had a really odd dream this morning. I had a very bizarre encounter with the Sakyong's father, Chogyam Trungpa Rinpoche. The dream occurred at what seemed to be a Shambhala retreat, possibly the Shambhala Center in Boulder, but I didn't recognize it. I walked up a flight of stairs to attend a talk. It was an older building, with wooden stairs that creaked as you walked up them. I was running late, and when I arrived, the doors were closed because the talk had already begun. Staring at the large grey doors, I decided not to intrude and began walking back down the stairs. For some strange reason, I was holding a machine gun in my right hand, the same kind that we used in Iraq. As I descended, the hard metal barrel thumped as it was dragged over each step. A long stream of grey mud trailed out the barrel's mouth as I walked back down the stairs. I could not see the bottom—the steps descended into darkness.

Suddenly, I was in a playground at a park. It was twilight, but children were everywhere. Then I noticed a solitary man nearby. Chogyam Trungpa Rinpoche sat on a wooden bench inside a small roofed picnic area, watching the children play, his attention focused on a swing set nearby. I walked over and sat down next to him. He grinned at me mischievously, like he was privy to some secret I would never understand.

Then he put his arm around my shoulders, pulling me close—acting as though he knew me. He didn't look at me directly, only showing his profile. I was taken aback by his sudden intimacy, but he radiated such generous warmth I felt instantly comfortable in his presence.

He seemed quite intoxicated, grinning at me in an odd, sidelong way. Suddenly I had a glass of beer in my hand. Seconds later, Rinpoche took it from me, had a sip, staring ahead without looking at me, and placed the glass behind us. Then I noticed a young girl with beautiful dark eyes and thick black hair, maybe five or six years old, playing on the nearby swings. She kept going up as high as she could and as fast as possible, as though trying to test herself in some way. She smiled gleefully, clearly having a wonderful time. I felt as though I recognized her somehow. Rinpoche's gaze was directed towards the girl. He asked me as he stared at her if I would go talk to her for him. I was a little shocked. I asked him if it was appropriate to approach a young girl in such a way in Tibet. He said matter-of-factly, yes, it was appropriate in Tibet. But I told him, no, if he wanted to speak to her, he would have to do it himself. He seemed pleased with my answer and began to get up. I helped him up and noticed that his legs were slightly withered, like he had polio as a child. As I helped him to his feet, he smiled at me and said it was nice of me to assist him, but he didn't need the help. He then walked off toward the little girl as if he had no physical problems at all.

Suddenly we were sitting at another picnic area in the park. Night had fallen on the playground, and a single bulb hung from the roof illuminating the scene. Rinpoche was talking to the young girl, who now had aged about twenty years. This made me feel better. She had a friend the same age with her, and we started a conversation when a third young woman appeared. I began telling her how this was not my first time here (wherever "here" was). I told her I'd visited Shambhala Mountain Center a number of times and had been there for the Dalai Lama's visit. She seemed interested in me and what I had to say. I looked over at Rinpoche in the soft glow of the light. He looked happy, smiling, and completely engaged with the young girl who had gone from five years old to twenty-five. His profile stood out clearly. As he spoke to her, she smiled, clearly enamored with him.

Then my cell phone went off, waking me. (Ironically, it was my ex-wife calling.) I called Margot to tell her about the dream while it was still fresh in my mind.

Having studied with Trungpa Rinpoche, Margot had known him as well as a student could. She told me a story about Rinpoche during the last years of his life, when his health was failing. One day she had helped him, like I had in my dream, with walking. She said he gripped her arm quite strongly, not weak in any way. He had allowed her to assist him even though he didn't need it, just to be kind—like he'd done with me. He had sat so close. His facial expressions were so vivid: intelligent, thoughtful, but very, very mischievous.

My dream made me feel as though I'd met him, bringing me closer to the dharma and certainly closer to him and the Shambhala lineage, a connection confirmed by Richard Reoch:

> Dear Paul,
> What an extraordinary and powerful dream sequence. All the elements of it seem so vivid, like extracts from living moments all strung together, like beads on a mala string. Maybe that's a way of thinking of it, not so much like a logical story, but more like a series of vivid, living encounters that come together in a way that transcends the conventional boundaries of the present, past, and future and transverses lifetimes and life experiences. I think a lot of our most moving experiences are like that, including experiences that might happen to us in meditation sometimes. It is obvious that you have a profound connection to the Shambhala lineage, both the Sakyong and his father. How that connection will continue to unfold, we have yet to see!
> Warmly,
> Richard

I'd tried to get into a lecture on the dharma, but the dharma I got instead was a descent down the steps into the darkness of suffering and death. There's a Shambhala teaching called the "self-existent playground," meaning the world itself is a training ground for the practice of spiritual warriorship, where young warriors can grow into mature ones. I emerged on the playground to find there the master warrior, Trungpa Rinpoche. A riveting and unforgettable character, it was like he'd been waiting for me all along, his eyes fixed on the little girl, pointing out to me something important. Back in Iraq, when I hadn't pulled the trigger, when I'd restrained my fear and aggression, the little girl's life had been spared, and now she'd grown up into a lovely young woman, just as a small, meaningful moment of kindness had developed into a much greater spiritual result. This was the light of human warmth shining in the night of so much delusion and hate.

CHAPTER TWENTY-ONE

THE WOLF I'LL FEED

Fear is a natural reaction to moving closer to the truth.
—Pema Chödrön
When Things Fall Apart

It was August 2007, a few months after signing the official papers ending my marriage and separating me from my children. I continued to teach part-time as an adjunct history professor to get by, but that's all I was doing—just getting by. Tension between me and my now ex-wife often ran high, usually over money. I spent as much time with my boys as I could, though I still had trouble dealing with the fact that I was no longer a regular feature of their lives. I'd become a weekend dad—not an easy thing to accept. I tried to focus on my time with the boys and nothing else, but it was hard. Fortunately, I had Margot and the sangha for support, and after a few months away from Boulder and Shambhala Mountain Center, I began to experience an urgent need to return to the place where I felt comfortable and accepted. I'd found my spiritual teacher in Sakyong Mipham Rinpoche, and in Richard Reoch, a trusted friend and advisor who taught me to look at the painful time following my return from Iraq in a positive light, and I had the friendship and support of Margot, the person responsible for making the journey possible. Nevertheless—though I'd been back from Iraq for over a year—I was still far from healed, both mentally and emotionally. An opportunity arose to attend a program at Shambhala Mountain Center entitled "Practicing Peace in Times of War" with Richard Reoch and Pema Chödrön—the Buddhist nun whose books I'd read in Iraq.

I'd arrived late due to rumbling over winding dirt roads at alpine altitude. I hustled from my car to the big white tent erected for the program, occupied by more than two hundred participants. Great I thought: I fly all the way from Jacksonville, Florida, only to reach Pema's first talk late. I walked in, removed my shoes, and looked around. Fortunately, Pema had yet to appear. I spotted an unoccupied meditation cushion at the back of the tent and navigated my way toward it. People were sitting patiently on their cushions, and I tried to be as inconspicuous as I could.

About ten minutes passed before Pema and President Reoch arrived. When she reached her seat at the front, Pema stood in front of her cushion, beaming a smile at everyone. She was dressed in traditional maroon-colored robes, and her hair was close-cropped. Behind her, above the shrine with its Tibetan offerings and incense, hung two large pictures of Sakyong Mipham and his father, Choygam Trungpa Rinpoche. She bowed; everyone in the room returned it, and only after she sat down did the audience follow suit.

Pema Chödrön is a world-renowned Buddhist teacher of the Tibetan Vajrayana tradition. She received her ordination as a nun in 1974 and studied with Chogyam Trungpa Rinpoche from that year until his death in 1987. *O, The Oprah Magazine* describes her as "one of the wisest women living in the world." She's a bestselling author, and people worldwide read her books in multiple languages for inspiration and support. Before Pema began to talk that morning, President Reoch spoke about war, the

Pema Chödrön with Richard Reoch.
—Photo by Andrea Roth

financial cost of which had become the world's single greatest monetary expenditure. He told us that Shambhala teachings talk about "dark ages" when societies become obsessed with aggression and materialism and that these periods also produce teachings on wisdom and compassion to benefit humanity. He also emphasized that we have a choice whether we want peace or aggression in our lives.

"An email message went around following the attacks on the World Trade Center," he continued. "The message spoke of a Native American grandfather who was speaking to his grandson about the real tragedy that the world was experiencing in the wake of 9/11.

"He said to his grandson, 'It's as if two wolves are fighting in my heart. One wolf is vengeful, violent, and angry; the other wolf is loving, forgiving, and understanding.'

"'Which wolf will win the fight?' asked the grandson.

"The grandfather answered, 'The one that wins will be the one I feed.'"

The program's goal was directed at finding the necessary tools for feeding the right wolf, the loving, non-violent, and forgiving wolf, rather than the one full of vengeance and anger.

Following her introductory talk, Pema turned to the senior staff at the program, including President Reoch, and stated, "I hear there is a service member from Iraq, one that I wrote about, who is actually here. His name is SGT. Kendel. He's supposed to arrive today."

The spotlight hit me.

I raised my hand from the back of the tent and said sheepishly, "Actually, I'm right here." Everyone in the tent turned to look at me, including Pema.

"Hey!" she exclaimed. People laughed and a number of them began to clap in honor of my service in Iraq. I hadn't planned on such a reception, especially since I'd just arrived a short time earlier and hadn't yet begun to relax.

"So I'm going to retell one of his stories," she began without warning. She found the following war experience particularly poignant and heartbreaking and referenced it, as well as others, a number of times throughout her talks over the weekend. Her retelling of the incident differed slightly from mine, but the essence was the same.

"This story is about a boy with Down Syndrome," she began. "This is a story of being in the war in Iraq, about him and his fellow soldiers, people he loved and cared about being blown up and killed—and the feeling of wanting revenge…and how he was so strong among all of them. One night they had the opportunity to actually find the people that were probably responsible for blowing them up. They went to the house. It could have been straightforward and simple, but what actually happened was the anger and frustration at being in such a claustrophobic situation where violence was the atmosphere you breathe and eat. Well, they messed up the people. It was in the dark, and SGT. Kendel put his flashlight on the face of a young boy. It turned out he had Down Syndrome."

She described how Ross's recognition of the boy's Down Syndrome reminded him of his brother, saying, "This shifted the situation just like that." she snapped her fingers for emphasis. "He felt so much compassion for the boy. The soldier began to see the whole situation differently." Pema choked up, holding back tears. "Women do this, they cry…The power of compassion has the power to cut through all the rage; the pent up—you could say justified—anger. Looking at it from the big picture, it's not justified, but when you're in the microcosm, you're just responding, and the basic teaching is that the capacity for love cuts through the aggression. It is more basic, more fundamental than the aggression.

"There's something called—" Pema laughed with tears in her eyes; the audience laughed with her. "I don't usually cry that much, but the energy of aggression—as I'll be talking about over the weekend—is actually not a problem. A lot of the teaching is about not denying, not turning against our own energy, but acknowledging it—without feeding it with a storyline—without turning it into something fixed and cold that depends on a lot of storyline. The underlying energy itself is not the problem, but when anger becomes fixated, it's poisonous. The energy within all of us can be transmuted into wisdom. Like the soldier who was able to see things from another perspective, everything shifts."

When she finished retelling my story, I felt a sense of release—a release from personal regret over the incident that night in Iraq when I'd dragged the Down Syndrome boy, frightened and whimpering, away from his home and family. And I thought about the innocent man standing in the street that I'd shot at and missed, how close he'd come to death because of the poisonous energy of anger and fixation. I saw him that day, not as a human being, but as a target for releasing my frustrations. Pema's words were soothing, straightforward, and resonated with me deeply, placing those terrible events into a bigger perspective. Listening to her recount the experience helped me release the negative energy that had created them.

Pema concluded the morning's talk by discussing the realities of the current war in Iraq and the public's response to it. She said that many people in the United States are numb and complacent as far as the war in Iraq is concerned and that they prefer to just cruise along, thinking they will have a good future. "I don't mean to belittle it," she said, "but ignorance about the suffering of other people in situations like Iraq is a problem. I would like to hear from people over the weekend who have been in war. That is the theme of the program."

Being the only person in the room that had served in the army and had actually fought in a combat zone, she obviously hoped I would speak. Damn, I thought, she just called me out. She's expecting me to stand up in front of the crowd and tell some Iraq stories. She'd done a fantastic job telling them for me, but I guess she wanted more words coming directly from my own voice and heart. I was scared of what I might say, how the story would be received, and just plain petrified at having to stand in front of such a large gathering of people. I was used to teaching history in front of fifteen to twenty students—this was a little different. I could simply ignore her request, of course, but that would be weak. Clearly the program needed something direct, something raw, to help invigorate it and stir a debate. Pema didn't expect me to speak right then— I would have time to stress out, thinking about what I should do or say.

While debating whether I had the courage to stand up in front of an audience and talk about Iraq, I began re-reading Pema's book, *Practicing Peace in Times of War*. Reading it previously during my winter visit to Colorado, I found the teachings incredibly profound and, to my surprise, found myself included within them:

> I recently read a letter from a U.S. soldier in Iraq. He wrote about the so-called enemy fighters, the unknown people who are so filled with pain and hate that they sit in the dark, waiting to kill foreign soldiers like him. When they succeed and his friends' bodies are blown into unrecognizable pieces, he just wants revenge. He said that each day, he and his fellow U.S. soldiers were also becoming men who wait in the darkness, hoping to kill another human being. As he put it, "We think that by striking back, we'll release our anger and feel better, but it isn't working. Our pain gets stronger day by day."

She goes on to explain the cyclical nature of aggression and the danger of letting anger consume us:

> Amid the chaos and horror of war, this soldier has discovered a profound truth: if we want suffering to lessen, the first step is learning that keeping the cycle of aggression going doesn't help. It doesn't bring the relief we seek, and it doesn't bring happiness to anyone else either. We may not be able to change the outer circumstances, but we can always shift our perspective and dissolve the hatred in our minds.

As the afternoon talk got going, it occurred to me that if Pema truly believed I'd discovered a profound truth in Iraq, the least I could do was share some more words and thoughts with her audience. I decided to muster up the courage to speak when the time came but remained unsure of the right story to tell.

The second talk of the day involved the *shenpa* teachings. This Tibetan word is usually translated as "attachment"; Pema interprets the word as "an experience of being hooked." When someone threatens you or says unkind things about a loved one, a tightness, an energy, grows within us, and we feel an urge to blame others, to strike back, to seek revenge. This is shenpa. As Pema explained to the audience, "Hate words of all kinds—racial slurs—it is the shenpa behind it that makes it worse." She mentioned the derogatory term Hajji, used widely by American soldiers to refer to the people of Iraq and other Arab countries. "When words are prompted by shenpa it dehumanizes—words such as Hajji or other racial slurs become the fuel of violence, the language of violence, the mindset of violence. The most poisonous thing about it is that it dehumanizes the ones that you're talking about to the point that you could kill them. It has so much power." Pema's answer to shenpa is to "let the storyline go, let the fuel of shenpa go. Now this is really hard to do. Shenpa comes along with an undertow that sweeps you away."

I was listening intently. Her words resonated deeply due to my experiences in Iraq. Suddenly, I heard my name. "So again, SGT. Kendel wrote in his letters about wanting to strike out because he felt, 'If I strike out, it would relieve this pain inside of me.' His observation was—it didn't do that; it just made you feel worse. He tells a story—I feel funny telling your stories." Pema looked over at me and smiled. "But he tells a story of an experience again of warmth overcoming the shenpa, the knee jerk reaction. And this was actually probably pre-thought really, without even feeding a storyline, but this was of somebody in a car coming to a checkpoint…soldiers turning their guns on this person and then realizing it was just someone on their way to work who was not a terrorist or anything, and how that completely stopped you in your tracks, and you realize just what you were about to do."

In retrospect I remember feeling what I now understand as shenpa—the tension, the energy, the anger building within me as the car came too close. It was shenpa that had fueled the anger over the death of SSG. Mercer earlier that morning. As Pema explains, "When shenpa arises, you acknowledge that you're hooked; and you already know it's going to have consequences."

Her retelling of my stories and discussion of dehumanization inspired me to choose a story about the way many of my fellow soldiers in Iraq had viewed the Iraqis. She finished her talk and opened it up for questions. Two microphones stood at both ends of the tent. While she was adjusting herself on her cushion in preparation for answering questions, she asked the audience, "If any of the people who have been in a war would like to come up and say anything, please do." There was my cue. Taking a deep breath, I stood up and nervously made my way to the nearest microphone. I stood there and looked at Pema and President Reoch. Pema was still arranging herself when she looked up and saw me standing a few feet away.

"Ah, hello!" she exclaimed, clearly pleased that I'd made the decision to speak. "This is SGT. Kendel," she announced to the audience.

"I just want to thank you for sharing my stories," I told her. "I think you tell them better than I ever could.

"You spoke about the word 'Hajji' as a derogatory term," I began, "but for U.S. soldiers it was also an easy way to lump all Iraqis together. Seeing the Iraqis as simply Hajjis became a defense mechanism for many soldiers—you didn't have to see them as human beings, so when you shot them or killed them, you didn't have to suffer the emotional consequences—they were just amorphous figures. They weren't really human; they were just Hajjis." I talked about how we fired on cars. "The patrol would just ride on even though there may have been women and children inside.

"I tried to convince some friends to see the bigger picture—that not all Iraqis were bad and they were not all trying to kill us. One soldier told me all he cared about was his piece of the pie—not the cultural or religious conflicts going on around us—he was just concerned with going home alive. And if that meant potentially killing innocent Hajjis in the process, so be it.

"Do you mind if I tell one brief story?"

"Please," responded Pema, who seemed to be listening intently. I had President Reoch's attention, as well. For a moment I felt I'd spoken too much already and considered sitting down, but I'd yet to tell the story that needed to come out. I talked about the night the innocent Iraqi husband had been shot in the testicles, bleeding out on the floor while the television ran an Arabic game show. I told the audience how his young wife stood shaking in fear while holding their young child in her arms, comforting the baby while it cried—how the young woman looked me straight in the eyes, blaming me for her husband's death. I may not have been the person responsible for killing her husband, but that didn't really matter—to her all Americans were the same.

"They're Hajjis in a way," Pema interjected, as I explained the young wife's view of me and fellow soldiers.

"Yeah," I agreed with her. I guess we were. I never really thought about it that way, but the Iraqis must have lumped Americans, soldiers and civilians, together just as we did with Iraqis. To the average American soldier or Marine, it didn't really matter whether someone was Sunni or Shia, Kurdish or Arab—they were just Hajjis. I concluded my story by describing how my fellow soldiers doubled over guffawing at the photos of the dead Iraqi's ripped genitalia.

Pema spoke: "One thing I've heard from a growing number of people is that the situation of war is so dehumanizing that people do such things, but then the post-traumatic stress occurs when they're back.... They start remembering things in a different light, from a point of view of humanity, and that's the cause of the post-traumatic stress rather than bombs going off. It's what they've actually done—they've denied their own humanity."

"Exactly," I said, agreeing with her. "Thank you."

As I turned to walk away from the microphone, I looked about the room. A number of women were crying. Most had shocked looks on their faces. Suddenly I felt panic. Had that story been too much? The program was about peace, not about a graphic description of an Iraqi man's ripped testicles and the loss of a child's father. A lot of elderly women sat in the audience, and most people only know about the war in Iraq from the sanitized stories they got from the media. Had I gone too far?

A woman walked up to the microphone to speak. "I don't really know what to say after that," she began. "I'm sorry that that happened to you… and to all those other people…that's horrible."

"Well, it's still happening," interjected Pema, cutting the woman off. Her demeanor and words intensified: "It's happening all the time, and it's not an isolated event—it's continual."

"I know," the woman agreed, crying.

"Because it's not happening in this room within your view, you need someone who comes back and tells you in order for it to even slightly penetrate. Even then, for a lot of us, we're not going to want to keep thinking about it. We have the luxury of being surrounded by fresh air, normal American situations. It needs to motivate us, in this case, to work with our own shenpa because it would be easy to not be SGT. Kendel or the medic, but to be the other people, doing that kind of thing, especially if you're young—the dehumanization and fear, the fear for your own life being threatened."

Pema paused for a moment.

"This is not some cute little retreat we're doing in the mountains. It's really how we relate to something as trivial as someone cutting in front of us in the car—and then with bigger and bigger shenpa-provoking situations."

Her words and tone had become more impassioned, more emotional. Of course, she was right. Programs and retreats at SMC are not designed to be self-help/feel-good activities. The teachings are designed to break one out of one's normal habitual patterns and ways of thinking, to encourage one to drop the "storyline."

The rest of the program continued in much this way, with many people sharing their innermost fears and pain with complete strangers. As I was told later by President Reoch, the whole program seemed to shift after telling the tragic story about the Iraqi man. Dozens of women hugged me over the course of the weekend in appreciation for the courage they believed I'd shown in telling my story; men wanted to shake my hand. It was all very overwhelming.

During that first morning talk, Pema said that she would like to meet with those of us who'd served in Iraq. At the close of the afternoon talk on the second day, I was told to meet her at her house, a short distance up an unpaved road from the shrine tent. When I knocked on the door, Pema's assistant greeted me and took me upstairs into a small, sparsely decorated room: a single bed, neatly made; a small table with a lamp in one corner; two chairs—a room fit for a monk. When I walked in, she stood and smiled. We bowed. My interview with the Sakyong was one of the most memorable encounters of my life, but somewhat intimidating. Pema's unassuming presence and demeanor made me feel warm and comfortable.

"Thank you for taking the time to meet me," I said. "It's a real honor."

"You're very welcome."

"When I read *Practicing Peace in Times of War*, I was shocked when you mentioned one of my emails from Iraq."

She smiled. "Yes, I was sitting, working on the book, and happened to pick up a copy of *The Dot* and read your emails from Iraq...I found them very moving. I was deeply touched by the one about the young Iraqi boy with Down Syndrome."

"Thank you," I said, a little embarrassed.

"How have you been adjusting since your return from Iraq?"

I knew this question would come. My adjustment had not been good. I repeated for her how my mother had died and my marriage had ended in divorce. I paused for a moment and added, "But I guess you're familiar with such things. Your story from *When Things Fall Apart* about throwing a rock at your husband after he told you about his affair really resonated with me."

She lowered her head and looked a little solemn for a moment. I was afraid I'd been a little too personal, bringing up her own painful past and then linking it to mine.

"It was just a marriage," she said flatly as she looked straight at me. I was taken a little aback. In America, at least in theory—minus the fifty percent divorce rate—marriage is supposed to be a sacred institution. The way she said it, emotionless, she seemed to dismiss it as if marriage was simply a job that one could easily change. But she quickly explained herself.

"If I hadn't gotten divorced, I wouldn't be where I am today," she said, smiling, holding her arms up slightly to emphasize what she'd accomplished. She was now a loved and revered teacher, a Buddhist nun with a number of bestselling books to her credit. I suddenly understood her attitude about marriage: everything's impermanent. Sometimes painful events can actually lead one to his true calling, as it had for her. Maybe my own pain and suffering, my wife's betrayal and our divorce, would lead to something better in my life.

"I'm slowly getting over my wife, but it's the issue of the children that really hurts. Not being able to see them on a regular basis, knowing some other man gets to be with them more than I do."

"Yes," she said sadly, "when there are children involved, it always makes it harder."

I lowered my head in thought for a moment and looked at her again. Her manner and her words were soothing, comforting. She broke the moment of painful reflection.

"I really appreciated you coming up and talking today," she said.

"Thank you," I said, pausing for a moment. "But I think maybe I should apologize for the story I told about the Iraqi man being shot in the testicles. It was probably a little too graphic."

"No, no," she said emphatically. "It was perfect. People need to hear stories like that—it makes it real."

"Thank you," I said. "But women were crying afterward. I felt it might have been a little over the top."

"No," she reiterated, "it was just what was needed."

"Thank you." I felt a sense of relief.

"About the shenpa teachings," she began. "What do you think? Did they have an effect on the audience?

I sat back in my chair for a second. She was asking my opinion of her own teachings.

"Yes," I told her, "the shenpa teachings are great, except…" In the larger scheme of things, my entire experience with Buddhism and Shambhala was a grand total of about two seconds, and here I was about to offer advice. "Maybe you need to be more blunt with people when you give the shenpa teachings, as I was with my story about the Iraqi man."

I thought of her reaction and response to the woman who had followed me during the question period. "This is not some cute little retreat we are doing in the mountains," she had said.

"Maybe some people need a kick to the head to make them wake up," I said. Iraq had done it for me, at least at a basic level.

Pema sat back in her chair and seemed to take in what I said. A few seconds of silence passed between us, and I began to think she might say something in a gentle way like, "I appreciate your advice, but you can leave now, and don't let the door hit you in the ass on your way out."

Instead she said, rather thoughtfully, "You're right. Maybe some people do need a kick to the head sometimes."

I felt relieved and happy that she'd actually considered my advice, but I figured that was probably enough for the day. We moved on to my current status as a member of the National Guard. "Do you think you will have to go back to Iraq?" she asked.

"Not Iraq, but we may be going to Afghanistan. I don't really want to go, but I still have a few years left before I retire."

"Can't you just tell the Army that you don't want to kill anymore?" she asked matter-of-factly. She must have assumed that I'd actually shot and killed someone while in Iraq. I'd shot at Iraqis and at numerous cars while driving around that may have been suicide bombers, but to my knowledge, I did not kill anyone.

"If I do have to go to Afghanistan," I told her, "I don't have any intention of killing anyone, not if I can help it."

In *When Things Fall Apart*, Pema asks the question: "Am I going to add to the aggression in the world?...Am I going to practice peace, or am I going to war?" For me, at least at that moment in time, this question was not so easy: war was a fact of life. I'd been deployed to Saudi Arabia after 9/11, Iraq in 2005, and now a deployment to Afghanistan loomed.

"If I do have to go to war again," I told her, "I would take the advice that the Sakyong gave me in a personal email while in Iraq: 'Since the purpose of your being there is wrathful compassion, the more force you have to apply, the greater your compassion should be.'" Those powerful words had aided me greatly through some very difficult times in a hostile place. I told her how valuable her teachings had been for me and how I'd read a number of her books, and even carried a small paperback copy of *Awakening Loving Kindness* with me every time I went outside the wire with the risk of being killed. She thanked me.

At this point our interview had run long enough, and it was time for me to leave. We both rose from our seats, and I bowed to her. Without warning, I felt suddenly compelled to give her a hug. As I embraced her, she seemed a little surprised, but she returned my embrace and squeezed my arm. I turned and left.

Pema taught that anger isn't necessarily a bad thing that needs to be expunged, that it can manifest itself positively, such as a reaction to the human suffering in Darfur. When it is infused with hate directed toward an individual or a people, however, it becomes a destructive force. To prevent anger from overwhelming us, we should try to "know it so thoroughly that we see its transparency, see its insubstantial nature." A common instruction in Buddhism, she said, teaches that when we get caught up in whatever is causing us stress or harm, we should pause for a moment and just "look at the sky." Many people, she explained, "when they've been in desperate situations such as a concentration camp, sometimes just look at the sky." She spoke about connecting with natural openness, connecting with the bigger perspective.

"It is easy to lose your perspective in the difficult situations in the office, at home, in Iraq, in prisons, anywhere. Sometimes, just looking at the sky can give you a bigger perspective, an outlook that there's the whole world, the whole universe, time without beginning; this is just a moment in time."

Everything I was hearing at SMC and in the meeting with Pema confirmed that the thread of dharma is consistent and true. We can hold onto it so we don't drown, so we don't fall into the camps of bias, prejudice, and judgment. For me, the dharma truly was a lifeline from a bloody, dismembered, desert nightmare to Buddhist meadows up against the Milky Way high in the Rockies.

* * * * *

On the final day of the program, Pema attended a fundraising event for Shambhala Mountain Center. Assisting the program as staff, I operated as a chauffer for President Reoch, driving him from his lodging, not far from Shambhala Mountain Center. He told me some great stories of his time working for Amnesty International and an early meeting with the Dalai Lama. I reciprocated with an anecdote about the summer when I helped support the Secret Service as a member of the Georgia National Guard during the G-8 conference on Sea Island, Georgia. As a security measure we had a humvee blocking the main entrance to the conference area in case someone tried to break through the fence and past the armed Secret Service members.

I sat in the hot sun and moved the humvee back and forth whenever a presidential motorcade needed to come through. By the second day, boredom set in. Resting over the humvee steering wheel, I fell asleep. I don't know how long I slept. When I looked up, I saw President Bush's motorcade waiting on me. They must have idled there at least five minutes before I woke up and moved the humvee out of the way. They didn't honk at me, nothing. The most embarrassing thing was that the humvee had no door, so they could easily see me slumped over the steering wheel, fast asleep, drooling in the hot sun. As I finished the story, President Reoch said, "Uh, Paul, I think you missed our turn." Dozens of people stood, awaiting our triumphant arrival, and I'd just driven right past them!

I circled back, and we got there safely.

While Pema and Richard sat with refreshments, I stood around the fundraiser crowd. The weather was perfect, warm with a light breeze, when near tragedy struck. An unexpected gust of wind suddenly blew over the large umbrella placed near Pema's seat to block the sun, nearly striking her. I heard someone ask out loud if anyone was willing to stand and hold the umbrella in order to prevent it from falling over again. That's when I jumped into action, volunteering for the post of standing stoic for the next hour in an effort to keep the sun off Pema.

I began to worry: what if the wind blew harder, and I accidentally let go of the umbrella? What if I couldn't prevent it from hitting her in the face? I'd be expelled from the sangha, branded an inept loser, and forever immortalized as the guy who let a large umbrella smack Pema Chödrön in the head. Talk about accruing bad karma! I could almost guarantee my next life as a fish stuck in an aquarium, spending my days floating around mindlessly and staring at children as they tapped on the glass in front of me. Fortunately for Pema and my own personal karma, I managed to keep the umbrella from physically abusing her.

The program had certainly turned out to be far more than I'd expected. The handshakes and hugs I received from dozens of people continued to affect me, but their words of encouragement made me reflect again on the advice from the Sakyong. According to a number of program participants and others who'd followed my emails, my actions in Iraq and attempts at compassion toward the Iraqis made me a true "Shambhala Warrior." But a "warrior" in traditional terms implies someone who engages in violence. Chogyam Trungpa Rinpoche said:

> The warriors of Shambhala do not create war. The word warrior, by itself, may mean a creator of war or a warmonger, but the warriors of Shambhala are the opposite—of course. The Shambhala warrior does not create war at all, but is somebody who creates peace. The warriors of Shambhala are those who are interested in subjugating their own desires for war and for aggression... We talked about sadness. That quality is precisely the heart of warriorship. The warrior is completely in tune with people and with their various levels of emotionality. We are the opposite of warmongers.

But what does it mean to be a Shambhala warrior on the battlefields of Iraq or Afghanistan, where violence is an everyday affair? Could I possibly be both a Shambhala warrior, as some people claimed, and a warrior in actual combat? When I received the Sakyong's email referring to "wrathful compassion," I gleaned from his advice a need for increased compassion, no matter how horrible or painful an incident might be. Nevertheless, the "wrathful compassion" statement by the Sakyong puzzled me and others.

Gary Allen, Education Director of the Ratna Peace Initiative, later wrote to me, offering an explanation:

> We should say that "wrathful" here is closer to vigorous. Since it's not about aggression, it's about doing something that destroys the ego of the situation, undermines the toxicity when situations can't continue without being harmful. Fearlessness also comes to mind as a synonym for wrath. "Wrath" implies that there's no

deception, no hesitation, and whatever must be faced and sub-
jugated as generally harmful and samsaric is faced and subju-
gated—the wrathful principle isn't concerned whether or not your
feelings get hurt. It's more concerned with taking action with the
greatest possible precision and effectiveness and without the issue of cowardice, so that a given situation is liberated from deception, aggression, confusion, whatever it is.

Seeking further guidance and clarification on what it means to be a
Shambhala warrior in actual combat, Margot asked meditation master
and scholar Thrangu Rinpoche about taking a life by shooting someone
to protect one's friends. She also asked him about shooting to protect
my own life. As further demonstration of the complexity of this issue,
Rinpoche sighed and said, "I don't know." Then just as quickly, he sat
forward, and with an attempt at ensuring that he understood the language accurately, he said, "There is danger, right?"

"Yes," Margot replied, "war—killing."

After some reflection, he said, "If he has to shoot someone to save
many others, that is okay."

"And if he has to shoot someone to save himself?"

"Yes, that's alright, too." But, he emphasized, as he sat in his elegant
gold and maroon robes, holding an imaginary machine gun, spraying
imaginary bullets back and forth, "But this is not good—not good!"

Later, Margot asked another monk, Lama Tenpa, for guidance in the
situation of war. "The most important thing," he said, "is to go with the
very clear intention that he is going as a protector, not just for his friends,
but also the enemy—a protector for all people—a wrathful protector. It
takes wisdom and judgment, and the danger to this is that the fear that
arises could cloud those qualities. He must be aware of that all the time,
as much as possible."

* * * * *

The final event of the program included a walk up to the Great Stupa of Dharmakaya. It was the first time I'd seen the stupa lit up at night—an impressive sight with a nearly full moon enhancing the atmosphere. A sense of energy seemed to permeate the entire space. The whiteness of the stupa glowed brightly from the illumination. Deer wandered peacefully nearby, immune to any human threat. Above the entrance, the large bronze figure of a standing Buddha greets visitors. A multitude of Tibetan symbols painted beautifully in blue, red, gold, and yellow decorate the outside, standing out boldly in the light. The program's participants were expected to circumambulate the stupa before entering. Once inside, the marvelous paintings and art often stun visitors. The Kalachakra mandala, painted on the first floor ceiling, represents the sacredness of reality itself. Small niches around the room contain photos and offerings honoring revered Tibetan teachers such as the Dalai Lama and Choygam Trungpa. I've traveled to numerous sacred places around the world that were influenced by Buddhism, such as Angkor Wat in Cambodia and Pagan in Burma, but a visit to the Great Stupa of Dharmakaya had a more personal resonance for me.

The program's participants filed slowly inside, allowing for prostrations in front of a large golden statue of the Buddha that contains Choygam Trungpa's relics. Loud gongs echoed as people prostrated and offered incense and white offering scarves to the Buddha. Incense smoke hung in the air and floated silently out the stupa's doorways. Before participants left the stupa, President Reoch presented them with a picture of Pema Chödrön. My staffing duty included keeping people moving, circumambulating around the stupa until the ceremony concluded.

When nearly all the participants had left, I waited with President Reoch outside the stupa near the entrance while he talked with a few lingering acquaintances. It was a scene of tranquility and peace without the large numbers of people, but I was ready to leave. It had been an eventful day, and I wanted to drive President Reoch home so that I could return to my own quarters and get some sleep.

After a time he announced his readiness to go. Before we got to the car, he stopped and said, "Look up at the sky—it's a beautiful night, a perfect night." I stood there in silence for a time, gazing up at the starry sky with the magnificent Rocky Mountains surrounding the Great Stupa as a backdrop. I'd been thinking about just getting to the car and finishing my duties, but President Reoch had the presence, the patience, and the awareness to stop and notice the world's beauty for a moment. Having forgotten the present moment for a time, I'd been caught up in the habitual pattern of rushing around, thinking about where I wanted to be, what I wanted to be doing.

We must have stood near the stupa in silence for at least five minutes, staring up at the moon and the Milky Way. I thought about a similar evening with the same moon in a place thousands of miles from Shambhala Mountain Center, a place called Iraq that was filled with people who hated me and wished me dead. During a routine convoy mission out in the desolate expanses of Al-Anbar province, I'd sat in the gunner's hatch of a humvee, looking up at the clouds moving back and forth across the moon, casting an eerie glow over the landscape. I'd suddenly felt a sense of peace; for a brief moment, contentment and happiness replaced the threat of death. As Pema had suggested in her talks, I'd taken a moment to "look at the sky," connecting with my natural openness, seeing the bigger perspective and appreciating my surroundings, realizing just how good life really was. As we rode along in a far off land that had once been the cradle of civilization, a land full of beauty and possibility, I had no clue it would take me on a journey that would lead me here on a warm evening high up in the Colorado Rockies, standing next to this superb monument of awakened mind. A true spiritual journey never ends, but experiences come of greater understanding and awareness. Looking up at the night sky, the feeling was unmistakable—a state of natural openness—a state of peace within myself.

Epilogue

Graveyards. I have always considered them a waste of good dirt, except in special situations. If the grave held someone who lived a life that influenced others, say, Beethoven, Winston Churchill, Ernest Hemingway, or even Jim Morrison, it would be fascinating to visit. But for the rest of interred humanity, most are soon forgotten.

I'd been at a typical National Guard weekend drill not long after my return from Iraq. While researching this book, I discovered that SSG. Mercer had been buried in Waycross, not that far from Valdosta, only an hour's deviation from my normal route back to Florida. I decided to travel to Waycross and visit Mercer's grave.

A sign in front of the church read Kettle Creek Cemetery. I found myself driving by gravestones on both sides of the road. I turned off and drove around a small, old section, noticing mostly grey and faded stones—not a place for someone recently buried. I remembered some of the graves on the other side of the road looked new. I left the older section and crossed the road, stopped my car, and got out. Walking toward these new graves, I recognized the name Mercer carved on the back of a shiny black marble bench and the name of his children carved on the back of the headstone: Alanna, Amber, and Gavin. For a moment I felt myself back in Iraq on that hot, sultry evening, holding Mercer's hand, looking up at the night sky over Baghdad, watching the medivac helicopter circle around and around. *Just land, goddammit! Why don't you just land?* My frustrations over that evening came back in a sudden rush of emotion and pain.

I had never met SSG. Chad Mercer, never listened to his voice, or appreciated his sense of humor. Never listened to him talk about his wife and his children. No. I never knew Mercer, but I did try to save his life on that evening that now seemed so long ago—a simple mistake that should have been avoided. Unfortunately, a good man died, and he won't be the last. There will be another SSG. Chad Mercer making the ultimate sacrifice.

The warm sun reflected off the shiny new marble of Mercer's grave. Black marble surrounded the headstone and grave as well. Around the marble slab in front of the headstone, thousands of small white rocks decorated the enclosure. To the left of the headstone lay a small vase holding plastic flowers, knocked over by the wind. On the right stood a marble container with plastic flowers and two American flags hanging limply over the edge. At the base of this container was a picture of the Mercer family. Mercer's wife held their young son in her arms. Placed lovingly in front of the headstone were small toy trucks that must have belonged to three-year-old Gavin, a small painting set from one of his daughters, a can of Mountain Dew and a cigar left by a friend. SSG. Mercer had clearly been a Florida State Seminole football fan. In the headstone's right hand corner was a large Seminole Indian portrait.

I sat on the bench and looked at the grave.

I suddenly realized I wanted to place something there as well, but hadn't thought to bring anything in particular. I walked back to my car to look in the trunk. Maybe I could find something appropriate. Searching through a box, I found the small copy of Pema Chödrön's *Awakening Loving Kindness*, which I'd carried with me every day while out on patrol. I also discovered a copy of *The Dot*, the Shambhala newspaper in which my emails to Margot had been published. Perfect, I thought. I walked back to Mercer's grave and sat down on the black marble bench. I held the small pocket book edition in my hand and thought about how it had aided me while in Iraq. I wanted to keep it. If I left it here, it would get

WALKING THE TIGER'S PATH
PAUL M. KENDEL

blown away or ruined in the rain. But no, it had served me well, and like the gift I'd given the Sakyong, it was time to let it go.

I placed the book at the base of the headstone next to the small toy cars and other items. I set the small vase with plastic flowers upright, and poured some of the small white rocks into the marble container holding the American flags. I rearranged the flags with enough rocks to hold them erect. I reread the article in *The Dot* entitled "Contemplating Anger and Aggression in Iraq." The first email presented described the death of Mercer. I left it opened to that page and placed *The Dot* alongside the copy of *Awakening Loving Kindness*.

Final resting place of SSG. Chad Mercer, Waycross, GA.

It was unlikely *The Dot* would last long exposed to the weather, but maybe, just maybe, it could be helpful in some small way if someone— Mercer's wife, family members, or a friend—discovered what I'd left. I rose, took one last look at Mercer's grave, and returned to my car. After an eventful day, it was time to return home. Not the home I had before I left for Iraq—that one was gone—but it was home, nonetheless, where my two young boys waited for their father to return.

ABOUT
THE AUTHOR

Photo by Moreland Nicholson

Paul Matthew Kendel was born in Hawthorne, CA in 1967. He grew up in Orange County, attending Fountain Valley High School, and after graduating in 1986, he went into the Army for three years, stationed at Fort Benning, GA. Completing his active duty service, he returned to California and began college, as well as continuing his service in the California National Guard. He graduated in 1994 from California State University at Long Beach with a bachelor's degree in history. He then entered California State University at Fullerton, graduating in 1999 receiving a master's degree in history with an emphasis on the Middle East. Following the 9/11 attacks, he deployed in early 2002 to Saudi Arabia. He later continued his education, getting a secondary teaching credential and completing a further master's degree in anthropology in 2003. After this, he moved his family to Jacksonville, FL, where he began teaching special education and joined the Georgia National Guard. In January 2005, he started his training for deployment in Iraq.

Subsequent to his return from Iraq in 2006, he worked as an adjunct professor teaching American history. In 2008 his unit was called up again, this time for deployment to Afghanistan. Promoted to platoon sergeant, during the course of training for combat he aggravated a previous injury sustained in Iraq and did not deploy with his men. Released from active duty in March 2010, he is currently teaching world history and special education at Andrew Jackson High School and working on a second book.

ABOUT THE
RATNA PEACE INITIATIVE

*We're accustomed to living a life based on running
after our wild mind... Through meditation we begin...to
see that we have to work with these intense emotions
because if we don't, they'll grow. Once they grow, we act on
them. When we act on them, they create our environment.*

—Sakyong Mipham

The Ratna Peace Initiative teaches meditation to prison inmates as well as military veterans suffering from post-traumatic stress disorder.

Tens of thousands of vets suffer psychological damage from their service in war. Ratna's Veterans Peace of Mind program trains veterans in mindfulness meditation techniques, providing personal instruction, peer support, and equine-assisted therapy to help them stabilize emotionally, and cultivate peacefulness and clarity.

Over two million people are incarcerated in America every year, with a recidivism rate as high as 70%. Regardless of one's past, Ratna Peace Initiative regards individuals as worthy of respect and compassion, and is dedicated to supporting them in the recovery of their sanity and humanity. Ratna writes to inmates throughout the United States. It runs meditation programs in prisons, and offers personal instruction through correspondence, study courses, and free distribution of meditation materials.

For more information, write or call:
Ratna Peace Initiative
1507 Pine Street
Boulder, CO 80302
1.800.75.RATNA (1.800.757.2862)
Or go to:
www.VeteransPeaceofMind.org
www.RatnaPeaceInitiative.org

DA ✓ APR 2 5 2012

NEW RELEASES AND TOP SELLERS
FROM TENDRIL PRESS

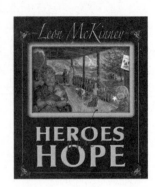

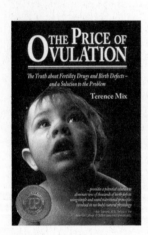

Tendril Press, LLC, is an Independent Press,
publishing thought provoking, inspirational, educational
and humanitarian books for adults and children.
Our highly-selective process is paying off, with multiple
award-winning books and an accepted entry for the Pulitzer Prize
We are changing lives worldwide, one book at a time.
Visit us often at *www.TendrilPress.com*
For Quantity orders of any title please call
303.696.9227